D

D1012843

IN THE HEAT
OF BATTLE

A history of those who rose to the occasion
and those who didn't

IN THE HEAT
OF BATTLE

A history of those who rose to the occasion
and those who didn't

DONOUGH O'BRIEN

First published in Great Britain in 2009 by Osprey Publishing,
Midland House, West Way, Botley, Oxford OX2 0PH, United Kingdom.
443 Park Avenue South, New York, NY 10016, USA.
Email: info@ospreypublishing.com

© 2009 Donough O'Brien

All rights reserved. Apart from any fair dealing for the purpose of private study, research, criticism or
review, as permitted under the Copyright, Designs and Patents Act, 1988, no part of this publication
may be reproduced, stored in a retrieval system, or transmitted in any form or by any means, electronic,
electrical, chemical, mechanical, optical, photocopying, recording or otherwise, without the prior
written permission of the copyright owner. Enquiries should be addressed to the Publishers.
Every attempt has been made by the Publishers to secure the appropriate permissions for
materials reproduced in this book. If there has been any oversight we will be happy to rectify
the situation and a written submission should be made to the Publishers.

A CIP catalogue record for this book is available from the British Library.

Donough O'Brien has asserted his right under the Copyright, Designs and Patents Act, 1988,
to be identified as the author of this book.

ISBN: 978 1 84603 464 0

Page layout by Myriam Bell Design, France
Index by Alan Thatcher
Typeset in Minion Pro and Futura
Originated by PPS Grasmere, Leeds, UK
Printed in China through Worldprint Ltd

09 10 11 12 13   10 9 8 7 6 5 4 3 2 1

Imperial War Museum Collections
Many of the photos in this book come from the Imperial War Museum's huge collections which cover
all aspects of conflict involving Britain and the Commonwealth since the start of the twentieth century.
These rich resources are available online to search, browse and buy at www.iwmcollections.org.uk.
In addition to Collections Online, you can visit the Visitor Rooms where you can explore over eight
million photographs, thousands of hours of moving images, the largest sound archive of its kind in
the world, thousands of diaries and letters written by people in wartime, and a huge reference library.
To make an appointment, call (020) 7416 5320, or email mail@iwm.org.uk.
Imperial War Museum www.iwm.org.uk

US Front Cover: John F. Kennedy, General Custer and George Washington. (TopFoto)
UK Front Cover: Douglas Bader and Field Marshal Montgomery. (Getty Images)

For a catalogue of all books published by Osprey please contact:

NORTH AMERICA
Osprey Direct, c/o Random House Distribution Center
400 Hahn Road, Westminster, MD 21157, USA
E-mail: uscustomerservice@ospreypublishing.com

ALL OTHER REGIONS
Osprey Direct, The Book Service Ltd., Distribution Centre, Colchester Road, Frating Green,
Colchester, Essex, CO7 7DW
E-mail: customerservice@ospreypublishing.com

Osprey Publishing is supporting the Woodland Trust, the UK's leading woodland
conservation charity, by funding the dedication of trees.

www.ospreypublishing.com

CONTENTS

4 – A CONSTANT THREAD OF VALOUR

5 – WITHOUT FAME AND FANFARE

PART 2: . . . AND THOSE WHO DIDN'T

1 – TOO CONFIDENT BY HALF

PREFACE

It is a sobering thought that out of the last 3,500 years of our 'civilized' world, only for 230 have we been at peace. Moreover, war imposes a unique kind of stress on its participants. Any normal fear of failure or disgrace in civilian life is immeasurably increased by the omnipresent danger of being killed, wounded or facing capture. This surely explains the great number of books written about battle, and those exploring the lives of the brave and cowardly.

However, this book examines a slightly different phenomenon: those who rose to the occasion and those who did not, viewed in a somewhat wider context.

Sometimes it is the junior ranks that seize the initiative and save the day, often with extraordinary acts of heroism. Often those who fail are senior and experienced, making their behaviour even more disgraceful. In their position of privilege, they should have known better.

'Seizing the Moment' includes familiar battlefield heroes like Audie Murphy or 'H' Jones, together with less well-known characters like Corporal Graham, 'the bravest man at Waterloo', and the young Erwin Rommel, one world war and two decades before he became famous as the 'Desert Fox'.

Those 'Bucking the Odds' have to include Douglas Bader, Britain's flamboyant aircraft ace flying with his artificial legs, George Washington daringly crossing the Delaware, and John Paul Jones challenging the might of the Royal Navy. Joan of Arc was certainly one of those who had the 'Courage of their Convictions', while Sergeant York had to overcome his pacifist views in World War I France. There have been few better examples of the 'Constant Thread of Valour' than Joshua Chamberlain, the saviour of the Union position at Little Round Top at the battle of Gettysburg, Michael Wittmann, the ultimate tank ace, or Albert Jacka, the Australian who many feel deserved not just one but three Victoria Crosses.

Among those who rose to the occasion, I have felt it only right to pay homage to those on the fringes of the actual fighting, 'Without Fame and Fanfare' – like the brilliant code breakers Alan Turing and Captain Reginald Hall RN, photographic experts such as Constance Babington Smith, and medical pioneers like Napoleon's great surgeon Baron Larrey or 'Weary' Dunlop, Australia's hero of the Kwai railway. All had an influence on warfare as great as any warrior.

And those who didn't rise to the occasion?

Many were 'Too Confident by Half', like Saddam Hussein, who was to lead his country to ruin, the corpulent and boastful Hermann Goering, wrecking the plans of others at Dunkirk and Stalingrad, or even the inexperienced Jack Kennedy during the Bay of Pigs fiasco.

Others simply display 'Fatal Inattention', like France's Constable Charles D'Albret at Agincourt, or General Ledlie at the battle of the Crater. 'Flaws and Obsessions' can wreck the reputations of otherwise great men: Douglas MacArthur in Korea, Napoleon in Russia, Montgomery and Patton, due to their jealous feuding, and even Mark Antony who risked everything for such a non-military notion as love. Worst of all in warfare must be 'Treachery and Rank Disobedience': Mark Clark vaingloriously capturing Rome instead of trapping the Germans, Lord Sackville refusing to charge at Minden, Mountbatten persisting with his disastrous raid at Dieppe, and Benedict Arnold changing sides to try to hand over West Point, becoming America's symbol of the ultimate traitor.

And nothing can unravel all the best military and political efforts faster than 'A Streak of Cruelty': witness the results created by unfeeling generals like John Maxwell at Dublin's Easter Rising, Reginald Dyer at Amritsar and young Lieutenant William Calley at My Lai.

Here are those who rose to the occasion and those who didn't: the recipients of lavish praise or quite the opposite. The ultimate judgement must be left to the reader.

PART 1

THOSE WHO ROSE TO THE OCCASION ...

1

SEIZING THE MOMENT

AUDIE MURPHY AND HIS THREE CAREERS

It was only by unflinching determination that America's most decorated hero ever came to fight.

Audie Murphy was one of 12 children, born to an impoverished farming family in rural Texas. His father abandoned them and Audie had to drop out of school at 12 to help support the family, and his skill with a rifle became vital in supplying rabbits and other game to supplement their meagre diet. So desperate did they become that when his mother died, Audie and his elder sister were forced to place three of their siblings in an orphanage.

Everything changed with the Japanese attack on Pearl Harbor. A mustard-keen Audie went straight to the recruiting station and was bitterly disappointed to be turned away because he was only 17. A few months later he was back, but his first choices, the rugged US Marines and the paratroopers, now rejected him because he was so short, only 5ft 5in., and slight, only 112lb. (He would not have been consoled by the thought that Nelson had been even smaller.)

Even when the US Army accepted him, his commanders were so worried about the small baby-faced boy that they tried to make him a cook.

They need not have worried. Audie Murphy took to combat like a duck to water. In Sicily, he was promoted to corporal after killing two Italian officers, then to

Still baby-faced, Audie Murphy, America's most decorated hero, could realistically act himself in a film ten years later. (Bettmann / Corbis)

sergeant when in Italy he overpowered a German platoon near Salerno. In southern France, his best friend was treacherously killed by a German pretending to surrender, and Audie Murphy exacted a swift revenge on the German and his comrades, earning the Distinguished Service Cross. Time and again, decisive and heroic action brought medals and promotion – and finally a battlefield commission.

So it continued, until as a 21-year-old second lieutenant he performed the act which earned him America's highest bravery award – the Medal of Honor.

In the freezing cold of January 1945, a German tank and infantry attack swamped his depleted unit. Murphy stayed behind directing vital artillery fire by telephone. When German infantry grew close, he leapt on to a burning tank destroyer and used its machine gun to hold off the attack. Wounded and with the blazing vehicle's ammunition always in danger of exploding, he fought alone for a full hour, destroying one German squad only ten yards away. As his citation said, 'his indomitable courage and his refusal to give an inch of ground saved his company from encirclement and destruction'.

Small wonder that his friendly, boyish face was soon smiling on the cover of *Life* magazine.

However, the wartime hero was to rise to the occasion several more times. First, he had the courage to admit publicly that he, of all people, suffered from Post Traumatic Stress Disorder, and was plagued with insomnia, depression and nightmares of bloody battle. This later helped the US government to understand similar sufferers in Korea and Vietnam.

The *Life* cover launched him into another career. Actor James Cagney saw it, realized Murphy's appeal and persuaded him to come to Hollywood. It took several years for his acting career to blossom, but his incredibly youthful appearance, once a hindrance, now helped him through the 1955 film version of his bestselling book *To Hell and Back*. He was able to play himself, acting out his exploits of a full ten years before. Not many of us can believably look 21 when we are ten years older. The film was Universal's highest-grossing release until *Jaws*, and Audie was to star in no fewer than 44 movies, 33 of them Westerns. He even made a career as a successful composer of 'Country' hits, many performed by the top stars.

Audie Murphy was killed in a plane crash when he was only 46. Now he is honoured not only in his native Texas but by the whole of the United States. His plain and undecorated (at his request) headstone at Arlington Cemetery is visited by so many people – only that of Jack Kennedy attracts more – that a special stone path had to be built.

Audie deserved his fame as an American who could always be relied on to rise to the occasion.

It is a curious fact that one of Britain's Victoria Crosses was awarded for a feat almost identical to that of Audie Murphy. Near the end of the war, Irish Guardsman Edward Charlton held off a German counter-attack by using the machine gun from the turret of his knocked-out, burning Sherman tank. He took down the heavy weapon and charged the enemy, firing from the hip. He was wounded in the arm, propped the gun on a gate post and continued firing, reloading with one hand until collapsing from a second wound. Amazingly, after he had died he was recommended for the Victoria Cross partly by a German officer, who came to the wire of his prison cage and insisted on getting recognition for 'that brave Irish soldier'.

CORPORAL JAMES GRAHAM AND HOUGOUMONT'S GATE

There were many brave men at Waterloo. Indeed, thousands of brave men of many nations. But there was one whom the Duke of Wellington decided had been 'the bravest man at Waterloo'. He was Corporal James Graham of the Coldstream Guards – one of the men who 'closed the gate at Hougoumont'.

On 26 February 1815, the exiled Napoleon had made his final and most decisive move. He felt affronted by the dishonourable way he had been personally treated, and he knew that France was seething under the misrule of Louis XVIII – especially the army. He secretly left Elba with just 1,100 men, landed at Antibes and began his legendary march into France. At Laffrey, he opened his overcoat to the blocking French troops. 'If there is in your ranks a single soldier who would kill his Emperor, let him fire. Here I am.' Then, at Auxerre, Marshal Ney – his 'bravest of the brave' – who had casually promised the king to bring Napoleon back 'in an iron cage', quickly fell under the spell of his old commander.

By 20 March, Napoleon was back in Paris. He offered the Allies peace, which was rejected, so he swiftly devoted his huge energy to rebuilding his veteran army into a formidable force, ready to strike at the foreigners invading France. When one thinks about it, it is truly extraordinary. It is as if Pétain and De Gaulle had decided that the Nazi terms in 1940 were unacceptable and had gone back to war. Or if the Confederates had rearmed and counter-attacked after Appomattox in 1865. Or if Hitler had re-emerged to throw the occupying Russians, British and Americans out of Germany in 1945.

In fact, if one wants a supreme example of rising to the occasion, Napoleon's next eight weeks, a surge of sustained energy and resourcefulness, provides it. Half a million men returned to the colours. Every French town and village worked round the clock to produce uniforms, boots, muskets, gun carriages, bayonets, swords and ammunition. A keen, experienced and well-equipped army rose, Phoenix-like, from the ashes of defeat and occupation.

But his enemies were on the move – the Russians with 200,000 men and the Austrians with 210,000. Much closer were 128,000 Prussians in Belgium under Marshal Blücher, as was a polyglot 'infamous army' commanded by the Duke of Wellington, of 106,000 Dutch, Belgians and Germans and fewer than 32,000 British, some of whom had served under him in the Peninsular War. Napoleon had a choice of conducting a defensive war or of attacking. He decided that if he could first destroy his most accessible enemies, he could then turn on the more distant Russians and Austrians. Above all, he must never let Blücher and Wellington combine.

Cleverly masking his intentions, Napoleon crossed the Sambre River at Charleroi on 15 June. It took some time for Wellington and Blücher to appreciate his line of advance, which was straight at the vulnerable hinge between them. Final confirmation came to Brussels during the glitter of the Duchess of Richmond's ball. 'Humbugged, by God!' admitted the duke, sending for maps and despatching his orders – almost too late.

Only the 'intelligent disobedience' of the commanders of the Dutch forces, who stayed at the crossroads of Quatre Bras, ensured that the French were opposed there long enough for a tough stalemate battle to develop. Three miles away at Ligny, the Prussians were badly mauled. Wellington had promised them 20,000 men, which now he could not spare. When they failed to arrive, it deepened Prussian suspicions of Wellington. But Blücher insisted that he had 'given his word', and so the Prussians retreated to Wavre, parallel to Wellington. But for this, both Allied armies might have been defeated piecemeal, as Napoleon had planned.

Wellington, after years of perfecting the defensive battle in the Peninsula, had chosen the ridge of Mont St Jean, south of Waterloo, a year before. He now arranged his forces on this ridge, anchored by three farmhouses, Hougoumont, La Haye Sainte and Papelotte. On the night of 17 June, it poured with rain. The waterlogged ground meant that the French could not deploy their heavy guns until it had dried, and for the Prussians – now intent on joining Wellington – it meant they would take many hours to arrive.

At 11.30am, Napoleon began the battle by sending Reille's Corps, spearheaded by his brother Jérôme Bonaparte, to attack Hougoumont, manned by Foot Guards, Dutch infantry and German riflemen. Napoleon always intended that this attack should be a heavy one, but only a diversion – to compel Wellington to shift troops and thus to weaken his centre. Owing to the courage of the defenders, the reverse occurred. It was Napoleon's precious reserves that were sucked steadily into the battle for this manor house.

The key to its defence would be some of Britain's finest troops, the 1st, 2nd and 3rd Guards, or what we now call the Grenadier, Coldstream and Scots Guards. Commanding the Coldstreams was Lieutenant-Colonel James Macdonnell, a huge Highlander, whom Wellington seemed to have selected for the task. When General Müffling, the Prussian liaison officer, appeared worried, Wellington drily remarked, 'You do not know Macdonnell'.

It is difficult to apportion the blame between General Honoré Reille or Jérôme Bonaparte for what now happened. Instead of isolating Hougoumont and using its wood or 'blind' west wall to gather troops to turn Wellington's flank, both made it a point of honour to capture the chateau. After losing 2,500 men in vicious fighting in the woods and orchards, another 8,000 French were sent against Hougoumont. The south gate having been successfully defended, the north gate was now threatened.

With an axe, a huge Frenchman, Lieutenant Legros, *l'enforceur* (the wrecker), smashed through the gate followed by 40 Frenchmen. Macdonnell saw the danger and, scattering the interlopers, rushed to close the gate with three officers and several Guardsmen, including James Graham and his brother. Macdonnell and Corporal Graham heaved their shoulders against the doors with screaming Frenchmen on the other side trying to resist them. Graham dropped a crossbar into place, but a Frenchman tried to climb over. Captain Henry Wyndham handed Graham a loaded musket and Graham calmly shot the intruder. The brave Legros and every other Frenchman lay dead in the courtyard, except one young drummer boy who was spared.

An impatient Napoleon now intervened and did something which should have happened earlier. He ordered the chateau to be shelled. Incendiary *carcasses* soon set Hougoumont ablaze, but the Guardsmen resolutely fought on from the burning buildings. Graham suddenly asked his colonel if he 'could be excused' from the firing line for a moment. Knowing his courage, Macdonnell was surprised, until Graham explained that his brother was lying wounded in a burning building and he requested 'permission to drag him to safety before returning to his post'.

After fighting for hours, apparently alone, in this 'battle within a battle' and after one more assault by Jérôme's troops, the defenders of Hougoumont were suddenly ordered to join in the general advance. The final assault on Wellington's unweakened centre by Napoleon's legendary Old Guard had failed and they had staggered back, broken. 'La Garde recule!' The astonished words echoed through the French ranks, then the dreaded 'Sauve qui peut.'

The stubborn defence of Hougoumont had exactly fulfilled its purpose, but at a frightful cost, especially for the French, with perhaps 8,000 of their corpses littering the orchard and woods, the shot-through trees bent over 'like weeping willows'.

The Duke of Wellington appreciated it only too well. 'No other troops could have held Hougoumont other than British – and only the best of *them*. The success of the whole battle turned upon the closing of the gates of Hougoumont.'

A few weeks later, John Norcross, the rector of Framlingham in Suffolk, wrote an unusual letter to the Duke of Wellington asking him to nominate a Waterloo soldier to receive an annual pension from his farm. After careful investigation, James Graham was chosen. Later, Norcross died and left £500 for 'the bravest man in England', and the duke was again consulted. This time he nominated Macdonnell, who, however,

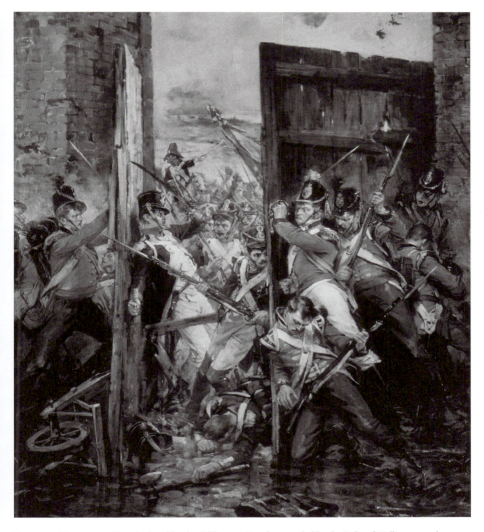

The gate at Hougoumont Farm is closed by the Coldstream Guards, regarded by the Duke of Wellington as the critical moment at the battle of Waterloo. (Trustees of the National Museum of Scotland)

decided to share it, 'because Graham, who saw with me the importance of the step, rushed forward and *together* we shut the gate'.

So, ironically, a Scotsman and an Irishman were honoured for being the bravest of Englishmen.

ERWIN ROMMEL AND HIS HANDKERCHIEF

Asked to name one German general during World War II, most Allied soldiers would have been stumped – with one exception, Rommel. Not only was he very well known, he was also admired. Winston Churchill even said in the House of Commons, 'We have a very daring and skilful opponent against us, and I may say across the havoc of war, a great General.' Small wonder that General Auchinleck, Britain's desert war commander, was moved to tell his officers, 'There exists a real danger that your friend Rommel is becoming a kind of magical or bogey-man to our troops, who are talking far too much about him. He is by no means a superman, although he is undoubtedly ever-energetic and able. Even if he were a superman, it would still be highly undesirable that our men should credit him with supernatural powers.'

Whether or not Rommel was indeed a *great* general is still open to debate. But there is absolutely no doubt that he was a past master at the art of rising to the occasion.

He was awarded the *Pour le Mérite*, Germany's highest decoration. He won it not for any of the exploits for which he became renowned in World War II but two decades earlier, in the mountains of what is now Slovenia. Nevertheless it set the scene for the type of brave, almost reckless resourcefulness that would later make him so famous.

Italy was an ally of Britain and France in World War I, but she had only just been holding her own against Germany's weaker ally, Austria. Suddenly, in October 1917, the Germans intervened and launched a stunning attack on the Italians, whose morale was already at rock bottom and whose pathetic commander, General Cardona, had decided that 120 miles from the front line was a nice, safe place to be. The battle of Caporetto saw the disintegration of the whole Italian 2nd Army, 800,000 men; it was, in fact, the most stunning victory of the whole war.

During the campaign, young Captain Erwin Rommel was serving with the Württenberg Mountain Battalion of the elite Alpenkorps. He had already served on the Western Front, had been wounded three times and had gained a reputation for lightning decisions, often ignoring the orders of senior and cautious commanders.

In the mountains near the Matajur Ridge, he saw 1,500 Italians milling about. Quite alone, waving a handkerchief, he marched towards them and, in Italian, ordered them to surrender. Any one of them could, and *should*, have shot him. But instead, they rushed forward shouting, 'Viva Germania', and hoisted him on their shoulders. One brave Italian officer tried to resist and was shot by his own men.

Erwin Rommel, ever daring and resourceful, became best known for his exploits in North Africa. Dubbed 'The Desert Fox', he was admired by his enemies as was no other German General. (Imperial War Museum)

Ignoring orders to fall back, Rommel then encircled a regiment of the Salerno Brigade and proceeded to pull off the same trick. He imperiously separated the slouching, dispirited officers, some weeping, and then made them and their 1,200 men surrender. Within 48 hours his tally had reached 150 officers, 9,000 men and 81 guns. It was for these actions that he received his *Pour le Mérite*, part of a pattern of quick-thinking courage, often against orders – and *always* taking the credit.

After the war, Rommel became an instructor and wrote *Infantry Tactics*, which became an international textbook. He became familiar to Hitler when he commanded the Führer's personal protection battalion during the Polish campaign in 1939. In spite of the fact that he had no tank experience, and to the irritation of fellow generals, he pulled strings with Hitler to be given command of the 7th Panzer Division, a rather weak division armed with light Czech tanks, but which he soon licked into shape.

Under fire, he led his division in rubber boats across the Meuse at Dinant, and soon his *Genspenster Division*, or 'Ghost Division', had broken through and was rampaging deep behind enemy lines, often out of touch with German High Command. Only one counter-attack halted him, but Rommel, with characteristic ruthless energy, personally directed some 88mm guns to beat off the British tanks. By the time he reached the sea at Cherbourg, he had, in just six weeks, captured 97,468 prisoners and destroyed 89 tanks, hundreds of guns and 9,000 vehicles.

It was proof he was ready for independent command, although his colleagues had mixed opinions about him, criticizing his lack of caution and, probably more justifiably, his unwillingness to share the credit with anyone else.

It was while in North Africa, between 1941 and 1943, that Rommel became 'the Desert Fox'. With characteristic speed and boldness, he won battle after battle against superior forces, often only held back by lack of supplies, while constantly arguing with his Italian allies and even his own superiors. At one stage, Field Marshal Halder sent Friedrich von Paulus (later infamous at Stalingrad) to 'head off this officer gone mad'.

In the desert, Rommel soon became renowned for his chivalrous behaviour towards his enemies, enhancing his personal aura. His Afrika Korps was never accused of any war crimes. He called it *Krieg ohne Hass*, or 'war without hate'.

In spite of a string of successes such as the capture of Tobruk, the tide would turn against Rommel, who found himself with his supplies in tatters, always short of fuel, ravaged from the air, with forceful new commanders like Alexander and Montgomery as well as the arrival of the Americans – though he did savage the latter at Kasserine Pass.

Now Rommel, once Hitler's favourite, was subjected to the same 'victory or death' orders, which hopelessly destroyed his freedom of manoeuvre and, ultimately, his army.

He was ill back in Germany when his Afrika Korps – no fewer than 130,000 valuable soldiers – finally surrendered in Tunisia. Now it became rather difficult for Hitler to know what to do with his erstwhile 'unbeatable genius'. Rommel certainly could not command Italy jointly with Albert Kesselring, who had begun to dislike him, and he was definitely no longer Hitler's 'golden boy'.

So he was put in charge of Army Group B in Normandy under Von Rundstedt. Feeling that Normandy was where the invasion would come, he vastly improved its defences. But he was once again soon at loggerheads with his superiors who felt the Calais area more likely.

The only senior commander with bitter personal experience of Allied air superiority, Rommel was convinced he must defend and counter-attack close to the beaches. The argument forced Hitler into a useless compromise. Rommel did not have enough armour and Von Rundstedt had lost his mobile reserve. So, a cohesive counter-attack never emerged.

Rommel was now disillusioned with his Führer's 'infallible judgement' and was at least on the fringes of the officers' plot against Hitler. 'I have given him his last chance,' he was heard to say. 'If he does not take it, we will act.'

But events were taken out of his hands by the airpower he feared so much. A prowling fighter-bomber, a Royal Canadian Air Force Spitfire, strafed Rommel's staff car and he suffered serious head injuries. Three days later in East Prussia, Claus von Stauffenberg's bomb went off, but failed to kill Hitler (see page 107). The Gestapo implicated Rommel in the plot. They had little real evidence, but they no doubt remembered his refusal to execute Jewish prisoners, or shoot captured commandos (even when they had tried to kill him), or his disobedience about handing French Jews to the SS, and his insistence on paying French construction workers properly rather than using them as slaves. They certainly would have heard of his disparaging remarks about 'incompetent Nazi leadership'. So, with his family threatened, he was forced to take poison. Hitler played a cynical leading role at his lavish state funeral.

How annoyed they would be, those fellow generals who regarded him as 'pushy and reckless', if they knew he was the only one of them now honoured with a museum in today's Germany.

YONI NETANYAHU AND ENTEBBE

How many 17-year-olds would write like this? Or would feel the need to?

Death – that's the only thing that disturbs me. It doesn't frighten me; it arouses my curiosity. It is a puzzle that I, like many others, have tried to solve without success. I do not fear it because I attribute little value to a life without a purpose. And if I should have to sacrifice my life to attain its goal, I'll do so willingly.

In spite of his good looks and playful disposition, Yonatan ('Yoni') Netanyahu had always retained a serious side. He was the son of a history professor at Cornell University and attended high school in Pennsylvania. He joined the Israeli Defence Force at 18 in 1964 and three years later was commanding a parachute company in the desperate fighting in the Sinai desert during the Six Day War. He then went on to Harvard, excelling at philosophy and mathematics, and was on the 'Dean's List' after only a year, but was sufficiently worried about what was going on back in Israel to return to study at Jerusalem's Hebrew University, his patriotism tinged with despair:

> The real cause is the sense of helplessness in the face of a war that has no end. For the war has not ended, and it seems to me that it will go on and on… This is the 'quiet' before the next storm. I've no doubt that war will come. Nor do I doubt that we will win. But for how long? Until when?… We're young, and we were not born for wars alone.

With these anxious views, it was hardly surprising that within months he felt that he should rejoin the army and he now opted for one of Israel's elite special forces units, *Sayeret Matkal*, and was soon its deputy commanding officer.

He was involved in many daring raids and operations, such as the destruction of the Palestine Liberation Organisation's (PLO) Black September leadership after their kidnap and killing of Israeli athletes at the 1972 Munich Olympics. It was a foretaste of Israel's determination to use a very long arm of retribution against those who harmed her.

'He went first, he fell first'. Yoni Netanyahu, the planner and leader of the spectacular rescue raid at Entebbe, was the only Israeli military casualty. (Netanyahu family)

After winning Israel's highest award, the Medal of Distinguished Service, during the Yom Kippur War in 1973, Yoni rebuilt and briefly commanded a tank brigade before taking over the leadership of his old Special Forces Unit, just in time for another intended atrocity against Israel.

The drama started in Athens, where a young woman and three young men, recently arrived from Bahrain, boarded Air France flight 139 on its way from Israel to Paris. Eight minutes after take-off, the four took over the aircraft with its 246 passengers at gunpoint, and forced it to land at Benghazi in Libya. Yoni was deployed with his unit to Israel's Lod airport in case it landed there, but it then, surprisingly, flew south towards Africa. With 77 Israelis and many Jewish tourists on board, it was a nightmare scenario for the Israeli government. Two of the hijackers were PLO terrorists and two were German: Brigitte Kuhlmann and Wilfried Böse, the overall leader.

The aircraft landed at Entebbe in Uganda, and it rapidly became plain that Idi Amin was an accomplice in the hijacking. A murderous and unpredictable dictator, he had expelled all Israelis from Uganda when Israel had understandably refused to lend him some Phantom jets to bomb Kenya and Tanzania in 1972.

Entebbe in June 1976 was an obscure small town, its international airport building the one reminder that only a few years before it had been the capital of Uganda. By great good fortune, an Israeli contractor had built Entebbe airport. The terminal's old blueprints were to prove extremely useful.

The hijackers were joined by three additional terrorists and were very obviously being supported by Idi Amin's forces. They demanded the release of 53 Palestinians held in Israel and other countries and threatened to start killing the hostages. The non-Jewish hostages were released and flown out, but Air France's Captain Michel Bacos and his crew honourably refused to leave with them, so now 103 hostages faced an agonizing wait.

The Israeli government tried to negotiate in good faith and did gain three more days before the executions started, during which time they interviewed the released hostages about the hijackers.

As one of the country's most resourceful commanders, Yoni was now directed in 'very general terms' to plan some kind of rescue. He quickly gathered his officers to brainstorm and together they planned one of the most audacious long-distance rescues in history. Six aircraft were to fly the 2,500 miles to Entebbe. Two were command-and-hospital Boeing 707s, while four C-130 Hercules would contain 100 Israeli commandos. One blocking group, with light armoured vehicles, was to protect the operation and destroy Idi Amin's parked MIG-17 fighters in case they intervened. The second, the actual assault group, was to be led by Yoni Netanyahu himself.

The team worked into the night. 'Yoni was very tired, you could see it by looking at him,' recalled his second in command. But it was Yoni who then remained awake to perfect the plan while his exhausted officers snatched some sleep. Early in the morning, he went over to present his plan to Defence Minister Shimon Peres, who had said he wanted to look Yoni in the eyes and say 'Can it be done?' 'My impression,' recalls Peres, 'was of exactness and imagination and complete self-confidence.'

Yoni went home to say goodbye to his girlfriend, Bruria, and then rushed back to inspect and brief his men. The aircraft then flew south to Sharm-el-Sheikh to await the final government go-ahead. There Yoni gave his final briefing. 'It was a speech I'll never forget,' said Alex, one of his soldiers. 'He gave us confidence that we could do it. His leadership and his ability to affect us were simply above and beyond anything.'

Then the word to go came at last and the planes took off. Yoni managed to get some sleep. 'Where did this calmness of his come from?' wondered the co-pilot. Over Lake Victoria and with Entebbe now near, Yoni went back to brief his assault group. 'In this reddish light, he spoke to the men, smiled at us, said a few words of encouragement to each one. It was as though he were leaving us, as though he knew what was going to happen to him. He acted more like a friend.'

They landed in the darkness just before midnight. To gain surprise, a large Mercedes (borrowed from a Tel Aviv car dealer) drove towards the terminal, escorted by two Landrovers – appearing just like Idi Amin on one of his frequent visits to tease the hostages. The assault team burst into the building, shouting 'Get down! Get down!' in Hebrew and English, shooting three of the terrorists.

'Where are the rest of them?'

The terrified hostages pointed to a connecting door. Grenades, then shots accounted for the last four hijackers. Sadly, three hostages had been killed in the cross-fire, but the rest were bundled gratefully on to the aircraft, in spite of increasing fire from Ugandan troops. It was all over in less than an hour.

But tragedy had struck. Yoni had been hit in the chest leading the assault and had died slowly on the tarmac, while his men obeyed his strict order not to stop for anything. As they lifted into the air, the excited soldiers soon fell silent in the planes when the news filtered in. Back in Israel's Ministry of Defence, the champagne and initial euphoria were soon forgotten as Chief of Staff Motta Gur had to break the news to his minister. 'Yoni's gone. A bullet hit him in the heart.' Shimon Peres wrote in his diary, 'For the first time in this whole crazy week, I cannot hold back the tears.'

As he had written all those years before, Yoni had indeed willingly sacrificed his life for a purpose.

LANCE-CORPORAL PATRICK KENNEALLY AND HIS BREN GUN

Prime Minister Winston Churchill paid tribute to the gallantry of the Irish during his famous May 1945 broadcast 'Five years of war', during which he told listeners of 'Lance-Corporal Kenneally and other heroes I could cite – and all bitterness for the Irish race dies in my heart'. He was making a laudable effort to be even-handed after his former pro-Unionist attitude to Ireland and the Irish struggle for independence.

However, the irony was that Kenneally was not Irish at all. 'John Patrick Kenneally' was an assumed name. He was actually more English than Churchill, being Leslie Robinson, the illegitimate son of an 18-year-old daughter of a Blackpool chemist. His father was apparently Neville Blond, later the chairman of the English Stage Company and husband of Elaine Marks, the Marks & Spencer heiress. So the young man was half-English, half-Jewish.

Always keen on adventure, Leslie joined the Royal Artillery on his 18th birthday and found himself in an anti-aircraft battery at Dollis Hill in London. He went 'absent without leave' and was detained at Wellington Barracks. He was so impressed by his gaolers, the Irish Guards, that he applied for a transfer, which the Royal Artillery refused. So he deserted and went back to civilian life. Working on a building site in Glasgow with a team of Irish builders, he was given the identity card of John Patrick Kenneally, a man who had returned to Ireland. Now he was free to turn up at the Manchester recruiting office to join the Irish Guards, a regiment formed in 1900 on Queen Victoria's orders because she considered the 'bravery and performance of my Irish soldiers' to be one of the few positive highlights of the Boer War. The Irish Guards, 'the Micks', became one of Britain's finest and best-loved regiments, famous for its disciplined bravery and acts of impulsive personal gallantry. So it was hardly surprising that 'Patrick Kenneally' should soon be fêted as 'a typical Mick, loving a good fight'.

Lance-Corporal 'Patrick Kenneally' receives his Victoria Cross from his commander in chief, General Alexander — who was also the colonel of his regiment. (Irish Guards)

In April 1943, General Sir Harold Alexander was planning his final assault on Tunis. The massive rock-strewn feature of Djebel Bou Azoukaz, 'The Bou', blocked his way. After two days of bitter fighting the Irish Guards had secured the central mile-long ridge. But they had suffered terrible casualties. Four companies of Guardsmen had been reduced to one and many of the officers and NCOs had been killed. Just 173 men were on their feet.

It was vital that they held off the vicious counter-attacks by the 8th Panzer Regiment. Kenneally saw below him a whole company of German Panzer Grenadiers forming up to attack. Leaping to his feet, he charged down the rocky hill, firing his Bren light machine gun from the hip. The German attack broke up in confusion (and probably disbelief).

What *is* unbelievable is that two days later he did it all over again, with the same victorious result. This time he was wounded, but continued to hop around the battlefield all day, supported by a Guardsman and firing his Bren gun, refusing to give it up 'as he was the only one who understood it'.

He proudly received his Victoria Cross from his army commander (who happened to be also colonel of the regiment), General Alexander.

Even 'Alex' probably thought he was giving it to a fellow Irishman.

CAPTAIN DANJOU AND HIS FIGHT TO THE DEATH

Each year, on 30 April, at their base at Aubagne in the south of France, the men of the French Foreign Legion are paraded, and the most decorated officer present reads out the story of Camerone. Then a wooden forearm and hand are solemnly carried out on to parade and the Legionnaires march past in salute.

The French Foreign Legion was formed in 1831 by King Louis Philippe. Its purpose was to use, for France's benefit, various volunteers like failed revolutionaries, footloose foreign soldiers and even those on the run for petty crimes, perhaps lovesick or just bored with civilian life. Few questions were asked about their past and many used false names. From such apparently unlikely material, the Legion became, and remains, one of the world's elite fighting units, with a unique 'Code of Honour' and great *ésprit de corps*. Based in North Africa, it was always led by the finest French officers and often found itself in some desperate situations all over the world. One of them was Mexico.

In April 1863, France found herself locked into an ill-fated attempt to impose the Austrian Archduke Maximilian on Mexico, ruled by Benito Juarez. France soon had 40,000 troops there, including 4,000 of the Foreign Legion. But even the Legion had been ravaged by dysentery, typhus and yellow fever, with many of its officers and men laid low by illness. On 29 April, the 1st Battalion of the Legion was guarding the road from Vera Cruz and was ordered to send a company to escort a vital convoy carrying three million francs and munitions to the troops besieging the town of Puebla. But all the 3rd Company's own officers were on their sick beds. So Captain Jean Danjou, the battalion's quartermaster, without hesitation decided to volunteer himself. He was a top graduate of the Saint-Cyr military academy and a seasoned Legion veteran of many wars. He had also lost his hand ten years before in battle and wore a wooden prosthetic replica. Together with two other volunteers, the pay officer, Lieutenant Vilain, and Second Lieutenant Maudet, Danjou led 62 Legionnaires out on to the dusty, dangerous road to Puebla.

Early in the morning of 30 April, soon after passing a deserted and ruined little hamlet called Camerón, they were suddenly attacked by 800 of Colonel Milan's Juarist Mexican cavalry, soon followed by 1,200 infantry.

The Legionnaires conducted a steady fighting retreat over the mile back to Camerón through the dense scrub that

The wooden hand of Captain Danjou, which is paraded and saluted every year by the French Foreign Legion to celebrate Camerone. (French War Ministry)

luckily protected them a little. But they had already lost 18 men and, almost worse, the pack mules with their spare rations, precious water and ammunition. Danjou's men desperately fortified Camerón's crumbling hacienda with its high corral walls. All that morning, they beat off assault after brave Mexican assault. They also refused Milan's demands for surrender. 'We have munitions, we will not surrender', Danjou calmly replied. He also swore to fight to the death and made his men, one by one, swear the same.

But with 2,000 Mexican rifles firing at them, casualties mounted steadily. At noon, Captain Danjou was shot in the chest, two Legionnaires vainly protecting his body until he died. Vilain stoutly continued the defence, refusing fresh Mexican demands to surrender. His men had not had food or water since the previous day, and were reeling from hunger and, especially, thirst, in the intense heat. Vilain was killed at 2pm and Maudet took command, even resisting an attempt to burn them out.

But by the evening only Maudet, a corporal and four Legionnaires were still standing, and with only one bullet left per man. So Maudet drew his sword and ordered them to fix bayonets. They charged the mass of amazed Mexicans. Maudet and two men were quickly shot down, but the last three were pinned down and spared. Even then they refused to surrender unless, in accordance with their Code of Honour, 'we can care for our injured men and retain our rifles'.

'Nothing can be refused to men like you', agreed the Mexican officer.

Colonel Milan did indeed make sure that his men cared for them and the other wounded (32 survived to fight in other campaigns). He even let them send back a message, 'The 3rd of the 1st has died, my Colonel, but it did enough to make those who spoke of it say, "It had nothing but good soldiers."'

Colonel Milan's chivalry and admiration were all the more impressive when you consider that he had lost 300 men killed and 300 more wounded. Moreover, by wasting time fighting the Legion, almost as a matter of honour, he had also lost the bullion convoy, which had used the time to escape back towards Vera Cruz. Three weeks later, a vengeful Legion duly took Puebla and then led the way into Mexico City.

The Emperor, Napoleon III, ordered that *Camerone*, in the French spelling, be embroidered on to the Legion's colours, and that the names of Danjou, Vilain and Maudet be engraved in gold in Les Invalides in Paris. And at Camerón itself, a monument was erected in 1892. Mexican troops salute it to this day.

And every year the Legion still carries out that strange ceremony of saluting a wooden hand.

CODE OF HONOUR OF THE FRENCH FOREIGN LEGION

- Légionnaire, you are a volunteer serving France with honour and fidelity.
- Every Légionnaire is your brother-in-arms, regardless of his nationality, race or religion. You will demonstrate this with strict solidarity, which must always unite members of the same family.
- Respect of traditions, devotion to your leaders, discipline and comradeship are your strengths, courage and loyalty your virtues.
- Proud of your status as a Légionnaire, you display this in your uniform, which is always impeccable, your behaviour always dignified but modest, your living-quarters always clean.
- An elite soldier, you will train rigorously, you will maintain your weapon as your most precious possession, you are constantly concerned with your physical fitness.
- A mission is sacred, you will carry it out until the end, respecting laws, customs of war, international conventions and, if necessary, at the risk of your life.
- In combat, you will act without passion and without hate, you will respect the vanquished enemy, you will never abandon your dead or wounded, nor surrender your arms.

GEORGE WELCH, KENNETH TAYLOR AND PEARL HARBOR

It was a beautiful Sunday morning at Pearl Harbor. Rows of proud battleships rode peacefully at anchor, in a low state of readiness that only required them to be able to get up steam in 12 hours and with only a quarter of their guns manned.

Fighter planes were crowded in neat rows, not only to make it easier to guard against local sabotage, but also to make room for the troops who had paraded for the previous day's Saturday Morning Inspection.

At 6.30am, the support ship USS *Antares* had spotted a midget submarine trying to enter the harbour. The destroyer USS *Ward* fired at it, depth charged it and sunk it. Nobody reacted to *Ward*'s report.

At 7.02am, young Lieutenant Kermit Tyler at the new Information Center decided that the very large and fast-moving blip reported by the radar operators at Opana Point was just some B-17s arriving from California and told them 'not to worry about it'.

At 8am, the band was starting to play on the deck of the battleship *Nevada* for the 'Colors' ceremony, when the music was drowned out by the snarl of aircraft engines and then explosions.

Many of the fighter pilots had been up all night dancing and playing poker at the Officers' Club. Their tuxedos hung on the backs of chairs while they slept. Suddenly they were woken by a plane roaring past. 'The damned Navy, buzzing us again to hurt our hangovers.' Then an explosion. 'My God, one of those idiots had crashed.' They rushed outside. The sky was full of planes. 'Japs, they're Japs!'

Japanese planes circle round the battleships moored off Ford Island, Pearl Harbor. (Tony Cowland)

Those neat rows of lined-up American fighters were being demolished by strafing Zeros, unfortunately helped by one courageous P-40 pilot, whose plane was hit on take-off and cartwheeled, blazing, down the line.

Second Lieutenants George Welch and Kenneth Taylor had just decided to have a nightcap after an all-night party. They took in the horrific scene at a glance. Their own planes were luckily parked for gunnery training at the little auxiliary grass airstrip at Haleiwa, 10 miles away. While Welch ran for Taylor's new red Buick, Taylor, without authority, shouted down the phone to Haleiwa, 'Get two P-40s ready. No, it's not a gag – the Japs are here!'

They drove at breakneck speed, dodging Japanese aircraft, leapt into their warmed-up fighters, still dressed in Tuxedo trousers, and, trailing dust, thundered down the runway. Over the Marine base at Ewa they caught up with 12 'Val' dive-bombers and each shot one down. Taylor chased another out to sea and it plunged into the ocean. Agile and deadly Zeros soon homed in on the American pair. Welch's P-40 was hit, he dived into the protective cloud, decided the damage was not serious and emerged to shoot down another 'Val'. Both pilots then landed in the burning chaos of Wheeler Field to rearm and refuel. Courageous mechanics had to fight their way into a blazing hangar to retrieve ammunition belts.

Just as they were about to take off, some senior officers started to lecture them on unauthorized behaviour. But the next wave of Japanese scattered the crowd and the two young pilots roared off straight at the enemy. Taylor reported, 'I took off towards them, which gave me the ability to shoot at them before I even left the ground.' After shooting down an enemy plane, Taylor was wounded in the left arm by a bullet which smashed through his canopy, missing his head by inches. He later revealed his main annoyance was that his 'new Tuxedo trousers had been ruined by the fragments'.

A handful of other pilots had managed to get into the air against the 350 Japanese planes to try to shoot

George Welch and Kenneth Taylor, the most famous of those who managed to get into the air to defend Pearl Harbor. (US Air Force)

them down or be shot down – one tragically shot down trying to join the slim P-40s in his tubby P-36, a fate shared by several others.

If just a little more time had been gained, the battle might have been less one-sided. The Japanese lost 29 aircraft, the Americans lost 188 with 159 damaged, while 19 ships were sunk or damaged.

Welch and Taylor were designated the first American heroes of the war. At the time, Welch was credited with four kills and Taylor with two, but Japanese records showed that Taylor had also downed four of the Japanese planes.

Both were nominated for the Medal of Honor, America's highest award for gallantry, supported by their Air Force Commander, General 'Hap' Arnold. But other officers, perhaps smarting from being caught out so badly, downgraded the awards to the Distinguished Service Cross – for the ridiculous reason that 'they had taken off without proper authorization'.

Thus, on that famous 'Day of Infamy', this was the rather shabby reward for two Americans who *did* rise to the occasion at Pearl Harbor.

Both pilots survived the war, Kenneth Taylor ending up a brigadier-general. George Welch, having notched up another 12 victories, became a test pilot. His friends and family feel he was cheated a second time out of a Medal of Honor. He broke the sound barrier secretly in a jet P-86 Sabre, one week before Chuck Yeager's historic flight in the Bell XS-1. However, as his Sabre was soon to be operational, the facts about its performance had to remain secret, and Chuck Yeager got the glory.

'H' JONES AND THE FALKLANDS

In May 1982, the brave action of 'H' Jones and many like him at Goose Green in the Falklands indirectly led to the previously unpopular Prime Minister Margaret Thatcher being branded 'the successful war leader' and to her easy victory in the forthcoming General Election. The Falklands War, however, had been instigated by the Argentinean Junta nearly two months earlier – with a naive and peculiar lack of military knowledge or political insight.

A public-relations friend of mine, Dan Murphy, used to work in Buenos Aires. He had been a signals officer in Vietnam before moving back to Argentina. On 1 April 1982 came a knocking on the door. Standing there was a captain of the Argentine Army who said, 'The Junta wish to see you immediately.'

At that time, when military cars came for you, it could be very frightening. All too often you might be joining *los desaparecidos* – the 'disappeared ones'. But, to his relief, he was driven to the 'Casa Rosada', the famous pink parliament building, and was ushered into a room full of officers, with General Galtieri and two other members of the Junta. One other foreigner was in the room, an Israeli called Cohen, who imported fruit. It transpired that he and Dan were the only people in the whole of Argentina, population 32 million, who had any combat experience.

A senior officer turned to Dan and said, 'Señor Murphy, tomorrow we attack the Malvinas. What do you think of that?'

Not knowing if the Argentineans celebrated April Fool's Day, Dan responded, 'If you attack with 2,000 children waving flowers or maybe 2,000 penguins, I think you will be all right. But if you attack with real troops, I think that Señora Thatcher will attack back.'

The officer stared coldly at him and exclaimed 'Ridículo!' Even though Mr Cohen agreed with Dan, they were ushered from the room while the High Command continued their ill-fated plans.

This farcical pattern of asking an American PR man and an Israeli fruit importer for their strategic advice – and then rejecting it – continued every few days throughout the Falklands War. It was also part of the Argentineans' complete misunderstanding of what 'that Señora Thatcher' would have to do. The first woman prime minister, the 'Iron Lady', as the Russians called her, was then very unpopular. So, there was no way she could now allow a piece of British 'sovereign territory', however remote, to be captured without a fight.

For the Argentineans, whose schoolchildren coloured maps of 'Las Malvinas' in their national colour, blue, it was about to be the 150th anniversary of their claim to the islands. The Junta, with an economic crisis and civil unrest, thought them a perfect, popular distraction.

By the 1980s, the British government had indeed been seeking to get rid of this strange outpost, with around 2,000 inhabitants, a number of whom were sheep farmers and fishermen, because it was considered 'impossible to defend'. It proposed that the Falklands should be handed over to Argentina with a long-term lease back to Britain. Perhaps new generations of islanders, less attached to British heritage, would eventually welcome becoming Argentine citizens. But the proposal coincided with an oppressive military regime in Buenos Aires. Thousands of citizens, men, women and children, were being kidnapped, tortured and murdered. Many were never seen again. The idea of being handed over to such a country was completely unacceptable.

With negotiations stalled, the Argentineans heard that, as part of defence cuts, Britain was going to scrap HMS *Endurance*, the ice patrol and electronic surveillance ship and Britain's only presence in the South Atlantic. They sensed Britain's waning interest and decided to seize their chance.

As tension increased, too late did Britain deploy submarines to the South Atlantic. The news pushed Argentina into mounting her invasion. On 2 April, thousands of Argentine troops attacked Port Stanley, overpowering the tiny Royal Marines garrison and forcing surrender on Governor Rex Hunt.

In fact, Argentina had decided to strike at the worst possible time. If they had waited, Britain's two aircraft carriers, *Hermes* and *Invincible*, would have been sold or scrapped. As it was, half the other ships involved were exercising off Gibraltar and were thus ready to sail south. Moreover, even though it was Easter, all the troops initially required were in the right place. So, to the amazement of everyone, Margaret Thatcher was able to send off a Task Force within 72 hours. It would eventually comprise 100 ships and 25,000 men. It was a very impressive piece of logistics.

'H' Jones, (centre) a Parachute Regiment commander who believed in leading from the front. (Parachute Regiment)

When, after 8,000 miles, the Task Force arrived off the Falklands, it faced a stiff task. The Argentinean Navy, which had pushed hardest for the invasion, was seemingly neutralized by fear after the cruiser *Belgrano* had been sunk by the submarine HMS *Conqueror*. But their air force was certainly not and, with great bravery, attacked with bombs and Exocet anti-ship missiles. HMS *Sheffield* was the first to be destroyed, but not the last. Without long-distance early-warning radar, the handful of vertical-take-off Harriers could not stop every attack.

For the actual invasion, the plan was to go into the sheltered waters of San Carlos inlet (a move predicted by Dan Murphy and Mr Cohen and, as usual, rejected as 'ridículo!'). A key element was the container ship *Atlantic Conveyor* and her precious cargo of big Chinook helicopters, which had to be unloaded quickly.

But now the Argentineans launched a deadly Exocet missile attack. The resulting destruction of the *Atlantic Conveyor* and its helicopters meant the loss of the means to move troops forward quickly to recapture Port Stanley. But Margaret Thatcher was putting pressure on the army commanders to get the soldiers moving quickly. The only option was to walk.

Before the forces began their punishing battle march to Port Stanley, their commander, Brigadier Thompson, had really wanted them to dig in at San Carlos and set up a bridgehead. But London disagreed. It felt that it was vital to move out of the bridgehead to bolster international opinion. The army was irritated by this political pressure, feeling there was no point in advancing until the logistics were in place. They might run out of ammunition or food and so be defeated unnecessarily. Thompson says: 'We needed to be balanced and ready to go and, until we were, I was not keen on rushing off to Stanley.'

But the War Cabinet in Whitehall wanted victory fast and ordered Thompson to advance. The Royal Marines duly 'yomped' off north, heading towards Port Stanley, 86 miles away. Meanwhile 400 paratroopers of the 2nd Battalion were ordered to attack the Argentine garrison at Goose Green, where the British would be outnumbered and outgunned by three to one. London itself then managed to remove any element of surprise. Keen to show off British military prowess and boost public morale, Whitehall briefed the British media on the precise route – a full day before the attack. The BBC's World Service was heard by the Argentineans.

The Goose Green attack began on the night of 27 May with a short naval bombardment. The plan was for a rapid advance, but with 400 British Paras now facing 1,500 Argentineans, and a serious malfunction in the naval gunfire support, progress was slow. Owing to lack of resources, the soldiers had only enough ammunition for a raid and very limited mortar fire. 'We were down to relying on courage, bayonets, machine guns and close gutter fighting.'

2 Para's Commander was Lieutenant-Colonel Herbert Jones, known as 'H'. Educated at Eton, he had transferred to the Parachute Regiment from the Devonshire and Dorset Regiment. He was an impatient, energetic leader who believed passionately in leading his men from the front. As they advanced they were held up, incurring casualties from 11 well-prepared trenches on a ridge. To maintain momentum, Jones took forward his reconnaissance party and continued to fight through, despite heavy fire. To gain a good viewpoint, he was now at the very front of his battalion. Feeling that desperate measures were needed, he seized the initiative by taking a sub-machine gun and with a small number of men charged up the slope. 'H' was shot in the back from a trench he had already passed.

Second in command Major Chris Keeble received the signal 'Sunray is down'. He assumed command of a battle that had already fallen badly behind, in broad daylight, across bare terrain. One in five of his troops had been injured or killed, but having witnessed the heroism of Lt Col Jones, Keeble lead the paras. The will of the hungry and conscripted Argentineans evaporated. They gave up – 1,200 of them.

'H' Jones was awarded the Victoria Cross posthumously. He joined the amazing number of 37 Old Etonians who have won the VC for outstanding courage in battle. Some criticized the idea of a senior officer taking such risks, leading from the front. But for others, such rising to the occasion was an inspiration.

Today, Goose Green – still surrounded by sheep – retains its lonely evidence of the conflict, including the Argentinean cemetery, the memorial to the Parachute Regiment and a simple stone memorial to 'H' Jones.

2

BUCKING THE ODDS

HORATIUS AND HIS BRIDGE

If there is one name that symbolizes a warrior selflessly rising to the occasion, it is that of Horatius. In its English version, Horatio, it was a name that the mothers of Lord Nelson and Lord Kitchener certainly thought appropriate for future heroes, as did Shakespeare for Hamlet's best friend, or C. S. Forester for his *Hornblower* – and even the scriptwriters of television's *CSI Miami*.

The action of Horatius in saving Rome, assuming that the Roman historian Livy's account is accurate, played a serious role in the growth of Europe and, above all, of its first powerhouse, Rome.

Lars Porsena of Clusium
By the nine Gods he swore
That the great house of Tarquin
Should suffer wrong no more.

In his famous poem (which Winston Churchill could recite in full), Lord Macaulay was being rather generous about Lars Porsena's motives in gathering an army to attack Rome. The man whom he was trying to help, Lucius Tarquinius Superbus ('Tarquin the Proud'), was one of the most unpleasant men to rule Rome, akin to brutal and mad emperors like Nero, Caligula and Commodus centuries later. He was to be the last Etruscan king of Rome – and indeed, the last king of Rome.

Horatius defends the gate while the bridge into Rome is being destroyed behind him. (After the engraving by John Reinhard Weguelin, 1879)

The Etruscans had been the dominant force in Italy for two centuries. Originally from Asia Minor, they had a strange language that has still not been translated. The largest of their city states was Clusium (modern Chiusi). They were good soldiers and sailors, and traded far afield. Women played an important public role and helped their artistic growth. But there was also a class conflict between the patricians and the working classes that would play a fateful role in their dealings with Rome.

'Tarquin the Proud', an Etruscan, seized power in Rome in 535 BC. He was furious that he had been passed over as king by his father in favour of his more deserving father-in-law, Servius Tullius. Tarquin managed to persuaded the Senate to remove Servius and then he assassinated him. His evil wife, Tullia, then rode her chariot repeatedly over her father's body, a vivid example of filial faithlessness!

Once consolidated in power by further killings, Tarquin employed relations and foreign mercenaries in his army, while forcing his own working class to dig drains, all part of his contemptuous Etruscan attitude that caused bitter and mounting resentment. He also instilled in his sons his own cynical approach to life. In his garden, he once cut the heads off some poppies, urging his son Sextus to kill the leading citizens of a captured city. Such a 'Tall Poppy Syndrome' would have had the full approval of Joseph Stalin and Adolf Hitler.

But it was his son's behaviour that would ruin Tarquin. Sextus went off and raped Lucretia, the virtuous wife of one of his best friends. When her distraught father and husband arrived to hear the tale, she killed herself with a knife. It was the last straw. A spontaneous revolt erupted, the resentful Roman working class joined it, and the gates of Rome were slammed in 'Tarquin the Proud's' face. So it was really for these rather unworthy reasons that Tarquin asked for Lars Porsena's support to get back his throne. Eventually, a huge and destructive army approached Rome.

> Now, from the rock Tarpeian,
> Could the wan burghers spy
> The line of blazing villages
> Red in the midnight sky.

The outer protective fort, the Janiculum, was captured by the Etruscans and it became apparent that, to save the city, the last bridge, the wooden Pons Publicius, would have to be quickly destroyed.

Obviously, this was going to take time, but the narrowness of the bridge gate meant that it might just be defended for long enough against an army. While many of the Roman citizens and soldiers fled in panic, a volunteer called Horatius Cocles (the one-eyed – 'Cocles' is a variant of the Greek 'Cyclops') rose to the occasion. Macaulay describes his reaction to the crisis:

> Then out spake brave Horatius,
> The Captain of the gate:
> 'To every man upon this earth
> Death cometh soon or late.
> And how can man die better
> Than facing fearful odds,
> For the ashes of his fathers
> And the temples of his Gods.
> Hew down the bridge, Sir Consul,
> With all the speed ye may;
> I, with two more to help me
> Will hold the foe in play.
> In yon strait path a thousand
> May well be stopped by three.
> Now who will stand on either hand,
> And keep the bridge with me?

Two companions, Titus Herminius and Spurius Lartius, stepped forward, and with them Horatius fought the finest that the Etruscans could send against them, until the bridge was collapsed behind him. Horatius plunged into the River Tiber and was saved, as was Rome itself. He was honoured by being given as much land as he could plough in a day, and by a one-eyed brass statue in the Temple of Vulcanus.

Tarquin never regained power and he and his wife died in exile. His rapist son Sextus was hunted down and killed.

The Romans understandably decided that having only one ruler was too dangerous, so they voted in two consuls (one of them Lucretia's widower), and declared Rome a republic. After Tarquin's thwarted attack, Rome went on the offensive, steadily capturing Etruscan cities and eventually eliminating their distinctive culture and identity. Rome became the dominant force in the ancient world for nearly 1,000 years, with its huge influence on every aspect of European life and culture.

DOUGLAS BADER AND HIS 'TIN LEGS'

The Bulldog fighter came across the airfield and began a slow roll, flying fast and low – too low. Its wing touched the ground and the biplane cartwheeled into a tangle of wood and metal. The shocked spectators watched the young pilot, with his legs hopelessly crushed, being pulled from the wreckage. What an end to a star career. What an end to a dream. And all for a dare! But they had not allowed for an extraordinary character called Douglas Bader.

It had been while staying with his aunt and her husband, the Adjutant of the Royal Air Force College at Cranwell, that the young Douglas Bader decided he wanted to fly. In 1928 he enrolled there, but his rebellious attitude nearly made him bottom of the class. Half way through his training, Cranwell's commandant, Air Vice Marshal Hanlahan, gave him a stinging rebuke. 'The Air Force wants men here, not schoolboys.' Bader's results and his flying improved dramatically. He played rugby and cricket for the RAF and he only just failed to be awarded Cranwell's 'Sword of Honour'.

So when he joined his squadron, all his dreams seemed to have come true – until that ridiculous, near-fatal crash. As he wrote later in his logbook, 'Crashed slow-rolling near ground. Bad show.'

Indeed it was. Both his legs had to be amputated, and none of the doctors expected him to live. But Bader had an indomitable spirit. He did live, and ruthlessly began to rebuild his life. He was the first customer of Marcel Desoutter, an aircraft designer who had lost his own leg and had turned to making aluminium ones.

After many agonizing months, Bader was able to walk again, always refusing a walking stick. 'I am going to start the way I mean to go on.' Then he was driving a car, and his thoughts turned to flying. Staying with the Under Secretary for Air, he was allowed to try out an Avro 504. He flew it perfectly. Then an RAF medical board passed him for 'restricted flying', but suddenly this was overturned because the situation 'was not covered by King's Regulations'. Invalided out of the RAF, Bader spent six bleak years behind a desk at Shell, his spirits kept up only by his devoted wife Thelma.

Then in 1939, Hitler intervened. With Britain now at war, all experienced pilots were needed, even 'crippled' ones, especially those vociferously volunteering. Pulling strings with Air Ministry friends, Bader then found himself at a selection board, once again facing Air Vice Marshal Halahan, who was much kinder this time, granting him flying duties and allowing the Central Flying School the decision to 'pass him or not'. Bader passed. What is more, he could actually fly even better than most fighter pilots because in tight turns he did not 'black out' due to blood draining to the legs – he had none!

Eight years after his accident he was in a Spitfire, a flight commander in 19 Squadron at Duxford, commanded by an old friend. He soon shot down a German fighter over Dunkirk, the first of many.

In June 1940, Bader took over a Canadian squadron. Badly mauled over France, the morale of its pilots was at a low ebb and they were naturally sceptical of their legless new squadron leader, who they assumed would be desk-bound. But half an hour of stunning aerobatics in a Hurricane convinced them, and he soon welded the squadron into a tough and effective unit, not least by his uncompromising attitude to everyone including his superiors. When he found out that they did not have enough spare parts, he sent a blunt signal to Group Headquarters: '242 Squadron operational as regards pilots, but not operational as regards equipment.' He refused to budge until the tools arrived 24 hours later.

Douglas Bader was either hated or loved. He could be arrogant, opinionated and dogmatic. Most of his immediate colleagues loved him. Johnny Johnson, another legendary pilot, later wrote of the way Bader bound them together with invisible threads of trust and comradeship.

Most pilots also agreed with Bader's three basic rules:

If you have the height, you control the battle.

If you come out of the sun, the enemy cannot see you.

If you hold your fire until you are very close, you seldom miss.

However, another of his concepts during the Battle of Britain was more controversial, the so-called 'Big Wing'. With the support of his group controller, Air Vice Marshal Trafford Leigh-Mallory, he advocated getting three or even five squadrons together to hit the huge German formations. In practice, it often did not work, taking too long to assemble.

But on one day, crucially, it did. On 15 September 1940, the German pilots had been assured by Goering and their other leaders that the RAF was 'down to its last 50 fighters'. But that day, as they lumbered towards London, the Luftwaffe formations were savaged by squadron after squadron of Spitfires and Hurricanes. Suddenly, they were faced by the awesome sight of five squadrons, 60 fighters of Bader's 'Big Wing' thundering in perfect formation out of the sky. They scattered, losing dozens of planes and finally convincing the German High Command that the battle was lost.

Two days later, Hitler postponed the invasion indefinitely and turned towards Russia, the daylight raids petered out and the assembled invasion barges in France drifted away. For that alone, Bader and his 'Big Wing' should be thanked.

The RAF then went on to the offensive, with Bader, in his Spitfire marked 'DB' ('Dogsbody'), becoming a legendary and rather eccentric wing leader. He would relax his pilots on the way out by commenting on the radio 'that 18th green could do with mowing, couldn't it?' On the way back, he used to light his pipe before

Douglas Bader lifts his artificial right leg into his Spitfire, DB (Dogsbody). Soon the plane would be cut in half, just behind the 'D', in a collision with a German fighter, but Bader would escape. (RAF Benevolent Fund)

landing. With 22.5 enemy planes to his credit, he christened his Tangmere Wing 'The Bee Line Bus Service. The prompt regular service – return tickets only.'

But one day, Bader himself did not use his return ticket, because in a dogfight over St Omer he felt his Spitfire lurch as if clutched by a great hand, then plunge straight down, the control column flopping loose in his hands. Glancing back, he saw that the tail and whole fuselage just behind him had disappeared, sliced clean off by a German fighter. The hood jettisoned, and using only his arms he struggled to get out, then stuck fast, his leg trapped, his face battered and torn by the 500mph slipstream. Suddenly, something below him snapped and he was free, leaving the false leg that had saved his life to smash into the ground with his Spitfire. He floated to earth and capture.

The Germans were quite amazed that they had been battling a legless pilot, and the German ace Adolph Galland sportingly allowed a new 'tin leg' to be parachuted in. Douglas Bader did not really return the courtesy, immediately trying to escape from St Omer hospital and later, time and again, from prison camps. Eventually, the exasperated Germans secured him in Colditz until he was liberated.

It was Douglas Bader who was given the honour to lead the RAF's 300-plane victory fly-past over Buckingham Palace. He then retired to devote himself to the cause of disabled people, for which he was knighted.

There cannot be many people who have risen to the occasion time and time again in such a way.

GEORGE WASHINGTON AND THE DELAWARE

We have become used to feeling it rather disrespectful or even unsporting for military attacks to be planned for the Sabbath. The list of 'sneak attacks' on religious holidays is a long one. Sunday 7 December 1941, the 'Day of Infamy' of the Japanese attacks on Pearl Harbor and the Philippines; Hitler's Operation *Barbarossa* against his 'ally' Russia; Egypt's war on the Jewish holy day of Yom Kippur; North Korea's Sunday morning invasion of the south, the 'Tet Offensive' in Vietnam.

However, if one has no strong religious scruples, a holy day is a perfect opportunity. The enemy's personnel are on weekend leave, and even those on duty may be suffering from the 'night before'.

So it comes as a bit of a shock to discover that the great George Washington, America's future first president, carried out his greatest coup to coincide with the religious festival of Christmas Day. It is also a shock to remind oneself that the War of Independence lasted longer than World War II.

George Washington was an experienced soldier, having fought for the British against the French for many years, before he settled down as a Virginia planter and politician, married to a rich widow.

When, after years of Townsend's and Lord North's foolish taxes, fighting broke out in 1775, George Washington appeared at the Second Continental Congress in military uniform. It was apparent to all that he had experience, military bearing, charisma and political support. There was no contest – he was elected Commander in Chief.

The British openly admired his courage, endurance and attention to the welfare of his troops and would compare him, rather favourably, to their own commanders.

This famous painting by Emanuel Leutze shows Washington in his daring attack across the Delaware River. In fact, it would have been even more difficult than portrayed, because the actual attack was in pitch darkness in the middle of the night. (Bettmann / Corbis)

Nevertheless, the British were undoubtedly experienced foes and the fact was that Washington won only three of the nine battles that he fought against them. But one of them, a tiny one, was to prove decisive, inspirational and a turning point in the whole war.

After the battle of Long Island was lost, Washington and his American army were forced to abandon both Boston and New York, and they retreated into New Jersey. The Declaration of Independence in the summer of that year, 1776, was beginning to have a hollow ring. The very survival of Washington's army was threatened, and in more ways than one, for, in addition to a lack of ammunition, weakened confidence and low morale, many of his troops might actually just leave on 31 December 1776 because their enlistment was due to expire. By the New Year, Washington might not have an army at all. He needed a victory – a 'spectacular' as we would call it today – and he needed it very quickly.

He decided to strike completely unexpectedly at the Hessians camped on the other side of the Delaware River. They were mercenary soldiers used by the British (the German state of Hesse had been furnishing troops for foreigners for generations). His choice of Christmas Day was also carefully planned. Of all the British forces, the Hessians were known to 'enjoy' their Christmas, and he counted on the likelihood that by Christmas night many of them would be drunk or out to the world.

Having been reinforced to about 6,000 fit-for-duty men, Washington resolved to use 2,400 of them on a surprise night attack in three columns across the Delaware River on 25 December, landing by boats at midnight. In the event, the conditions were appalling. A hail and snow storm and blocks of ice floating down the river delayed his landing until about 3am. Two of his columns were forced back by the dreadful weather, but he led his own forces to burst upon the Hessians and rout them, killing 22, wounding 98 and capturing 900. Only three Americans were killed, two of them from exposure.

Within days, the Americans had followed their success on the Delaware with a victory at Princeton, and the British were driven out of New Jersey. Washington's army was transformed.

The war would drag on for many more years, but after the British surrender at Yorktown, and the Treaty of Paris acknowledging the independence of the United States, George Washington would say goodbye to his soldiers on 23 December 1783 – almost seven years to the day after his famous attack across the river. However, the United States was not about to say goodbye to Washington. He became its first president, so popular and revered that he twice received 100 per cent of the electoral votes.

In modern terms, his daring attack across the river might be judged as little more than a raid, and his battle a skirmish. But its effects make it one of the decisive battles of history. Without it the American Army might have given up and dissolved, George Washington, perhaps demoted and disgraced, might have been a footnote of colonial history, and New York might still be the capital of Britain's largest colony.

ELIZABETH I AND THE 'INVINCIBLE' ARMADA

Looking out across the Atlantic near Limerick in the west of Ireland is a headland called Spanish Point. There, in September 1588, the *San Marcos* and other ships of the Spanish Armada foundered on the rocky shore. The survivors were all killed on orders of Sir Turlough O'Brien and Boethius Clancy, High Sheriff of County Clare, some at *Cnoc na Crochaire*, 'Gallows Hill'. And those orders came straight from Queen Elizabeth I, one of Britain's most resourceful and successful monarchs.

Even as a baby, Elizabeth was a part of the political and religious situation that would one day launch the Armada against her. Henry VIII's lust for her mother, Anne Boleyn, had caused him to reject the Catholic Church, pocketing the proceeds from the dissolution of its monasteries.

Elizabeth I defied the might of the apparently invincible Armada. (Bettman / Corbis)

By divorcing Catherine of Aragon, he had equally offended the Pope and Spain. In his desperate quest for a male heir, he executed Anne, and Elizabeth and her elder sister Mary were declared illegitimate.

Elizabeth was quietly and privately educated. Speaking and writing Latin, Italian, French and Greek, she became the best-educated woman of her age. She also became used to keeping her own counsel, when her fervently religious sister Mary became Queen and reinstated Catholicism at the point of the sword. Elizabeth just survived imprisonment in the Tower of London, suspected of complicity in Protestant plots against her sister.

In November 1558, Elizabeth became Queen at 25, welcomed by an ecstatic people now thoroughly disillusioned by the excesses of 'Bloody Mary'.

The new young Queen listened carefully to her sensible advisors and adopted a cautious and tolerant approach to religion and everything else. In spite of this, Pope Pius V eventually excommunicated Elizabeth and denied that she was the rightful heir, starting the long and painful saga of Mary Queen of Scots, whom Elizabeth was forced to execute in 1587.

This execution, together with repeated English attacks on Spain's American treasure routes and support for the Protestant rebels in Holland, all combined to resolve the mind of Philip II of Spain, who was 'Bloody Mary's' former husband and once King Consort of England.

He decided to send a huge fleet, or Armada, under the command of the Duke of Medina Sidonia, to pick up troops from Flanders, invade England and restore the 'true religion'. He had the full support of Pope Sixtus V, who blessed the Armada's banner and collected crusade taxes for what was called *La Grande y Felicisima Armada* ('great and most fortunate navy') or, tempting fate even more, *Armada Invencible* – 'Invincible Navy'. It consisted of 130 ships, 22 of which were warships and the remainder converted merchantmen. They carried 8,000 sailors and 18,000 soldiers and were meant to pick up 30,000 more from the Spanish Netherlands. It must have looked fairly *Invencible*.

News of Cornwall's first sighting of the Armada was relayed by a system of beacons to London. Elizabeth's naval forces were fully prepared, under the command of Lord Howard of Effingham and Sir Francis Drake. There were several inconclusive skirmishes up the Channel and the Armada reached Calais to find that the Duke of Parma's waiting army would take at least six days to assemble and then embark.

The trouble was that the Spanish were not to be given six days, because the very next night their tightly anchored, crescent-shaped formation was threatened by eight English fire ships drifting towards them.

While two of these were towed safely away, the remaining six, blazing in the darkness, so panicked the merchantmen that they cut their anchor cables to escape and scattered. Now the Spanish were to leeward of Calais and the English fleet attacked them off the small port of Gravelines. They were careful to close to about 100 yards so that their shot could penetrate the Spanish hulls, but not to get so close as to allow the Spanish to board. Indeed, unlike the English, the Spanish were not trained to fire repeatedly, but merely to fire one single broadside and then to rush to the rigging to board – an opportunity that never came.

Five Spanish ships were lost but many more were damaged. Any chance for the fleet to meet with Parma's troops had disappeared. However, this was not apparent yet to the English. Elizabeth visited the 4,000 troops waiting at Tilbury to resist any possible Spanish incursion up the Thames and made her memorable speech of defiance, including the immortal words: 'I know I have the body of a weak and feeble woman; but I have the heart and stomach of a King – and a King of England too, and think foul scorn that Parma or Spain, or any Prince of Europe, should dare to invade the borders of my realm.'

Medina Sidonia now realized that he must sail the Armada north, right round Scotland and back to safety in Spain. His ships were damaged, food and water were running low and the cavalry horses were cast overboard. He carefully briefed his captains not to try to land in Ireland 'for fear of the harm that may happen to you on that coast'. Rather, he told them to go right out into the Atlantic, 400 miles west of the Shannon.

In spite of the poor shape of the ships and crews, most of the Armada might have made it back safely to Spain but for something of which they were not even aware – the Gulf Stream flowing steadily eastwards under their keels. At least one ship's log noted that it was safely hundreds of miles out in the Atlantic the very day it hit Galway. Violent storms and those abandoned anchors meant that 28 ships and thousands of men were doomed to strike Ireland's rocky coast.

Faced by the possibility of a large and disciplined enemy force landing in pro-Catholic Ireland, Lord Deputy William Fitzwilliam in Dublin had been given clear instructions by Elizabeth and her ministers. All Spanish were to be executed – as were any Irish caught helping them. Even when it became apparent that, in reality, those landing were struggling survivors, the orders stood. 5,000 Spaniards were ruthlessly put to death by sword and axe on the beaches or on the gallows of the towns.

The once-proud and 'invincible' Armada limped slowly home. Only half the ships that had sailed made it. Spanish power was not broken by this setback because, fuelled by the gold and silver from the Americas, she continued to dominate the world for another century. But the defeat of the Armada was a huge boost for both Elizabeth and England's national pride. The Protestant cause seemed 'blessed by God', and it took new heart.

And the Royal Navy's use of expert seamanship combined with disciplined broadside gunnery would change the face of the world for the next two centuries, right up to Trafalgar and beyond, and help to create the British Empire.

OSMAN PASHA AND HIS RIFLES

Other countries called it, sneeringly, 'The Sick Man of Europe', but the Ottoman Empire had not been created by wimps, nor by its Turkish soldiers not knowing how to fight.

Twelve years after the American Civil War, the Turks had learned some lessons that other nations would take decades to absorb. One of them was the firepower of the modern rifle.

In 1869, Oliver Winchester had sent some of his famous 15-shot repeating rifles to senior generals in Turkey, and trials showed that Turkish soldiers adapted to them very quickly. So Turkey ordered thousands of Winchesters and about 60 million rounds of ammunition. For their long-distance rifle, the Turks had noted the success of Britain's Martini-Henry, so they ordered an American duplicate, the Peabody-Martini from the Providence Tool Company in Rhode Island – no fewer than 600,000 of them! This rifle could be fired fast, 17 aimed shots a minute, was very accurate up to 700 yards and could still be lethal at much greater distances. These two weapons and a brilliant and resourceful commander were to create one of the great military shocks of the 19th century.

In April 1877, Tsar Alexander II decided to attack the Ottoman Empire, and a huge army of 150,000 crossed the Danube and advanced into Bulgaria with his brother, Grand Duke Nicholas, at its head. A very experienced Turkish officer, Field Marshal Osman Nuri Pasha, swiftly took command of the 20,000 available Turkish troops in the area. Unable to reach the city of Nikopol before its capture, he placed his small force in the strategic town of Plevna. There his men built trenches, redoubts and gun emplacements. His officers then carefully marked out the yardage on the expected battlefields, using stakes with ribbons and also noting the range of prominent objects like trees and rocks. On 18 July, the first Russian cavalry arrived and, seeing nothing but a few Turkish skirmishers, sent back messages advising the immediate occupation of Plevna. A total of 7,500 Russian infantry walked confidently into the town. A bugle sounded, and the Russians were raked by Turkish Winchester fire and, as they retreated, by the Martini-Peabodys. In 15 minutes 3,000 were killed, including both commanders. The Turks lost a mere 12.

The shaken but courageous Russians decided to attack again on 30 July, supported by artillery, but the gun crews had to be withdrawn because of the deadly Turkish rifle fire coming from a mile and a half away.

The main Russian infantry attack was met with the same devastating fire as far out as 2,000 yards, with the sights of the Turkish rifles being constantly adjusted under the calm orders of the officers. At 600 yards, more and more of the attackers fell and the Russians were reduced to small groups, goaded by both the rifle fire and shrapnel shells. Then, at 200 yards, the Turks picked up their Winchesters and their rapid fire was akin to the machine guns of the future. They next withdrew to their prepared second position, where boxes of 500 cartridges waited for every man. The brave Russians stubbornly charged them, but with the same deadly result. General Prince Schachowskoi sent a desperate message back

Osman Pasha, whose Turkish defenders at the 'Plevna Delay' should have reinforced for the military world the harsh lesson of defensive infantry firepower. (Tim Ross)

to his commander, 'Extricate yourself as best you can. My companies of 200 are coming back 5 and 10 men strong.'

Grand Duke Nicholas was now being urged by his very impatient tsar to get the advance going past the town. A Romanian army of 32,000 arrived to help the 84,000 Russians. But it did no good. The third assault on Plevna, which ended on 11 September, resulted in no fewer than 13,000 Russian and 2,600 Romanian casualties. Some had even been hit by that deadly plunging rifle fire while they were forming up 1,000 yards behind their own lines. One more local attack by the Romanians saw 20,000 rounds a minute fired at them, leaving a thousand dead on the slopes and removing any enthusiasm to attack again. The effects of such rifle fire exceeded the level of losses experienced at Antietam, Shiloh and Gettysburg, and were a frightful omen of what was to come.

The 'Plevna Delay', which had electrified the world's newspapers and was wrecking Russian stocks and bonds on world markets, could, sadly for the Turks, not go on forever. Faced by unequal odds, Osman had sensibly asked for permission to withdraw, but had been overruled by headquarters in Constantinople. By December, the Turks, surrounded for several weeks, were running out of ammunition, food, fuel, clothing and medical supplies. Osman decided to try and break out and, on 10 December, he gave his men 150 rounds of ammunition, three days' food and a pair of sandals each. Mounted on his chestnut stallion, he advanced in two corps of 20,000. But eventually, after initial success, the Turks were stopped by Russian artillery and overwhelming numbers.

Osman's horse was killed and he himself was wounded in the leg by a shell splinter. He was finally forced to surrender. Lieutenant-General Skobeleff, whose troops had been the first to be ravaged by Osman's rifles, said, 'He is the greatest general of the age. I will offer him my hand and tell him so, personally.' As Osman lay on a cart, Grand Duke Nicholas accepted his surrender and said generously, 'I congratulate you on your success in defending Plevna. This is one of the most splendid exploits in history.'

The next day, the tsar asked him why he had not surrendered sooner and Osman replied, 'My state gave these weapons for fighting, not to drop them at the sight of the enemy. They sent me here to fight.' The tsar returned his sword as a mark of esteem.

After the brief war, which Turkey technically lost, Osman returned to be fêted as a hero, awarded the title *Gazi*, or 'Victorious', and served four times as Minister of War. A Turkish military anthem is still sung in his honour.

In the outside world, not enough people paid attention to what had happened at Plevna. If a tiny force of Turks could hold up a huge army for five months, inflicting terrible losses on the attackers, and just with repeating rifles, what, in the future, would larger armies do with machine guns?

The answer, of course, comes to us attached to the ominous names of the Somme, Verdun, Passchendaele and, again at the hands of the Turks, Gallipoli.

CAPTAIN LUCAS AND ADMIRAL NELSON

If, in the coming battle, Nelson could be likened to a Goliath and the man who slew him to a David, the analogy would be rather spoilt by how small they *both* were. Admiral Lord Nelson was just 5ft 5in. but Captain Jean Jacques Etienne Lucas was a mere 4ft 8in. One was already a famous hero, the other virtually unknown. But their meeting was destined to be as fateful as that of Wellington and Napoleon at Waterloo, Crazy Horse and Custer at the battle of Little Big Horn or Montgomery and Rommel at El Alamein.

On land, Napoleon was the master. Nearly every country in Europe had been beaten in battle – all except England, protected by 22 precious miles of water and the Royal Navy. But Napoleon was determined to invade, and thousands of his troops waited in Boulogne.

Of all the foreign invasion threats, including the Spanish Armada's (beaten by Drake and the weather in 1588) and Hitler's (beaten by the Battle of Britain in 1940), Napoleon's was probably the most dangerous and likely to succeed, though Napoleon was hampered by his own lack of knowledge of the realities of sea power. 'The Channel is a mere ditch, and will be crossed as soon as someone has the courage to attempt it.' Moreover he foolishly turned down the offer by the American inventor of steamboats, Robert Fulton, to use them in becalmed conditions to tow his invasion barges to

England: 'What Sir, you would have my boats fight the wind and waves by lighting bonfires under their decks? Pray you, excuse me. I have no time for such nonsense.'

Nevertheless, Napoleon ordered the French Admiral Villeneuve to join him and clear the Channel of British ships so that his army could cross. 'Come to the Channel. Bring our united fleet and England is ours. If you are only here for 24 hours, all will be over and six centuries of shame and insult will be avenged.' British Admiral Jervis dryly commented, 'I do not say they cannot come, I only say they cannot come by sea.'

As a feint, Napoleon ordered Villeneuve to sail to the West Indies, pursued there and back by Nelson. However, at a skirmish with Admiral Calder off Finisterre, Villeneuve lost his nerve and turned south not east, thus failing to fulfil his emperor's orders to join the French Navy at Brest. Instead he joined a Spanish Navy even more ramshackle, sick and ill trained than his own. He also knew that he was about to be replaced by Admiral Rosily and even that a frustrated Napoleon had struck camp to begin his march across Europe to conduct the brilliant Austerlitz campaign against the Russians and Austrians. The logic for a battle was gone, but Napoleon had ordered the humiliated Villeneuve out anyway, to make it into the Mediterranean. The scene was set for one of the most decisive battles in history.

Villeneuve's formidable adversary, Admiral Horatio Nelson, was already a legend. In a long and brilliant naval career, he had lost an eye before his victory at Cape St Vincent and later his right arm. Off Copenhagen he had ignored his vacillating superior's signals by famously holding his telescope to his missing eye. He had conducted a scandalous affair with Emma, the wife of Sir William Hamilton (albeit with her husband's acquiescence), and had a daughter by her, Horatia.

The problem for Napoleon was that while he had 2,000 ships, they had been blockaded in their ports for years by the Royal Navy which had nothing to do but watch and endlessly practise seamanship and gunnery to perfection. They could fire at twice the rate of the French.

There was one man in the French Navy who understood this problem perfectly. Captain Lucas commanded the 74-gun *Redoutable*. Only 4ft 8in. tall, even smaller than Nelson, he was brimming with confidence in his own abilities. Already regarded as the most efficient French commander with the best-run ship, he decided that his crew would be at least superlatively trained in the one skill they *could* practise –

HMS *Victory* sails slowly into the French line, where Nelson would find his nemesis — one of Captain Lucas' snipers. (Richard Grenville)

musketry. His 40 selected marksmen were also taught the age-old maxim of any sniper: it is much more effective to kill an officer, and preferably a senior one, than an ordinary soldier or seaman.

It was not as if his enemies were oblivious to the threat. Off Cape Trafalgar, the breeze on 20 October 1805 was so light that the two great fleets approached each other at walking pace. So there was plenty of time, six hours, to prepare – and to worry. On the *Victory*, Nelson stood with his staff, including Dr William Beatty, the surgeon, who quietly expressed his unease that the four shiny stars embroidered on the admiral's uniform would mark him as an obvious target when they were within range of rifle fire, and that he should change into a plain coat. 'Take care, Doctor, what you are about,' warned the admiral's secretary. 'I would not be the man to mention such a matter to him.' Beatty tried but failed to do so, hovering near the admiral, awaiting a chance to bring the subject up.

Eventually, it was the *Victory*'s captain, Thomas Hardy, who raised the question of the coat, suggesting that the decorations might catch the eye of a sniper. Nelson replied, 'I am aware it may be seen, but it is now too late to be shifting a coat.'

It was to be a brave, foolish and fatal decision. In fact, at 11am, Nelson did take the time to go below. He prayed and wrote letters and his diary for an hour. There he could easily have changed his coat in seconds.

An hour later, the *Victory* cut straight into the French line and was soon locked by collapsed spars and lines in a murderous embrace with the smaller *Redoutable*. This is when Captain Lucas' training came into its own. As he later reported: 'Then a heavy fire of musketry opened, in which Admiral Nelson fought at the head of his crew. Our firing, though, became so rapid, and was so much superior to his, that in less than a quarter of an hour we had silenced that of the *Victory* altogether. More than 200 grenades were flung on board her, with the utmost success, her decks were strewn with the dead and wounded. Admiral Nelson was killed by the firing of our musketry. Immediately after this, the upper deck of the *Victory* became deserted, and she again ceased firing, but it proved difficult to board her because of the motion of the two vessels.'

Nelson looking down from his column in Trafalgar Square. (Tony Eckersley)

Victory was in real danger of defeat and capture, but out of the smoke came the British *Temeraire*, whose devastating point-blank broadsides killed and wounded 300 of the *Redoutable*'s crew and reduced her, as Lucas reported, to 'a heap of debris'.

While the *Victory* was saved by the sudden intervention of the *Temeraire*, Nelson had indeed been hit by one of Lucas' well-trained snipers.

He was rushed below decks to the surgeon. 'Ah, Mr Beatty you can do nothing for me. I have a short time to live; my back is shot through.' After hours of long agony, Nelson was visited by Captain Hardy, 'We have got 12 or 14 of the enemy's ships in our possession.' 'I hope none of our ships have struck?' asked Nelson. Later Hardy returned to report. After his last orders, Nelson said, 'Kiss me Hardy.' After the captain had kissed his cheek, Nelson sighed, 'Now I am satisfied. Thank God I have done my duty.' Two hours later he was dead, one of Britain's great and tragic heroes.

Surrounded by ships, Lucas finally struck his colours and surrendered, and British and French sailors then struggled manfully together to save the brave *Redoutable*, but she finally sank, shot to pieces and having sustained the worst casualties of the battle, with no fewer than 300 killed and 222 wounded out of 643 men.

Of all Britain's opponents on that day, Captain Lucas had performed intelligently and courageously and thoroughly deserved the praise that Napoleon eventually heaped upon him.

ROBERT BADEN-POWELL AND MAFEKING

All over the world, there are boys who wear short trousers, a curious Stetson hat and a scarf – an incredible 28 million of them. They are, of course, the Boy Scouts, and they owe their existence to a classic example of a man who rose to the occasion, Robert Baden-Powell, and to his resolute defence of a little town in South Africa called Mafeking.

It was Baden-Powell's schooldays at Charterhouse that first set him on the road to scouting, when, against the rules, he hid from the masters in the woods, stalking and cooking game. But he was not just an outdoors enthusiast; he played the violin and piano, acted in plays and was an excellent artist, painting and drawing equally well with either hand.

He took up a military career, but always with extra enthusiasm for intelligence gathering. The legendary American scout Frederick Russell Burnham, attached to British forces, became a lifelong friend, taught him more about scouting and persuaded him to adopt the idea of the Stetson hat.

Now the youngest colonel in the British Army, Baden-Powell was raising forces in Rhodesia to counter the rising threat of the Boers in South Africa when President Kruger of the Boer Transvaal Republic declared war on the British on 12 October

1899. The same day the telegraph and railway lines into Mafeking, a railway junction town that Baden-Powell had been quietly and secretly preparing to defend, were cut. The next day, they were besieged by 8,000 Boers.

With only 1,500 white soldiers and civilians, including 630 women and children, the odds did not look good. Baden-Powell recruited Africans to help, prompting a strange and furious signal from Commandant Cronje, the Boer commander, 'You have armed Bastards, Fingas and Borsalongs – an enormous act of wickedness. Disarm your blacks, hereby acting the part of a white man in a white man's war.' Baden-Powell ignored him, eventually recruiting 500 Borsalongs as extremely useful soldiers.

Luckily, Mafeking was well stocked with food, because a supply had, by chance, been in transit to Rhodesia. But, while it had plenty of rifles and some Maxim machine guns, it was critically short of artillery, with just a handful of small guns. By contrast, the Boers had plenty of guns, notably a huge 94-pdr Creusot, soon to be known as 'Old Creaky'. On 16 October, Baden-Powell rejected Cronje's demand for surrender and the first Boer shells hit the town.

Outgunned, the British managed to bolster their firepower a little bit. One new gun, 'The Wolf', was hastily constructed from the steam pipe of an engine mounted on the wheels of a threshing machine. Another was an ancient 1792 cannon, being used as a doorpost. It fired a 10lb shot that was often described as bouncing along like a cricket ball. The makeshift artillery was rushed around the town and fired from as many angles as possible to give the impression of a large defensive battery.

The confident Boers attacked the town and were repulsed, then the British sallied forth and struck the Boers in their own lines. Both sides settled down for a siege. Baden-Powell now employed all his imagination and skills to bluff his opponents into thinking how strong he was.

The most pressing concern was to stop the Boers from storming at night, which would certainly have proved unstoppable. To prevent this, a visiting salesman of acetylene lamps was employed to construct a searchlight. Using biscuit tins as reflectors, the lamp was rushed around the town and shone out upon all areas of the Boer lines, giving the impression that the defenders possessed an entire array of searchlights, which would make a night assault difficult. Then there were the 'landmines'. His men buried metal containers all round the town as ostentatiously as possible. By the time that a 'test' was conducted, an explosion of a stick of dynamite, the Boers had been convinced that the landmine threat removed the possibility of a mass attack.

When the Boers had shelled the convent at Mafeking, their excuse had been that they 'lacked powerful field glasses'. So when the British ran out of barbed wire to protect their lines, Baden-Powell realized that at long distance they could pretend to lay it and then crawl under the 'wire' or clumsily lift their legs over it, and it would prove an effective deterrent. And so the Boers were convinced of the town's defensive strength and resorted to continuous shelling. Often they would seem to have struck a fatal blow, as their artillery fire destroyed one of the defending forts. But this was yet another bluff; the fort was a dummy, manned by dummies, whose movements were induced by pulleys and string. Time and again, the thin defences of the town were bolstered by bluff and deceit.

Robert Baden-Powell, at the time of Mafeking, whose defence was a resourceful mixture of courage and bluff. One can see where the Boy Scouts' hat came from.

The town was hit by 20,000 shells, of which 1,500 were big ones from 'Old Creaky'. And, as the siege dragged on, supplies were running low.

Raising morale was another of Baden-Powell's tasks and he organized everything from dummy-making competitions to baby shows, concerts and games of cricket. Eventually one of the most active of the Boer commanders, young Field Cornet Sarel Eloff, a grandson of President Kruger, became so bored and frustrated with the siege that he sent a sporting message:

To Colonel Baden-Powell, I see in *The Bulawayo Chronicle* that your men in Mafeking play cricket on Sundays and give concerts and balls on Sunday evenings. In case you would allow my men to join in the same it would be very agreeable to me as here outside Mafeking there are seldom any of the fair sex and there can be no merriment without their being present …

Wishing you a pleasant day. I remain your obliging friend,

S. Eloff. Commandant of Johannesburg.

And the reply – sent under the white flag:

Sir, I beg to thank you for your letter of yesterday … I should like nothing better – after the match in which we are at present engaged is over. But just now we are having our innings and have so far scored 180 days, not out, against the bowling of Cronje, Snijman, Botha … and we are having a very enjoyable game.

I remain yours truly, R. S. S. Baden-Powell

Together with the weekly truce on Sundays, this showed a chivalrous attitude which, sadly, was not to last out the war.

By the middle of January 1900, it was obvious that the siege was going to last much longer than anyone, Boer or British, had ever imagined. Rationing was introduced and meat was provided by the horses, every bit of which was used, as Baden-Powell later described in detail.

The donkeys, too, which were at first used to carry messages, soon found themselves in kitchen pots, as the food supply began to dwindle. To replace the donkey messaging service, young boys, mostly on bicycles, were employed as couriers. The responsibilities of these khaki-clad youths began to grow – replacing men in the front line. Soon, as well as message carriers, they were used as hospital assistants and lookouts. These boys were the prototype of the modern Boy Scouts. Mafeking was their baptism of fire.

All the time, striding confidently around and whistling popular tunes, even in the most pressing situations, Baden-Powell tried to inspire by example. He was famous for being awake almost all the time, snatching only a few hours of sleep a day. Furthermore, as the food crisis worsened, he and his staff had smaller rations than the rest, so as to show how little food was needed for survival. Spurred on by their commander, the locals never cracked, no matter how long the siege dragged on.

Mafeking was fulfilling its role of tying down many Boer troops. On 11 May 1900, the Boers, increasingly frustrated, finally made a direct attack on the town itself, under the command of the eager Sarel Eloff. At first it seemed that all of Baden-Powell's guile and heroics had been in vain, as the attackers pushed into the very heart of the town, even telephoning Baden-Powell in triumph. But they had overstretched themselves and soon found themselves surrounded. The British captured Eloff and 108 Boers. It was to be the besiegers' last attack.

Five days later, distant gunfire could be heard from the town, and on the next day the British Army arrived, and Mafeking had finally been relieved. The town, during the 217 days of the siege, had suffered 212 killed and 600 wounded. Three Victoria Crosses were awarded. The bravery and inventiveness of the inhabitants, and especially the talismanic Baden-Powell, became famous back in Britain. Crowds rejoiced in the streets at the happy ending of such an amazing tale, and thronged outside the house of Baden-Powell's mother to cheer and applaud. In fact, the word 'mafficking' was coined to describe such joyous scenes. Queen Victoria herself had been keeping a close eye on the siege throughout and sent Baden-Powell the following telegram: 'I and my whole Empire greatly rejoice at the relief of Mafeking after the splendid defence made by you through all these months. I heartily congratulate you and all under you.'

When he returned from South Africa in 1903, Baden-Powell found that one of his 35 books, his military manual *Aids to Scouting*, had become a bestseller. He rewrote it for younger readers. He experimented with a camp for a group of boys and then went on to found the Scouting movement and later the Girl Guides with his sister Agnes. His work for Scouting was judged so valuable that Field Marshal Kitchener refused to use him, 'as just another general' in World War I.

After seeing his movement spread throughout the world, Baden-Powell was honoured by America when a Californian mountain peak was dedicated to him with great emotion in 1931 by his old friend Frederick Russell Burnham, who, 20 years later, had the nearby peak also named after himself – a lasting and visible memorial to a great and influential friendship.

In 1941 Baden-Powell died. Forearmed with his motto, 'Be Prepared', he probably was.

ROMAN ORLIK AND HIS TINY TANK

For Adolf Hitler, the 1930s were a decade of deceit. He was a master bluffer, and he had to be, because Germany was much weaker than anyone realized. When Hitler was bullying Chamberlain and Daladier to sign away half of Czechoslovakia at Munich in 1938, the reality was that, apart from coal and steel, Germany had almost no strategic materials – oil, aluminium or rubber. She could not buy them because the Reichsmark was not even a convertible currency. During the Munich crisis, the Luftwaffe, for instance, had only 25 per cent of the fuel it would need in operations and only 6 per cent of lubricants. If it had been forced to go into action, its engines would have seized.

Throughout the coming war, German tanks were always more powerful, but their production, curiously, was almost pathetic compared with that of the British and Americans. They built 1,349 Tigers and 6,000 Panthers, but the Americans built no fewer than 49,000 Shermans. So one of the reasons Hitler needed to absorb his Czechoslovakian neighbour was to get hold of the huge Skoda works, second only to Krupp (see page 150), and its considerable tank production.

A year later, Hitler turned to Poland, once again marking his intentions with soothing words. In January 1939, he said in the Reichstag: 'During the troubled months of the past year, the friendship between Germany and Poland has been one of the most reassuring factors in the political life of Europe.'

But just weeks later he revealed his real attitude secretly to his generals: 'There is therefore no question of sparing Poland, as we are left with the decision to attack Poland at the first suitable opportunity. We cannot expect a repetition of the Czech affair. There will be war. Our task is to isolate Poland. The success of the isolation will be decisive.'

He had several reasons to attack Poland. He needed to create *Lebensraum* (living space') in the east, he had the firm intention of making the Poles into *Sklaven* (slaves), and he wanted to destroy Poland's huge Jewish population.

Those politicians like Britain's Neville Chamberlain who were still naïve enough to think that they could negotiate Hitler out of this crisis would have been shocked by his secret military briefing on 22 August: 'Now, Poland is in the position in which I wanted her. I am only afraid that at the last moment some *Schweinehund* will make a proposal for mediation!'

Nine days later, after a ridiculous charade of pretending that the Poles had attacked first, one million troops and 2,500 tanks crossed the border and sliced into Poland. One-third of the tanks were Czech, now called PzKpw 38(t) and 35(t); the 't' was for *tscheche*. The resulting *Blitzkrieg* or 'Lightning War' shook the world – the combined use of Stuka dive-bombers (to replace slow-moving artillery), infantry that could move in their vehicles as fast as tanks, and tanks each with radios that enabled them to manoeuvre with the great tactical initiative that a new generation of resourceful German officers would demonstrate.

Facing this onslaught was a large, proud and brave Polish Army, but of a previous age, traditional marching infantry, horse-drawn artillery and courageous cavalry. Poland did have a few tanks, but they were tiny, two-man tankettes based on a British design and weighing just 2.5 tons – less than Hitler's cars! And it was in one of these little vehicles that young Officer Cadet Roman Orlik of the Wielkopolska Cavalry Brigade rose to the occasion.

Just nine days into the war, Orlik knocked out three German 35(t)s. Then three days later, he ambushed three more in the forest, changing position each time to avoid being overwhelmed by tanks with four times his weight and armour thickness, and with much more powerful guns.

The next day, the Poles captured the village of Sierakow, but the Germans poured in a complete armoured brigade. Orlik, ordered to advance, looked at the frightening sight of a dark moving mass of 50 enemy tanks, again 35(t)s. He worked out a plan. He would emerge from some sunken gravel pits with his tankette, with its automatic 20mm gun, while his two comrades, their tankettes armed only with machine guns, would try to protect him. Time and again he would rush out, fire, reverse, change location and advance again. It worked. His enemies were confused in the dust clouds and could not get a fix on him. Orlik thought he had missed his third victim, but amazingly its crew surrendered. He knocked out three more but then faced sudden disaster. Caught in the open, he

The tiny Polish 2½ ton TKS 'tankette'. It weighed less than most of Hitler's motor cars. (Polish Ministry of National Defence)

was out of ammunition and desperately zig-zagged backwards to reach cover as shells from the German tank hit all around him.

After reaching safety once again, he looked out and saw that his enemy was now immobilized and its crew gone. He had knocked out seven Panzers, and the guns of his brigade had destroyed 13 more, forcing the German 1st Light Division to be withdrawn to recover. The Germans later described it as 'the toughest fight of the campaign'.

Soon Orlik was forced to retreat with the rest of the army, and his was the only tank to make it back to Warsaw. When Poland surrendered, he joined the Underground Army, becoming a successful architect after the war. He was awarded Poland's highest honour, the Virtuti Military Cross.

There are some who have compared his action, somewhat favourably, with the German tank ace Michael Wittmann's feats – especially in Normandy (see page 101). Because, after all, Wittmann's massive 57-ton Tiger was greatly superior to his enemies.

In his little tankette, Orlik was really much more of 'a David facing Goliaths'.

JOHN PAUL JONES AND HIS FIGHT

By 1905, the United States was becoming a major naval power, urged on by its swashbuckling president, Theodore Roosevelt. It was but a few years since the *Maine* had blown up mysteriously in Havana harbour, starting a war with Spain that saw Admiral Dewey destroy the Spanish fleet in Manila. Soon America's 'Great White Fleet' would circle the globe, demonstrating a new way of 'talking softly and carrying a big stick'. So now seemed a good time to try to find in Paris the remains of 'the father of the American Navy'.

It took six years and a great deal of detective work for the American ambassador, General Horace Porter (once General Grant's aide during the Civil War), to narrow down the possible resting place of John Paul Jones. Perhaps the special lead coffin that had been kindly donated by a rich French admirer over a century before might provide a clue. Eventually the search focussed on a long-forgotten cemetery, now used as a dumping ground for dead cats and dogs, and a place for illicit secret animal fights. It was the former royal 'St Louis Cemetery for Alien Protestants'.

John Paul Jones, the Scotsman who came back to haunt the Royal Navy. (George Bagby Matthews)

After probing the earth, it was discovered the third lead coffin found did indeed contain the body of John Paul Jones. Obscurity quickly changed to adulation. He was loaded with all due ceremony aboard the USS *Brooklyn* and was escorted across the Atlantic by three other American cruisers, to be greeted by seven battleships firing salutes. Eventually his body would be re-interred, with a rousing speech by President Roosevelt, in a magnificent bronze and marble sarcophagus at the United States Naval Academy at Annapolis.

John Paul was born in Scotland in 1747, the son of a humble gardener, John Paul (Senior). A boyhood friend described his childhood in a little port on the Solway Firth. 'He would run to Carsethorn whenever his father let him off, talk to the sailors and clamber over the ships. He taught his playmates to manoeuvre their little boats to mimic a naval fleet while he, taking his stand on the tiny cliff overlooking the roadstead, shouted shrill commands at his imaginary fleet.' It was hardly surprising that John Paul 'ran away to sea' at just 13, signing on in Whitehaven for a seven-year apprenticeship. He often sailed to Fredericksburg, Virginia, and visited his older brother, who had prospered there. He was also persuaded to undertake just one dreadful voyage on a 50ft slave ship, but he thought it an 'abominable trade', resigning in disgust.

On the way back in a Scottish ship, he took command when the captain and first mate both died of yellow fever and the grateful owners made him a partner on his next voyage. He was now a captain at just 21 – wiry, with a sharp nose and high cheekbones. He dressed smartly and was popular with the ladies. But he also had a violent temper. He flogged the ship's carpenter, who later died, but John Paul was judged entirely innocent of murder when he returned to Kirkcudbright. Indeed, he was respected enough by the local community to be accepted as a mason.

In the West Indies, trouble struck again. He was forced to kill the ringleader of a mutiny ('a prodigious brute thrice my strength'). He decided it wise to leave for Virginia, where he now adopted the lengthened name of 'John Paul Jones'.

In Virginia, revolution against British rule was stirring and John Paul Jones volunteered for the 'Continental Navy' of just five ships. Even when this rose to 30, it was dwarfed by the 800 ships of the Royal Navy – difficult odds indeed. Jones was the very first lieutenant to be commissioned and then, as a captain, advised Congress on the drawing up of Navy Regulations. Soon he was in Europe, making firm friends with Benjamin Franklin, American Commissioner in France, and sailing off to attack the British in his home territory. In fact he seemed to take extra pleasure in attacking familiar places, raiding Whitehaven twice. In Kirkcudbright, to raise ransom money to free American prisoners, he even tried to kidnap one of his former neighbours, the Earl of Selkirk. He later purchased back and then returned the Countess of Selkirk's silver, which his crew had looted.

He then sank HMS *Drake* off Northern Ireland and became a household name in America, where he was a hero, and Britain, where he was feared and vilified as a pirate. Years later, Prime Minister Benjamin Disraeli, one of his biographers, wrote, 'The nurses of Scotland hushed their charges by the whisper of his name.' He was about to become even more famous.

He was leading a five-ship squadron with his 42-gun *Bonhomme Richard*, which he had named after a book by his friend Benjamin Franklin. Off Flamborough Head on 22 September 1779, he spotted and decided to attack a large merchant convoy, escorted by the Royal Navy's 44-gun HMS *Serapis* and an armed escort.

Serapis and the *Bonhomme Richard* were soon locked together. At the height of the battle, the British captain shouted a question as to whether Jones was surrendering. He received the famous reply: 'I have not yet begun to fight.' For three and a half hours the two ships slogged it out, each losing half their crews as dead or wounded. Again, a more serious question as to whether he had 'struck' his colours was met by Jones' defiant 'I may sink, but I'll be damned if I'll strike.'

Indeed, he knew that *Bonhomme Richard* was sinking beneath his feet, holed ironically not by *Serapis* but by mis-aimed shots from the *Alliance*, one of his own ships. However, Jones' luck held. Some gunpowder cartridges left by *Serapis'* young 'powder monkeys' on her deck were suddenly set off by his grenades and the explosion and fires settled the fate of the British ship. Her captain, Pearson, the only one who was brave enough, climbed his rigging to pull down the flag he had previously nailed to the mast. Jones put out the fires on the *Serapis*, and transferred to her because his *Bonhomme Richard* was about to sink. He returned in triumph to Holland with 500 prisoners.

He was made a 'Chevalier' by Louis XVI, the King of France, and a gold medal was struck 'for valour and brilliant services'. Congress also passed a vote of thanks to him for the way 'he had sustained the honour of the American fleet'.

He had been destined next to command the 74-gun *America*, but she was given in gratitude to the French, so after the War of Independence had ended, he devoted his time to the establishment of the US Navy and the training of naval officers.

When he was once again in Paris, the new ambassador, Thomas Jefferson, suggested he offer his services to Catherine the Great. As a Russian rear-admiral, 'Pavel Ivanovich Jones' was his usual forthright success. One night, he personally reconnoitred the enemy Turkish fleet in a rowing boat, which enabled him to destroy 15 ships the next day, killing 3,000 Turks and taking 1,500 prisoners at a cost of a frigate and 18 men.

But glory slipped away. Three years later, ill with nephritis, jaundice and pneumonia, John Paul Jones died face down on his bed in Paris. He was just 45. A tiny group of friends escorted his body to the royal cemetery where the grateful King Louis XVI had agreed that he could be buried. Weeks later, however, the French Revolution would sweep away the king. His cemetery would decline into a forgotten ruin and John Paul Jones' grave would disappear under the weeds, to be rescued more than a century later by an American nation now fully convinced of the importance of sea power.

John Paul Jones' 'I have not yet begun to fight' is one of many famous defiant responses over the ages. When Philip II of Macedon threatened in 338 BC, 'If I enter Laconia, I will raze Sparta to the ground', the suitably laconic reply was 'If'. A century earlier, Leonidas and his men, just before their last stand at Thermopylae, had been ordered by the Persian Emperor Xerxes to lay down their arms. For a Spartan, Leonidas was quite talkative, 'Come and get them'. When Mussolini in 1941 sent an ultimatum to Greece, Prime Minister Metaxas kept up the tradition, sending back a simple 'Óhi', or 'No'. Every year, Greece celebrates 'Óhi Day'. The Germans besieging Bastogne during the 1944 Battle of the Bulge were thoroughly confused by US General Anthony MacAuliffe's response to their demand that the 101st Airborne should surrender: 'Nuts'.

3

COURAGE OF THEIR CONVICTIONS

JULIUS CAESAR AND THE PIRATES

When the pirates told their young Roman prisoner that they were going to ransom him for 20 talents, he roared with laughter. He told them he was worth *much* more than that, and that they should ask for 50. Even though they thought this overconfident youth was simple-minded, they took his advice, releasing his companions to go off to try to raise the money.

During the next 38 days, Julius Caesar became really quite friendly with the bloodthirsty Cilician pirates. He joined in their games, acting more as an assured leader than an anxious prisoner. He scolded them when they kept him awake and even teased them as ignorant illiterates when they failed to appreciate his poetry. He also smilingly told them that he would kill them when he was released – all of which they thought highly entertaining and amusing.

When the money arrived, Julius Caesar was duly released. He quickly gathered a fleet, captured the pirates and, when the local Roman governor failed to punish them, removed them from prison and crucified them all.

All through his eventful life, Julius Caesar would rise to the occasion, seizing the initiative, moving swiftly and decisively, leading from the front and acting with a boldness close to recklessness.

Julius Caesar crossing the Rubicon. (Corbis)

In the blood-stained emergence of Rome as *the* world power, politics and war were inextricably linked. Julius Caesar would develop as a virtually unique combination of soldier, politician, orator and writer (in history, probably only Winston Churchill compares). As a soldier, he is certainly regarded as one of the greatest of all.

Born into a noble but not rich family, Caesar was always connected with the 'Popular' political faction. His first run-in with their rivals, the aristocratic 'Optimates', was when Sulla, the Optimate dictator, ordered him to divorce his young wife. Caesar refused and went into hiding until pardoned.

After being awarded Rome's highest award for gallantry for saving a man in battle, Caesar's first political success came in obtaining a fleet of ships from King Nicomedes of Bithynia, aged just 21. Unfortunately this was somewhat marred by gossips maliciously attributing this to Caesar's willingness to share a bed with the King.

After his escapade with the pirates, it was not surprising that Caesar backed another rising star, Gnaeus Pompey, to lead Rome's efforts to rid the Mediterranean of them.

It was the beginning of a strange love/hate relationship between the two men. Caesar, already a handsome, imposing figure, tall and clean-shaven, was also rumoured to have had affairs with several men's wives, including Pompey's. He cynically divorced his own wife, Poppeia, for a supposed indiscretion, stating with some self-importance, 'The wife of Caesar must be above suspicion'.

After a successful stint in Spain, Caesar returned and persuaded Pompey and Crassus to work with him in a coalition called the First Triumvirate. To cement the relationship, he gave his daughter Julia to Pompey in marriage. Through these alliances, he became consul with a powerless Optimate nonentity called Bibulus. From now on, his furious political opponents in the Senate planned to prosecute him as soon as he left office and became a private citizen.

But Caesar now left Rome for nine years of brilliant campaigns, defeating the Helvetii (modern Swiss), the Sueli (Germans), the Belgi (Belgians) and the Venetii (Maritime Gauls in Northern France), with the help of Marcus Brutus. He extended Roman rule to the Rhine. He also invaded Britain twice, before returning to fight much tougher campaigns against a rejuvenated Central Gaul under the redoubtable Vercingetorix.

In 52 BC, Caesar won the most decisive battle of his career. With 70,000 troops, he besieged Vercingetorix in a natural hill fortress at Alesia, surrounding it with a very cleverly designed 11-mile ring fence, with ditches, traps and towers. He was not only able to counter any sorties that Vercingetorix could mount, but, showing great leadership, he turned to defeat a huge Gallic army of over 300,000 under Commius, which arrived to try to lift the siege. Alesia surrendered, Julius Caesar became a hero and 20 days of thanksgiving were celebrated in Rome.

What is more, Caesar, having left Rome badly in debt, was now enormously rich from the booty and slaves captured in his campaigns, enabling him to buy the fervent loyalty of his troops.

The uneasy arrangement of the Triumvirate then began to disintegrate. Crassus, the financier, decided that he, too, would like some military glory, but he was killed by the Parthians (see page 218). This now left just one rival for power, Pompey, called 'the Great' because of his own military successes. His tenuous links with Caesar were suddenly loosened by the death of Julia in childbirth, and his links with the Optimate Senators were rapidly strengthening.

Faced by an enemy Senate that was about to acquire dangerous military backing, Julius Caesar took one of his most decisive steps. Against Roman law, he led his troops across a small stream separating Cisalpine Gaul from Italy, the Rubicon. 'Alea iacta est,' he remarked – 'the die is cast'.

With his loyal and well-trained legions, he forced Pompey out of Italy, defeated Pompey's lieutenants in Spain, then followed him to Greece. At Pharsalus, with just 21,000 men, Caesar beat the 43,000 of Pompey, who was forced to flee to Egypt. Caesar then pardoned all the Romans who had fought against him – including Brutus. It was a generous form of rising to the occasion that would prove fatal a few years later.

Caesar pursued Pompey to Egypt but found that he had been murdered. There, in Alexandria, the joint ruler, Cleopatra, smuggled herself into his presence wrapped in a rug. Caesar was captivated by her and started an emotional and political alliance, with huge consequences. For six months, they were besieged by her brother Ptolemy's army. At one battle, attempting to capture the Pharos lighthouse, Caesar was forced to jump into the water and swim to safety holding important documents above his head and gripping his general's purple cloak in his teeth.

Eventually Roman reinforcements arrived, Caesar beat Ptolemy, who was killed, and Cleopatra was secured as sole ruler. Caesar then left for Asia Minor, where one battle gave us his famous phrase, 'Veni, Vidi, Vici' – 'I came, I saw, I conquered', which rather encapsulates his style of rising to the occasion.

Julius Caesar returned to Rome to celebrate four magnificent 'triumphs'. He sent for Cleopatra and installed her and their son Caesarion in a villa across the Tiber from Rome.

Apparently unchallenged, he listed his political aims as 'tranquillity for Italy, peace for the provinces, and security for the Empire'. He had an ambitious but thoroughly sound and farsighted programme to achieve all this, but his autocratic, high-handed attitude towards the Senate, still containing many enemies, was storing up trouble and danger.

He conducted one last campaign, against Pompey's two sons in Spain. When he returned in October 45 BC, he was heaped with honours. He was called 'Father of the Country', made 'Dictator for Life' and consul for ten years, his person was declared sacred, his statutes placed in temples, his portrait struck on coins and a month named after him, July. At his last triumph, celebrating victory over Gnaeus

Pompey, one wonders if he listened to the traditional slave riding in the chariot and quietly warning the hero that he was 'only human and fallible'.

'Beware the Ides of March', a soothsayer had told him, and others had warned him of a conspiracy. On that fateful day, 15 March 44 BC, a Senator had even slipped him a note, which he did not bother to read. Those old enemies of the successful – hubris and overconfidence – now played their part in the coming tragedy, preventing him from rising to the occasion in his usual decisive way.

Sixty conspirators had gathered at the Senate's temporary home, ironically a theatre built by Pompey. Suddenly, they attacked with their hidden daggers, striking no fewer than 23 blows. Caesar stared with disbelief at one of the leaders, the man he had commanded in Gaul and had pardoned after Pharsalus: 'Et tu, Brute?'

The assassins had no long-term plans. They allowed Caesar's friend, Mark Antony, to survive, who would soon hunt them down. Rome was plunged into another round of civil war, which finally destroyed the Roman Republic, allowing it to become, under Caesar's great-nephew, Octavian, later Augustus Caesar, the mighty Roman Empire.

MICHAEL COLLINS AND THE LAST SHOT

Michael Collins is regarded as one of the most attractive, charismatic and tragic figures in Irish history. He was a complex character, a mixture of infectious, warm enthusiasm and ice-cold calculation.

He was born in West Cork, the youngest of eight children. His father had been a member of the republican Fenian movement, pledged to rid Ireland of the British, as was his first schoolmaster. Michael was a bright, precocious boy, good at sports and a passionate nationalist. But that did not stop him leaving for London aged 15, studying at King's College and even passing the Civil Service Examination, in which he had to praise Britain's 'great Empire'. So he knew Britain and the British and it was in London that he joined the Irish Republican Brotherhood (IRB), quickly becoming the IRB's treasurer of London and the South East, through his tireless energy, financial and organizational skills. The IRB would provide his power base in the years to come.

In May 1914, after years of negotiation, the Home Rule Bill for Ireland had passed the House of Commons. It seemed that 700 years of English dominance was about to end. But, within weeks, the outbreak of the Great War would fatefully ensure its postponement. Staunch resistance to Home Rule by Ulster's Protestants had not gone away and they had even been importing guns from Germany to fight the British, if necessary. The Irish Volunteers saw no reason why they should not follow suit.

In January 1916, under threat of conscription into the British Army and hearing of clandestine activity in Ireland, Collins set sail for Dublin in time for the doomed 'Easter Rising'. At the General Post Office, he fought alongside Patrick Pearse, but thought his ideas of a 'blood sacrifice' were foolish, and he was furious at the 'hand-fisted amateurism' of the whole tragic event. Never again, he vowed, would he allow his men to be 'sitting targets'.

When they surrendered, luckily the British did not recognize him and he escaped General Maxwell's firing squads (see page 253). He soon became a most formidable enemy. Released from prison in England, he returned to Ireland to start his war. There, the threat of extending conscription to Ireland, coupled with restrictions on Irish language and sports, was once again hardening resistance against Britain.

When the Great War ended, Collins was elected in 1918 as Member of Parliament for Cork South, but he refused, like the other Irish MPs, to take his seat at Westminster. The Sinn Fein MPs, those not in English jails, set up their own Parliament, Dáil Éireann. On the day of its first sitting, the first shots of the Anglo-Irish War were being fired, far away in Tipperary.

Michael Collins masterminded the brilliant escape of his colleague Eamon de Valera from Lincoln Jail, who then decided to go to America to raise support. Collins was now president of the IRB and director of intelligence of the IRA, and in 1919 Eamon de Valera made him Sinn Fein's Minister of Finance. This may sound rather ridiculous for a government on the run but, unlike other ministries that only existed in name or in a back room, Collins' finance ministry organized a large bond issue in the form of a 'National Loan' to fund the new Irish Republic. Such was his reputation that even Lenin heard about his spectacular National Loan and sent a representative to Dublin to borrow some money to help fund the Russian Republic, offering some of the Russian Crown Jewels as collateral. The jewels remained in a Dublin safe, forgotten by all sides, until the 1930s when they were found by chance.

But it was his military role that set Collins apart as he began a sophisticated intelligence war, with spies in the British headquarters in Dublin Castle, where he even had the nerve to spend the night himself, sifting through British files. He also recruited the 'Squad', hand-picked trained assassins, and they began the killing of informers and the more brutal policemen.

1920 was a year of terror, with killings and counter-killings, and the introduction of British volunteers to fight in Ireland, dubbed the 'Black and Tans', and the more effective ex-officer 'Auxiliaries'. Murder and atrocity escalated. By the end of the year, 50,000 troops and 15,000 policemen were in conflict with 15,000 Volunteers.

Michael Collins, still an unknown and invisible figure to the British, coolly cycled round Dublin visiting his girlfriend, Kitty Kiernan, meeting his men and plotting his next moves. He was tall, good looking, vivacious and popular, now affectionately named 'the Big Fella'. But he had a hard, cold streak when it was needed. Eventually, once they realised who they were dealing with, the British put a bounty of £10,000 on his head – £120,000 today.

The British now brought in a special group of intelligence officers, the 'Cairo Gang', to try to counteract Collins' great advantage. But he coldly used his 'Squad' to track them down and kill them in their beds one morning, the so-called 'Bloody Sunday'. Panicking Black and Tans vengefully reacted by shooting 14 dead at the Croke Park football stadium, with many more wounded. (They did *not* drive on to the pitch and machine gun players and spectators from an armoured car, as depicted in the otherwise excellent film *Michael Collins*.)

Bearing in mind that it had always been planned to give Ireland Home Rule, Britain now began to realize the cost of an almost full-scale guerrilla war in terms of lost lives, money and international reputation. The first peace feelers went out and led to a truce.

De Valera now came back from America. He was a difficult man, of Spanish origin. Willie Cosgrave once accused his ancestors of 'bartering budgerigars in the back streets of Barcelona'. He was plainly jealous of Collins, snarling as he arrived, 'We'll see who's the Big Fella'. When he first went to London, he pointedly excluded Collins from his group of negotiators.

Then, in a move that astonished observers, De Valera in 1921 made the Dáil upgrade his office from prime minister to president of the Republic, to make him the equivalent of King George V in the negotiations – then announced that as the king would not attend then neither should he as president. Instead, De Valera nominated a team of delegates headed by Arthur Griffith with Collins as his deputy. With heavy misgivings, Collins agreed to go to London.

They were being trapped into signing a treaty that would, because of Ulster's opposition, be forced to partition Ireland. Britain's Lord Birkenhead said to Collins, 'I may have signed my political death warrant tonight.' Michael Collins replied prophetically, 'I may have signed my actual death warrant.'

After the treaty was signed, it was Michael Collins as effectively the Irish Free State's prime minister who took over the reins of government from the Lord Lieutenant of Ireland, Viscount Fitzalan at Dublin Castle. When Fitzalan complained that Collins was seven minutes late for the ceremony, he retorted, 'You had to wait seven minutes, but we had to wait 700 years.'

In spite of Collins' best efforts at reconciliation, De Valera duly rejected the treaty, the Irish split and a civil war erupted. To avoid the return of the British, Collins was even forced to borrow field guns from them to shell his anti-treaty former comrades holed up in the Four Courts. The tragic civil war lasted 11 months and killed many more Irish than the war with Britain ever did.

Michael Collins, shown here during his time as the head of the Irish Free State Army, was only weeks away from being killed in an ambush in his native Cork.

And so it was that the Irish Free State's Commander in Chief, Michael Collins, feeling confident and at home, decided to do an inspection tour of his native West Cork. Many think his real purpose was to meet Republican leaders to end the civil war.

After meeting friends and supporters at various pubs, Collins drove off, supported by an armoured car. On the road to Bandon, at the village of Béal na mBláth (the mouth of the flowers), Collins' column stopped to ask directions. Unfortunately, the man they asked, Dinny Long, was a member of the local anti-treaty IRA. An ambush was prepared for the convoy when it returned. After a long wait, most of the ambush party had repaired to the nearby pub. When Collins and his men came back, the remaining five ambushers opened fire.

Tragically, Michael Collins, after a lifetime of quick decisions, now rose to the occasion just once too often. As Commander in Chief, as a minister and as probably the future president of Ireland, he should have taken the urgent advice of his sensible companions and retired 'in good order' to play his role in history.

But, no. Behaving more like an eager young corporal, he grabbed a rifle shouting, 'Let's fight, boys!' After half an hour, rashly standing up away from the cover of his armoured car, he was hit, in the failing light, by a last parting shot – ironically by a former British Army marksman, Sonny O'Neil.

His death caused an outpouring of grief which has never been seen before or since in Ireland, resembling that shown after the deaths of Princess Diana and Mahatma Gandhi. The sense of loss was shared by friends and foes alike, Irish and British. Had he lived, Ireland might have been a different place under Michael Collins than under the colder, fanatical Eamon de Valera. Who knows?

PRINCE BLÜCHER AND HIS HORSE

Even today in Germany, they still use the admiring phrase *Ran wie Blücher*, 'on to it like Blücher', about someone taking a direct and courageous course. A whole century on, they are commemorating the style of Prince Gebhard von Blücher, *Marchall Vorwärts*, 'Marshal Forwards', one of the two men who finally vanquished Napoleon. His actions the day before Waterloo would change the course of history.

Blücher was born on the Baltic near Rostock to a family who had been farming landowners for 500 years. Strangely, his first fighting was actually for the Swedes *against* the Prussians in 1760. He was captured by a Prussian colonel, who was so impressed by the fiery young hussar that he enrolled him in his regiment – unusual to say the least.

He was a typical young cavalryman, reckless, brave, proud – and sometimes unthinking. His excesses and pranks led to disciplinary action and he impetuously and foolishly wrote a rude letter of resignation to his King, Frederick the Great, who understandably ordered 'Der Rittmeister von Blücher kann sich zum Teufel scheren!' ('Cavalry Captain von Blücher can go to the devil!'). So young Blücher had to retire to the country for 15 years, take up farming and raise seven children. And there he might have quietly stayed, passed over by history. However, Frederick's death ended his exile and he rejoined the Red Hussars in 1787, winning Prussia's highest award for courage, the *Pour le Mérite* two years later.

Time and again he distinguished himself against the French, but often with the old touch of impetuosity, even when he became a general. At Auerstädt he charged too early, at Lübeck he was captured, but then exchanged for a French marshal. Napoleon wanted to meet such an exceptional enemy commander and visited the captive Blücher. They disliked each other on sight. Blücher's innate aggressiveness would be supplemented by a personal hatred of Napoleon – for the humiliation heaped on him, his army and his monarch. He would become a formidable enemy.

Soon he was a field marshal leading the Army of Silesia, 40,000 Prussians and 50,000 Russians in the 1813 'War of Liberation'. Napoleon was beaten at Leipzig, 'The Battle of the Nations'. He turned to maul Blücher twice, but was finally beaten by him at Laon and then at Montmartre, right at the gates of Paris.

With the war won, Napoleon exiled and a Bourbon king restored, Blücher once more retired to his estates, having visited England, where, among many honours, George Stephenson named his second steam locomotive *Blücher* after him.

But suddenly in February, Napoleon had escaped from Elba and had in weeks raised new armies from scratch. Prussia, Russia, Britain and Austria each pledged huge armies to defeat him – but only Britain and Prussia were close enough to intervene. Napoleon knew he must strike them first, before the other armies arrived. Moreover, he absolutely had to drive a wedge between the British and the Prussians and keep them separated at all costs.

The Duke of Wellington, interrupted by messengers at the Duchess of Richmond's ball in Brussels, knew full well that he had been 'humbugged' by both the speed and direction of Napoleon's approach. He rode to meet Blücher at the windmill at Brye to promise him a corps of 20,000 men. But he was then very nearly beaten himself at Quatre Bras, and it was a promise he just could not keep.

Napoleon next attacked Blücher at Ligny, starting quite late in the day, about 2.30pm. Hard pressed, Blücher was very lucky that, through faulty orders, D'Erlon's whole corps marched back and forth between the two battles – helping at neither Quatre Bras nor Ligny.

However, at 7.45pm, Napoleon, with a barrage of 60 guns, launched his final overwhelming assault on Ligny and the Prussians reeled back. Blücher, a white-haired old field marshal aged 72, saved the day by *personally* leading repeated cavalry charges. His horse was shot from under him and the old warrior was trapped under its body for some hours, until he was dragged out, semi-conscious, by his aide de camp (ADC).

In his long and inexplicable absence, General August von Gneisenau, his chief of staff, assumed command of the retreating Prussians. He personally disliked and distrusted Wellington, who he knew had, at the Congress of Vienna, been party to a secret treaty against the Prussians. He was also furious that the British help had not arrived as promised. As effectively the joint Prussian commander, he was about to give orders for his army to withdraw to safety towards the east, away from Wellington. Napoleon's dream of destroying his two enemies piecemeal was about to come true. But suddenly, a muddy, blood-spattered Blücher returned. He at once insisted on a retreat due north, to keep in touch with Wellington, 'to whom he had given his word'. So the Prussians withdrew towards Wavre in good order, unmolested by the exhausted French. Eight miles away, Wellington took up a new position that he had scouted a year before, on a ridge south of the village of Waterloo. It started to rain heavily as night fell.

Because of the rain, Napoleon had to wait next day at Waterloo for the ground to dry and only attacked Wellington at 11.30. The battle raged with Wellington playing a masterly defensive role. And all the time Blücher's men were struggling through the muddy 8 miles from Wavre to Waterloo. Even as Napoleon's troops were at last victorious at one of the two key farmhouses, La Haye Sainte, he could see that Plancenoit to his rear was suddenly in danger, because, after 11 gruelling hours, the Prussians had arrived. The emperor was forced quickly to throw in eight precious battalions of his reserve, the Young Guard, then two more of the Old Guard. They just held Plancenoit, but their absence fatally weakened by ten battalions the final uphill assault on Wellington, which failed. Blücher had indeed kept his promise and Napoleon was beaten at last.

When they met at a farmhouse called La Belle Alliance, Blücher suggested that was a good name for *their* battle. Wellington, however, insisted on 'Waterloo', making sure that it appeared a British victory.

It was perhaps a somewhat churlish attitude in view of the way that Blücher had more than risen to the occasion.

ALVIN YORK AND HIS RELUCTANT HEROISM

It is highly unusual for someone who believes that killing is a sin to become a war hero, just as it was unusual for his exploits to become a Hollywood hit, when his religion deeply disapproved of the movies. But both happened to Alvin York.

If you said to someone in England that you had been born in Pall Mall, an immediate picture of London's elegant Mayfair and high society would come to mind. But Alvin York was American and he was born in a very different Pall Mall, in a two-room log cabin in a rural Tennessee backwater. He was one of 11 children, and the way that he helped their precarious farming existence and supplemented it by shooting small game to feed his family is very reminiscent of that other American hero Audie Murphy, 40 years later. Except that Alvin York often used a muzzle-loader.

Alvin York received only a few months of formal education but many years of perfecting the use of a rifle. Unfortunately, as a young man he became a heavy drinker and a gambler in some very rough bars. Most people thought he would come to nothing.

Then in 1914, his best friend was killed in a bar fight, which shook Alvin to the core, and that event coincided with his attending a revival meeting of a strict religious sect, the Church of Christ in Christian Union, which existed in only three states, Ohio, Kentucky and Tennessee.

He enthusiastically embraced its teaching, which forbade drinking, dancing, swimming, going to the movies and popular literature, and also its stern attitude towards violence and war. All seemed fine with his new life.

However, in April 1917 the United States declared war on Germany. Two months later, nearing his 30th birthday, Alvin received his call-up papers. They were delivered by his friend the postman, who also happened to be his church's pastor, and who advised him to declare himself a 'conscientious objector' based on his religious beliefs. 'Dont want to fight', he wrote on his draft card. The authorities viewed his church as unofficial and would have none of it. Alvin York found himself, very reluctantly, in a Georgia boot camp in the 328th Infantry Regiment. There, he was regarded with something

A homespun, backwoods hero, Alvin York had to be persuaded that, in some circumstances, it was right to kill. (Bettmann / Corbis)

more than curiosity, a crack-shot who did not want to fight. However, both his company commander and his battalion commanding officer took the time patiently to engage him in religious debate, and eventually he became convinced that *some* warfare could be justified in God's eyes.

In October 1918, Alvin, now a corporal, found himself on the Meuse-Argonne front in France. The events that would make him a household name were about to unfold.

His battalion advanced to try to cut a railway line supplying the Germans in the Argonne Forest. In a funnel-shaped valley they were hit by machine gun and artillery fire from all sides. Alvin York described it in his own homespun style:

The Germans got us and they got us right smart. They just stopped us dead in our tracks. Their machine guns were up there on the heights, overlooking us and well-hidden and we couldn't tell for certain where the terrible heavy fire was coming from ... And I'm telling you they were shooting straight. Our boys just went down like the long grass before the mowing machine at home. Our attack just faded away. And there we were, lying down about half way across, and those machine guns and big shells getting us hard.

Seventeen men under Sergeant Early and Alvin York then managed to infiltrate the German lines and came across a large body of Germans and captured them. However, the Germans in the front line realized how tiny the American group was, and turned down their machine guns, pinning down captors and captives alike. Sergeant Early was hit with 17 bullet wounds and soon only eight men remained in action. York realized that he must silence the enemy:

> Those machine guns were spitting fire and cutting down the undergrowth all around me something awful. And the Germans were yelling orders. You never heard such a racket in all your life. I didn't have time to dodge behind a tree or dive into the brush… As soon as the machine guns opened fire on me, I began to exchange shots with them. There were over 30 of them in continuous action, and all I could do was touch the Germans off just as fast as I could. I was sharp shooting… All the time I kept yelling at them to come down. I didn't want to kill any more than I had to. But it was they or I. And I was giving them the best I had.

Indeed he was, taking out one German after another with his deadly rifle fire. One German officer, after emptying his pistol at the implacable York, finally opted to surrender his men too. York and his seven comrades now marched 132 prisoners to the rear. Asked by an amazed officer how many there were, he replied 'Hell, Lieutenant, I ain't had time to count them.'

York never claimed to have done it all on his own, but he was awarded the Medal of Honor. The American public latched on to him as a symbol of someone from a simpler past. A humble, self-reliant, God-fearing, taciturn country boy and still a very reluctant hero: 'A higher power than man guided and watched over me and told me what to do.' His similarities with Audie Murphy ended after the war. He was shocked by his celebrity and his welcome in New York, and struggled to get home to marry his sweetheart. He rejected all advances by Hollywood and advertisers, rather devoting himself to bringing education to the mountain children of Tennessee.

But he was to come back from self-imposed national obscurity and rise to the occasion again at the end of the 1930s. He had spent years as a Christian isolationist, questioning any American involvement in a future war. But the twin threats of genuinely evil German and Japanese warmongering now changed his mind completely.

First, he at last allowed a film to be made about his exploits, specifying that only Gary Cooper should play the role. Against Alvin's initial wishes to focus on his local good works, *Sergeant York*, released in 1941 and enormously successful, ended up as a call for patriotism and, with Pearl Harbor weeks away, it came out at just at the right moment.

York also publicly abandoned his isolationism and threw his weight and prestige behind the 'Fight for Freedom' committee, battling against another American hero, Charles Lindbergh, and his isolationist 'America First' movement (see page 225).

However brave his actions in the Argonne Forest may have been, his later use of his fame was probably much more important.

JOAN OF ARC AND THE SIEGE OF ORLÉANS

France in 1428 was in a desperate state. The Black Death had devastated her population the previous century. Then the longest war in history, the Hundred Years War, against the English over the succession to the French throne, had wrecked France economically. She had repeatedly lost too many of her ruling noble elite at defeats like Crécy, Poitiers and Agincourt. The victor of the last of these battles, Henry V, had been determined to unite England and France – under English rule (see page 193).

France's forces had also been fatally weakened by the rivalry between two factions, the Armagnacs and the Burgundians. The dire result was that nearly all northern France, including Paris, was now in English hands and the rich south-west was under the control of her allies, the Burgundians, who also controlled Rheims, the traditional site of French coronations. So her king, Charles VII, the Dauphin, had not even been properly crowned.

Now the English were besieging Orléans, the last loyal French city north of the Loire, the key to the remaining French heartland and, indeed, to the very future of the kingdom. Who were the demoralized French to turn to? Who would rise to the occasion?

It was not to be a battle-tested, noble veteran. It was, amazingly, to be a teenage, illiterate peasant girl, 'who saw visions'. It was as unlikely a scenario as a failed artist and ex-corporal, with staring eyes and a curious moustache, dominating the German officer corps and leading his country and much of the world to disaster. But, as with Adolf Hitler, Joan of Arc was only too real and was about to become a legend.

Joan was born in Domrémy, a little village in Lorraine and a loyal Armagnac speck in a sea of Burgundian countryside. Her father, Jacques d'Arc, a poor farmer, was the local tax collector and policeman. It was when she was 12, alone in a field, that Joan first heard voices. St Michael, St Catherine and St Margaret told her 'to drive out the English and bring Charles the Dauphin to Rheims to be crowned'. For four years the voices continued. She approached the local garrison commander, Count Robert de Baudricourt, to ask him to take her to see Charles at the royal court at Chinon. Not surprisingly, he merely laughed at the suggestion. But, ever persistent, she returned and this time made a remarkable prediction that there had been a serious reverse outside Orléans, a failed attempt to intercept a food convoy – the so-called 'Battle of the Herrings'. Now Count Robert listened and she was smuggled through Burgundian lines dressed as a man. At court, she was subjected to moral and religious examination and allowed, at last, to see the Dauphin.

We will never know what she whispered to Charles VII, but it impressed him enough to allow her to join a relief column heading for Orléans. Her horse, sword, escort and distinctive white armour were donated by friends. On the way she now sent the first of two extraordinary letters to the English besiegers:

> King of England and you, Duke of Bedford, who call yourself regent of the Kingdom of France ... Settle your debt to the King of Heaven. Return to the maiden, who is envoy of the King of Heaven, the keys to all the good towns you took and violated in France.

The second threatened 'to raise a war cry against you that will last forever. I shall not write any further.'

For years there had been strange prophesies that 'an armed maid from Lorraine' would rescue France. So when the virginal Joan, in her white armour, arrived at Orléans, the soldiers and citizens greeted her warmly. Not so the city's commander, Jean de Dunois, who proudly called himself the 'Bastard of Orléans' to show his noble blood relationship to Charles. He was cautious and conservative, had conducted no attacks except the failed 'Battle of the Herrings' and was now certainly not going to rise to any occasion. The arrival of this aggressive girl, who had somehow achieved royal support, was not welcome at all and he repeatedly blocked her from war councils and tried to forbid any aggressive moves. However, he was to be no match for the doggedly persistent Joan, who promptly carried out a proper reconnaissance.

Orléans, the seat of the Duke of Orléans the Armagnac leader, could expect little mercy from the English. But their cannons could not batter down the walls, nor had they enough men to make the siege watertight, so some meagre supplies and reinforcements could still get in – as Joan had done.

She quickly worked out that the key was the repossession of the various forts abandoned by the French early in the siege and she resolved to attack them. On 4 May, when Jean de Dunois was away, she led the assault on the fort of St Loup, which fell with 100 English dead. The next day she took over the fort of 'Jean le Blanc'. At a war council next day, Jean de Dunois refused further attacks, but Joan summoned the townspeople and soldiers, who forced the town mayor to unlock the gates. She took over the monastery fortress of St Augustines with just one captain at her side. However, another weak-willed war council, from which she had been excluded, decided to wait for reinforcements.

Undeterred, Joan prepared to attack the last key fort, Les Tourelles, a building on the 1,312ft, 400-metre, bridge into the city. Leading the assault, she was wounded and the English, who could only attribute Joan's charisma to magic, danced with premature joy, 'The witch is dead!' Once again, Jean de Dunois tried to call off the attack, but Joan insisted and that evening Les Tourelles fell. Next day the whole English Army paraded in battle formation. But after an hour they turned and marched away. The siege was over.

The effect was electrifying. Joan was made joint commander of French forces with the Duke of Alençon. Even Jean de Dunois now supported her. The army, transformed, won victory after victory, the battle of Patay being an Agincourt in reverse, a disaster for the English. Charles VII was crowned in Rheims on 17 July, and Joan was wounded again in the successful assault on Paris.

But vacillation by Charles and his courtiers once again made them back off and make a negotiated peace, promptly broken by the Burgundians.

Then disaster struck. In May 1430, Joan was captured commanding a rearguard by the Burgundians near Compiègne. Her family did not have the money to ransom her and Charles made no attempt to help the girl who had put him on his throne. So, after several daring escape attempts, she was sold to her enemies, the English.

They decided to destroy her dangerous myth with a trial for heresy. Joan was so measured and intelligent in her subtle replies to her inquisitors that the court had to be closed to the public and the records falsified.

After a trumped-up political trial, Joan, aged just 19, was burned at the stake and her ashes scattered.

But if her enemies thought that the legend of Joan of Arc would go away, they were mistaken. The last years of the Hundred Years War went badly wrong for England, and Joan herself became a symbol of fierce national liberation.

The statue of Joan of Arc in Orléans, the city that she relieved, thus starting Britain's decline in the Hundred Years War. (Orléans Tourism)

French politicians ever since have invoked her memory, and Charles de Gaulle adopted the 'Cross of Lorraine' as the symbol of the Free French Forces and the French resistance against German occupation. Innumerable writers, artists, composers and film makers have used her remarkable story.

In 1920, she was made a saint – surely the only time that a woman warrior has been given such an honour.

GÉRARD LEMAN AND HIS FORTS

Lieutenant-General Gérard Leman was a brave and resourceful officer, who had been the military tutor to his king, Belgium's Albert I. By August 1914, he had few illusions that Belgium's neutrality would be respected and he knew just how important the town of Liège, and even more important its railway line, were likely to be.

In many ways, the legendary German 'Schlieffen Plan' was a railway plan. The American Civil War had proved that railways, with their ability to move masses of men and supplies rapidly, were going to transform future warfare. Germany had so embraced the concept that only her best military graduates ('our finest horses') were allowed to go to the all-important Railway Department.

General Count Alfred von Schlieffen, the chief of staff, had personally spent 15 years studying in great detail both Germany's and her neighbours' railway systems for his proposed great sweep through Northern Europe, designed to defeat France in weeks, before turning on Russia – as the Kaiser overconfidently boasted, 'Lunch in Paris, dinner in St Petersburg'. Schlieffen had plotted out the role of every station, signal box, switch, bridge and wagon, to move with precision four million men and their horses, supplies and ammunition.

Liège was always going to be the key to such an assault. It not only blocked the best way into Belgium, but it also lay on the main railway line from Germany to Brussels and Paris, a line that Schlieffen had planned to use.

The Belgians, even if theoretically protected by neutrality, fully grasped the strategic significance of Liège. So, they had built a defensive ring of 12 forts round the town. Their overlapping fields of fire meant that, if one fort fell, its neighbours could still dominate the gap.

The forts, each manned by 80 men, had big 6in. guns in retractable steel cupolas, together with 4.7in. guns, heavy mortars and machine guns, and were surrounded by ditches and barbed wire. Their 400 heavy guns were not quite as formidable as they sounded, because they were contracted to be replaced, bizarrely, by modern German Krupp guns. Of course these were never to be delivered; moreover the Germans, because of their sales visits, were now also fully briefed on the design of the forts.

General Leman was put in charge of the 25,000 men who manned this defensive system. In addition to the forts, he energetically organized 18,000 labourers to dig trenches and earthworks to strengthen the defences round the town itself. A nervous visiting minister worried that it might 'compromise Belgium's neutrality'. Leman retorted that Belgians would thank him if war broke out, and if it did not, 'they can take away my stars'.

The Germans had assigned an elite force of 30,000 men, led by General Otto von Emmich and with General Erich Ludendorff as an observer. They smashed through 'neutral' Belgium's border on 4 August 1914, and next day attacked Leman's defences. However, they were bloodily repulsed time and again, in front of both the forts and the town, which was even bombed by a Zeppelin – the first air raid in history.

The clock was ticking, and after two days of costly failed assaults, Ludendorff took command of a brigade and infiltrated between two forts, capturing Liège itself. It made no difference to Leman. Only one of his forts had been captured, one had suffered a cupola mechanical failure, but the rest valiantly held out and still interdicted the all-important railway.

The over-rigid Schlieffen Plan was now being fatally delayed. The Germans had to turn urgently to Krupp in Essen, where huge 14.5in. howitzers (called *dicke Bertha*, 'Big Bertha', named after the owner, Bertha Krupp) were waiting. They were rushed off by rail, but delayed by a tunnel cleverly blocked by the retreating Belgians.

But eventually the squat, black 93-ton guns were hauled by road into Liège and their teams, 200 men for each, went to work. With a shattering roar that broke windows for blocks, their 1-ton shells left their muzzles, went a mile into the sky, sliced down through the forts' concrete roofs and exploded with devastating force. So horrible and inexorable was the shelling that the commander of one fort went mad and shot at his own men. Leman himself had both legs crushed by masonry, but was patched up and continued to be driven between the forts by car to encourage his men. But finally a Big Bertha shell hit Fort Loncin and its magazine. Colossal blocks of concrete crashed back down to earth, burying the garrison, who were all wounded or killed. Leman was dragged, asphyxiated by fumes, from under a beam by his orderlies. 'Respectez-vous le General, il est mort,' they entreated a German captain. But Leman came to, murmuring, 'It is as it is. Please put in your dispatches that I was unconscious.'

'Big Bertha', the massive Krupp howitzer that battered the forts of Liège to pieces.

One of the German officers, plainly moved by the bravery of General Leman and his men, reported:

> We brought him to our commander, General von Emmich, and the two generals saluted. We tried to speak words of comfort, but he was silent.
>
> Extending his hand, our commander said: 'General, you have gallantly and nobly held your forts.' General Leman replied: 'I thank you. Our troops have lived up to their reputations.'
>
> With a smile he added: 'War is not like manoeuvres' – a reference to the fact that General von Emmich was recently with General Leman during the Belgian manoeuvres. Then, unbuckling his sword, General Leman tendered it to General von Emmich. 'No,' replied the German commander, with a bow, 'keep your sword. To have crossed swords with you has been an honour,' and the fire in General Leman's eye was dimmed by a tear.

On his way to captivity, Leman wrote to his old pupil, the king:

> I am convinced that the honour of our arms has been sustained. I have not surrendered either the fortress or the forts.

Deign, Sire, to pardon my defects in this letter, I am physically shattered by the explosion of Loncin. In Germany, whither I am proceeding, my thoughts will be, as they have ever been, of Belgium and the King. I would willingly have given my life the better to serve them, but death was denied me.

His stubborn defence of the forts imposed a vital extra delay to the great German sweep through Belgium and Northern France, a delay that probably spoilt the whole enterprise. France was not knocked out of the war, the French and British counter-attacked on the Marne near Paris and trench warfare began. Germany's troops were not 'home by Christmas' and she was condemned to a long, bloody war that ruined her.

After the war, General Leman returned from four years' captivity to a hero's welcome in Belgium. It was well deserved.

ELAZAR BEN-YAIR AND MASADA

Nearly 2,000 years after the event, Israelis, especially soldiers, use the exhortation 'Masada must never fall again'. Masada is not far from Jerusalem, overlooking the Dead Sea, an isolated mountain standing 1,200ft above the Judean Desert with steep rocky sides – a natural fortress. And there King Herod, patronized by the Roman Empire, between 37 and 31 BC built such a fortress, but with luxurious palaces, with pools and bathhouses and a 1,412,586 cubic feet cistern supplied by an intricate water system using winter flood water, in an otherwise arid wasteland.

'Fortified by Heaven and man alike against any enemy who might wage war against it.' Thus was Masada described by Yossef Ben-Matityah, a Jewish historian who later joined the Romans as Josephus Flavius.

In AD 66 a Great Revolt against Rome broke out and the Zealots occupied Masada. The Zealots' extreme faction was the Sicarii, or 'Daggers', as they were called after their chosen tool of assassination (Judas Iscariot's name may have come from the sect).

Gradually more and more Zealots and Sicarii and their families arrived in this last refuge. Three years after the 'Destruction of the Temple' by the Roman Procurator Flavius Silva, *c.* AD 70, he turned to Masada, arriving with 15,000 men including the 10th Legion. They surrounded the mountain with eight camps and laid siege, thinking at first that the 967 men, women and children would quickly surrender, faced, after all, by impossible odds. It was not going to be as easy as that.

So formidable was the desert fortress that it would need the most sophisticated use of battering rams and siege engines to breach the defences. With typical thoroughness, the Romans first built a 2.5 mile wall with towers round Masada to seal it off. Then, to get their weapons close enough, the Romans forced thousands of Jewish prisoners of war to construct a huge 328ft-high earth ramp, topped by a 82ft stone platform on which was a timber tower armoured with iron plates. It took them three months, and the ramp can be seen to this day. The moment of reckoning had come. Under a hail of missiles, the ram breached the wall, but the assault team then found an earth-filled second wooden wall that they partially burned down.

Elazar Ben-Yair was the Jewish leader, and it became painfully obvious to him that the final assault was to be the next day, an assault that could lead only to the death and enslavement of everyone in the fortress. So he took a calculated and terrible decision. On the final evening, he gathered his people together and made this moving speech:

Brave and loyal followers! Long ago, we resolved to serve neither the Romans nor anyone other than God himself, who alone is the true and just Lord of mankind. The time has now come that bids us prove our determination by our deeds. At such a time, we must not disgrace ourselves. Hitherto we have never submitted to slavery, even when it brought no danger with it. We must not choose slavery now, and with it penalties that will mean the end of everything if we fall alive into the hands of the Romans... God has given us this privilege, that we can die nobly and as free men.

In our case it is evident that day-break will end our resistance, but we are free to choose an honorable death with our loved ones... Let our wives die unabused, our children without knowledge of slavery. After that, let us do each other an ungrudging

The desert fortress of Masada, still to this day surrounded by the visible traces of the camps and the assault ramp of the Roman besiegers. (Israeli Tourist Board)

kindness, preserving our freedom as a glorious winding-sheet. But first, let our possessions and the whole fortress go up in flames. It will be a bitter blow to the Romans, that I know, to find our persons beyond their reach and nothing left for them to loot.

One thing only let us spare – our store of food: it will bear witness when we are dead to the fact that we perished, not through want but because, as we resolved at the beginning, we chose death rather than slavery ... Come! While our hands are free and can hold a sword, let them do a noble service! Let us die unenslaved by our enemies, and leave this world as free men in company with our wives and children.

According to Josephus Flavius, the renegade Jew, the Jews then calmly and methodically committed suicide.

They then chose ten men from amongst them by lot who would slay all the rest; every one of whom laid himself down by his wife and children on the ground, and threw his arms about them, and they offered their necks to the stroke of those who by lot executed that melancholy office, and when these ten had without fear slain them all, they made the same rule for casting lots for themselves, that he whose lot it was should first kill the other nine, and after all, should kill himself ... and he who was last of all, examined the mass of those who lay on the ground, and when he had perceived that they were all slain, he set fire to all corners of the royal palace, and with the great force of his hand ran his sword into his body up to the hilt, and fell dead beside his kinsmen. Thus they all died believing that they had left no living soul behind to bear the Roman yoke.

The next day, the Romans at last breached the strangely silent, undefended and deserted ramparts. They were at first relieved, then puzzled, shocked and finally moved to find nothing but an eerie silence, dead bodies in little family groups and burned buildings and belongings. Hiding in a cistern were some children and two women who had lived to tell the terrible tale, a tale since confirmed by relics – pottery, coins, clothing, armour and even skeletons – perfectly preserved in the arid desert for 2,000 years.

The sacrifice at Masada did nothing to affect how the revolt would end, but it has acted as an icon for Jewish resistance ever since, from the Warsaw ghetto to Israel's many wars.

KEMAL ATATÜRK AND HIS WATCH

If you visit Turkey, something strikes you at once. In every public building, every office and even most homes you will be confronted by a portrait or a sculpture of one man – handsome, high cheekboned and with penetrating eyes. He is Kemal 'Atatürk' – 'father of the Turks'. And at 9.05 in the morning of each 10 November, the exact time of his death, vehicles stop and people observe one minute of respectful silence. The amazing thing is that he died in 1938. So it would be the unlikely equivalent of every public building in Britain still displaying to this day pictures of Neville Chamberlain or, in America, Franklin D. Roosevelt! No other military *and* civilian leader has ever earned such national respect – and one of the ways he earned it was by constantly rising to the occasion.

He was born in Salonika in Macedonia, then part of Turkey's sprawling and crumbling Ottoman Empire. His father was a minor civil servant and his mother a sturdy peasant. But Mustafa Kemal looked different, blue-eyed, fair-haired, almost blonde and he seemed to be different from other children. His teacher called him 'Kemal' or 'Perfection' because of his excellence at mathematics.

Although his mother wanted him to attend religious school, Kemal was determined to become an army officer, the only shortcut to social acceptance for someone of humble origins, and at 12 he joined a junior military college.

As he grew up, he developed a dislike of Arabic calligraphy and also of religious fanaticism of any kind. With his distinctive looks, he was highly attractive to women but was never dependent on them.

Mustafa Kemal, who became Kemal Atatürk, 'Father of the Turks'. (Hulton Getty)

A fervent nationalist, hating to see the Ottoman Empire (the 'Sick Man of Europe') in decline, he refused to participate in bribery and other scams practised by his fellow officers, recognizing that an honest approach was the only answer. Once he was mocked by urchins in Sicily, and he even began to hate the fez as a symbol of faded decline. It joined the long list of the things that he would one day change.

But Turkey itself *was* changing. Kemal joined a movement of young officers sworn to reform, and in 1908, a group of officers, the 'Young Turks', forced the sultan to abdicate in favour of his brother and brought in limited reforms. A key figure emerged, Major Ismail Enver (Enver Pasha), trim, polished and dapper – the image of a young Turkish officer – and one with whom Kemal would have a long rivalry. Kemal found himself constantly being exiled to obscure parts of the empire, to 'get him out of the way'. He fought in several defensive wars with distinction, becoming a highly efficient, brave and imaginative officer. A journalist noted: 'A very blond young officer was sitting on a chair. He was handsome and very well dressed, he had keen eyes and he was very proud. He attracted the attention of everybody, but he did not speak much. But it was obvious that he was far more important than his rank suggested.'

But something much bigger was brewing – quite close by. Bismarck had once prophesied, 'the next great war will start with some damn stupid thing in the Balkans.' Sure enough, in July 1914, the Austrian Archduke Franz Ferdinand was assassinated by Serbs at Sarajevo.

Enver, now heading a Triumvirate, had desperately searched for an ally against Turkey's great foe, the 'Russian Bear'. He secretly signed an alliance with Germany, offering, as a bribe, two battleships being finished in British shipyards (hiding the fact that Winston Churchill had already purloined them).

Often, Kemal had publicly come out against any alliance with Germany, reasoning that if Germany won Turkey would become a mere satellite and that if she lost Turkey would lose everything. As usual, he would be proved right. As usual, Enver ignored him and precipitated war.

Once the war that he had opposed broke out, Kemal threw himself into it with his usual energy and patriotic fervour. It would both make him famous and turn him into one of the great figures of history.

Enver Pasha, vainglorious and incompetent, tried two offensives. One, against the Russians, lost a whole precious army. The other, towards the Suez Canal, merely alerted the British to the danger.

Kemal was kicking his heels, deliberately blocked from significant command by the jealous Enver. Then at last in 1915 he was given the 19th Division and, under the overall command of the German General Otto Liman von Sanders, it was sent to Gallipoli. Colonel Mustafa Kemal was suddenly to be in the right place at the right time.

Gallipoli was a campaign thought up by the ever-imaginative Winston Churchill, Britain's First Sea Lord. To try to break the horrific, bloodletting deadlock on the Western Front, why not sidestep and knock out Turkey, the Central Powers' weak ally? The British and French first tried to force, with ships alone, the narrows of the Dardanelles by which they could reach the capital Constantinople, but they lost their nerve when three battleships were sunk by Turkish mines. Then land attacks began, the British at Cape Hellas and the Australians and New Zealanders (Anzacs) at Gaba Tepe. Hearing the guns, Kemal galloped almost alone to the point of danger, finding Turkish troops fleeing from the vital ridge overlooking the landing beaches.

He asked why they were running away, and they replied that they had no ammunition left. 'You have your bayonets,' he calmly replied, ordering them to fix bayonets, face the enemy and lie down. Amazingly, the Anzacs then also stopped and lay down. Vital moments had been gained, moments that decided the fate of the whole campaign. Now the Turkish 57th Regiment came scrambling and panting to the summit, dragging mountain guns that Kemal himself helped to manhandle into position.

An Australian soldier at Gallipoli, running with his wounded comrade. (Imperial War Museum)

Kemal wrote a memorable order for the counter-attack: 'I don't order you to attack, I order you to die. In the time it takes for us to die, others can come and take our place.' Under the furious Turkish assaults, the Anzac troops fell back from the ridge, only just saving themselves by digging in near the beach. Their chance of a swift advance to victory was gone.

Fresh British landings in August prompted Kemal to ask Von Sanders for 'unified command'. He was helped by British irresolution – the British were bathing in the sea! But Kemal, in spite of days without sleep and suffering from malaria, was everywhere in action, galvanizing his troop, who only needed proper leadership. Once again, a ridge, Tekke Tepe, was the key, and Kemal and his Turks once again won the race and reached the summit first, pushing back the British. That night, before dawn, the Turks attacked silently, using only the bayonet – only naval shells later saved the British from total collapse.

Suddenly, Kemal was struck in the chest by shrapnel. Seeing the blood, his ADC rushed to help him. 'Sir, you're hit!' 'Nothing of the sort,' he calmly replied, silencing the young officer. His watch, in his breast pocket, had shattered, but had saved him. 'Here's a watch that's worth a life!' he mused. At the head of 'Johnny Turk' as the Turks were now respectfully known, Kemal's personal leadership blunted the British attacks, and indeed the official British historian would write, 'Seldom in history can the exertions of a single divisional commander have exercised, on three separate occasions, so profound an influence not only on the course of the battle, but perhaps on the fate of a campaign and even the destiny of a nation.'

Indeed. The British, after months of cruel losses, finally withdrew.

After the war, Kemal erected a monument at Gallipoli to the hundreds of thousands of the fallen of both sides with the moving and generous words:

> Those heroes that shed their blood and lost their lives, you are now lying in the soil of a friendly country. Therefore, rest in peace. There is no difference between the Johnnies and the Mehmets to us where they lie side by side, now in this country of ours. You, the mothers who sent their sons from far away countries, wipe away your tears; your sons are now lying in our bosom, and are at peace. After having lost their lives on this land, they have become our sons as well.

Mustafa Kemal was now famous and went on to fight, as best he could, in campaigns that Turkey was bound to lose, in the east against Russia and in the west against Allenby and Lawrence's 'Arab Revolt'.

When peace came, just as he had predicted, the Ottoman Empire did lose everything – dismembered and occupied (imagine how powerful Turkey would be today if she had remained neutral, controlling half the oil-rich Middle East).

Intensely patriotic, Kemal was appalled at what had happened. But he acted decisively once more. A friend, the Chief of the General Staff, persuaded the sultan to send Kemal to the heartland of Anatolia as an 'inspector' to supervise the disarming of Turkish troops. Instead at 38, and as the 'hero of Gallipoli', he began to organize resistance, helped enormously by Lloyd George's encouragement of the Greeks to land 20,000 troops at Smyrna and invade inland. Here was a familiar common enemy. Deep in Anatolia, Kemal became the master of the telegraph, persuading troops and local governors to join him, and then making them swamp the sultan's government with cables demanding 'justice'.

As more and more of Turkey's hinterland joined Kemal, the British became thoroughly alarmed. Soon the Ottoman government ordered his recall, next his arrest and even finally condemned him to death.

The Greek armies nearly reached Ankara, Kemal's new 'capital', but he smashed them at the Sakarya River and then later drove them into the sea at Smyrna. There, he was helped by his opponent, General Hajianestis, a political appointee, who did not rise to the occasion and indeed did not rise at all, deciding that he should not get out of bed on his yacht in Smyrna harbour because his legs were made of glass and might shatter. With the foreigners expelled or persuaded to leave, Kemal became not just a military hero but a political giant. He abolished the sultanate and the last sultan left for exile on a British battleship. Turkey became a republic and Kemal, aged 43, its first president.

He then embarked on one of the greatest eras of change in any country's history. He built a genuine democracy, liberating women, giving them the vote and political power. Turkey became a secular state by law, no longer dominated by the Muslim religion. The veil was banned ('The Law Relating to Prohibited Garments') together with his old pet hate, the fez ('The Hat Law', 1925).

Arabic writing was changed to Western, Roman script to improve both education and business communication, huge railway and road networks were built and modern new industries like car-making and aircraft construction encouraged.

Kemal ruled as president from 1923 until 1938, 15 years in which he really earned his title 'Atatürk'. His death, at the age of 57, was mourned deeply, his funeral procession 2 miles long, senior officers and ministers openly weeping.

What a good thing for his country that Kemal's watch saved him.

4

A CONSTANT THREAD OF VALOUR

MICHAEL WITTMANN AND HIS TIGER

The view was both enticing and intimidating. SS-Sturmführer Michael Wittmann stared down into the village of Villers-Bocage. There below him was a long column of tanks and other vehicles, the spearhead of the British 7th Armoured Division, the famous 'Desert Rats'. Wittmann was not one of the people they should want to meet. He was already one of Germany's Panzer aces, with 88 destroyed tanks to his credit. He had risen from the ranks to campaign in Poland, Greece, the Balkans and Russia, being wounded twice. During the battle of Kursk, the largest tank battle in history, he and his crew had, time and again, knocked out many Soviet tanks and guns. On just one day, 13 January 1944, they had destroyed no fewer than 19 T-34s and three heavy assault guns, a feat for which Wittmann was personally decorated by Adolf Hitler. He married his sweetheart, and his best man was his superb gunner, Balthazar (Bobby) Woll.

Now his handful of heavy Tiger tanks were all that was in position to try to stop a massive thrust by Montgomery's forces towards Caen. The British were totally unaware of their forthcoming nemesis. The commanding officer of the 4th County of London Yeomanry, Lieutenant-Colonel Lord Cranleigh, had asked headquarters if he could do a proper reconnaissance, but had been told to press on regardless.

Michael Wittmann atop his Tiger. He was probably the most daring and successful tank ace of all time.

Wittmann could not radio for reinforcements for fear of detection, and he had only six serviceable Tigers, but he knew what he had to do. 'The decision was a very, very difficult one. Never before had I been so impressed by the strength of the enemy as I was by those tanks rolling by. But I knew it absolutely had to be and I decided to strike into the enemy.'

One reason for his confidence against such odds was the Tiger tank itself. Weighing 57 tons, it looked like a steel blockhouse of thick armour and mounted the legendary high-velocity 88mm gun that could destroy any Allied tank up to a mile and a half away. By contrast, the thinly-armoured, small-gunned Shermans were called 'Tommy-cookers' by the Tiger crews, and 'Ronsons' by the cynical British because they lethally lived up to the cigarette lighter's famous advertising slogan: 'Lights up first time, every time'. The Cromwells were not a lot better.

Wittmann now briefed his other crews to attack in another direction and then burst from cover and rumbled down alone towards the British column. Having met nothing but cheering French villagers, the confident British troops had decided to stop and make tea. They stared aghast at the approaching monster. 'Clang'. The first Sherman, then a Cromwell went up in flames. Gunner Woll then carefully took out the vehicles at the front of the British column to block any escape. Most of the British crews could do nothing but hide, unable even to reach their doomed tanks, some still with their engines running. Woll's loader, Boldt, had to work like a crazy man with the 30lb shells as Woll slammed them into three more tanks and then the thin-skinned vehicles. They stopped wasting shells on these and reduced them to wrecks using just the Tiger's machine guns. Then the big gun started again, and three light tanks were destroyed.

Wittmann was not finished. Leaving the blazing wrecks littering the road, he now entered Villers-Bocage. The great tank rocked back on its suspension as four Cromwells in the village square went up in flames. Then he collapsed a house onto a Sherman. Another Sherman tried to stalk Wittmann from a side street. It was a 'Firefly', which was the one tank that the Tigers feared because it mounted the excellent British 17-pdr. But its two shells just bounced off the Tiger, whose turret then inexorably turned and its massive gun blew the British commander straight out of his turret, killing his crew.

Once surprise was lost, Wittmann knew that narrow streets were no place for a huge and unwieldy tank to remain too long, but leaving town he was stopped, ironically, by a humble 6-pdr anti-tank gun which managed to hit and jam his sprocket drive wheel. So he and his crew had to walk back to his unit. His exploit had been amazing. He alone had destroyed 27 enemy vehicles, including 12 tanks. Together with his little group of Tigers, he had completely blunted Montgomery's great attack.

He was now a hero throughout Germany and could now have gone on to the Staff or become an instructor at tank school – but once more he volunteered to fight. He was killed just weeks later, carefully stalked from the side by one of those 'Firefly' Shermans.

He would probably have admired the way they did it.

COLONEL CHAMBERLAIN AND HIS GETTYSBURG CHARGE

Like so many officers in the American Civil War, Joshua Lawrence Chamberlain had no formal military training. When war broke out he was living a quiet life as a professor at Bowdoin College, Maine, teaching modern languages, rhetoric and oratory.

When he volunteered to enlist, against his college's wishes, his only qualification for command was that he was 'a gentleman of the highest, moral, intellectual and literary worth'. So he was made a lieutenant-colonel. But unlike some other such untrained officers, like General Ledlie (see page 190), Chamberlain was to rise time and time again to the occasion and, on one such occasion, he was to alter the course

Joshua Chamberlain, the college professor whose defence of Little Round Top and desperate charge probably won the battle of Gettysburg. (Library of Congress)

of a battle, a campaign and, indeed, a whole war.

His regiment, the 20th Maine, was made up of local farmers and lumbermen, seamen and trappers. They were bloodied at Antietam, and they bravely assaulted at Fredericksburg:

The 20th Maine … coming across the field in line of battle, as upon parade, the great gaps … plainly visible as the shot and shell tore through… It was a grand sight and a striking example of what discipline will do for such material in such a battle.

But, like all the other regiments, they were shredded by devastating Confederate gunfire and were forced to hug the ground. Fourteen assaults were beaten back and 9,000 men fell. Confederate General Robert E. Lee, victorious, murmured sadly, 'It is well that war is so terrible, or we should grow too fond of it.' Chamberlain and his men endured a frozen night and a terrible day trapped under fire among their dead and dying.

A year later, Chamberlain, now a colonel, approached Gettysburg and he first had to deal with a sensitive problem. 120 soldiers of the 2nd Maine were handed to him in a state of mutiny. 'I am told that I'm allowed to shoot you – but you know I won't.' His quiet oratorical skill with words now persuaded nearly all of them to forget their grievances and join the 20th, adding a third to the depleted little regiment.

A crisis loomed as soon as they reached the battlefield. The Confederate 15th Alabama Regiment had scrambled up the 300ft hill, Big Round Top, and saw the opportunity to reach the next hill, Little Round Top, which dominated the whole Gettysburg battlefield and had on it only a few Union signalmen. Union troops were rushed to fill the gap, as Private Theodore Gerrish recalled:

It was a critical moment. If that line was permitted to turn the Federal flank, Little Round Top was untenable, and with this little mountain in the Confederates' possession, the whole position would be untenable. It was a most fortunate fact for the Union cause that in command of the Twentieth Maine was Colonel Joshua Lawrence Chamberlain.

As they advanced, a shell fell near them and Chamberlain sent his two brothers to different parts of his line. 'Boys, another shot might make it difficult for mother.'

Their orders were to hold the hill 'at all hazards'. Just in time he despatched his Company B across the defile, before the Confederates hit them minutes later. His little regiment was now all that could stop the 80,000-strong army from being outflanked. Now assault after assault by thousands rushed up against Chamberlain's 350 men, as he eloquently recalled:

> The edge of the conflict swayed to and from, with wild whirlpools and eddies. At times I saw around me more of the enemy than of my own men; gaps opening, swallowing, closing again; squads of stalwart men who had cut their way through us, disappearing as if translated. All around a strange, mingled roar.

A bullet struck Chamberlain on his thigh but he was saved by his sword scabbard. 40,000 rounds were fired on those wooded slopes, cutting right through trunks of trees. With a third of his men down, soon ammunition was running out, and so the next assaults would overwhelm them. He decided on a bold and desperate action. He was going to charge.

> Not a moment was about to be lost! Five minutes more of such a defensive and the last roll call would sound for us! Desperate as the chances were, there was nothing for it but to take the offensive. I stepped to the colors. The men turned towards me. One word was enough – 'BAYONETS!' It caught like fire and swept along the ranks.

Then, while the right of Chamberlain's regiment held straight, he had his left plunge down the hillside, all the while wheeling to the right – 'like a great gate upon a post'.

The 2,000 Confederates, expecting imminent victory, were taken completely by surprise. Some of those in front dropped their weapons. 'An officer fired his pistol at my head with one hand,' Chamberlain remembered, 'while he handed me his sword with the other.'

Others turned and ran. They had gone only a few paces when they received another horrifying surprise. Chamberlain's Company B, which had survived the earlier fighting by taking shelter behind a stone wall, rose and fired into the retreating rebels.

It was too much for the brave and exhausted men of 15th Alabama. They broke and ran 'like a herd of wild cattle', as their colonel, William Oates, frankly admitted.

It was one of those decisive moments in warfare and Chamberlain had more than risen to the occasion.

He was to fight on in the same style for the rest of the war, six times wounded, once so severely that he read his obituary in the newspapers.

At the end of a tragic war that had killed 600,000 Americans, it was Chamberlain, now a general, who received the formal surrender of the Confederate Army of Northern Virginia on 12 April 1865. Twenty thousand men in a tattered grey column, headed by General John Gordon, himself wounded five times, approached Chamberlain, who was lost in admiration:

> On they came, with the old swinging route step and swaying battle flags. In the van, the proud Confederate ensign… Before us in proud humiliation stood the embodiment of manhood; men whom neither toils and sufferings, nor the fact of death … could bend from their resolve; standing before us now, thin, worn, and famished, but erect, and with eyes looking level into ours, waking memories that bound us together as no other bond.

A magnanimous Chamberlain called his victorious army to attention, 'a token of respect from Americans to Americans'. The gesture was at once appreciated by his former enemies:

> At the sound of that machine-like snap of arms, General Gordon started, then wheeled his horse facing me, touching him gently with the spur so that the animal

slightly reared and, as he wheeled, horse and rider made one motion, the horse's head swung down in a graceful bow, and General Gordon dropped his sword-point to his toe in salutation.

Chamberlain went on to be governor of Maine four times and to devote himself to education. But his scholar's example of the very best of 'officer qualities' will always be remembered for that little hill.

CLAUS VON STAUFFENBERG AND HIS BOMB

In the future when people look back, they will be incredulous. 'We don't believe it. A little Austrian corporal with a funny moustache managed to get and keep absolute control of something as hierarchical and conservative as the German officer corps, and lead it to its obvious doom. It's impossible and ridiculous.'

But of course that is exactly what happened. When the scruffy and brutal Nazi Party, led by Adolf Hitler, tried to take power, the venerable Chancellor, Field Marshal Hindenburg, commented acidly, 'Him for Chancellor? I'll make him a postman and he can lick the stamps with my picture on them!' But, like others, he had underestimated Hitler and soon they were driving together to open parliament.

Once in power, Hitler forced his officers to swear an oath of loyalty to him *personally*. With rapidly expanding armed forces and plenty of new jobs, they went along with it. They also went along with the destruction of the rival *Sturmabteilung*, Ernst Röhm's three million SA 'Brownshirts', and the murder of its leadership, in what has become known as the 'Night of the Long Knives'.

As Germany edged towards war, there were anxious officers willing to remove Hitler. But such conspiracies evaporated after his stunning and bloodless political successes, the re-occupation of the Rhineland, the *Anschluss* with Austria, and the Munich Agreement which obtained half of Czechoslovakia while the Allies sat on their hands.

And again any thought of a coup against Hitler was removed by the generals' brilliant successes in Poland, Norway and France. It was only when things started to go wrong and Germany's vulnerability became obvious that anyone honourable in the officer corps would emerge to rise to the occasion.

And so in July 1944, a staff car wound its way through the sultry, dank forests of Poland, carrying a one-eyed colonel with a yellow briefcase. He had come to kill Hitler.

An aristocratic, religious and family man, the handsome Count Claus von Stauffenberg's military ancestry went back to the 13th century. He had fought bravely and loyally in all of Hitler's campaigns, but the atrocities he had seen in Russia had appalled him and convinced him that Hitler was the 'anti-Christ', an incarnation of evil. 'Is there no officer in HQ capable of shooting that beast?' In North Africa fighting the

At the Wolf's Lair at Rastenburg, Stauffenberg (left) watches Hitler and plans his assassination attempt.

British, he had lost an eye, a hand and two fingers. He was now the key figure in one last conspiracy to get rid of Hitler and the Nazis before it was too late.

Germany was in real trouble. By that fateful day, 20 July 1944, the Allies were advancing from their Normandy beachhead and the Russians were only 60 miles from German soil. In deep despair, hundreds of army officers were now at last part of Operation *Valkyrie*, a plan to take over Berlin, Paris and Brussels, arresting the SS and Gestapo and making peace with the Allies. This was their third attempt to kill Hitler with a bomb.

A fatal complication was that Stauffenberg was no suicide bomber or merely the assassin. He had to survive: because, as chief of staff of the 'Replacement Army,' he also had to lead the revolt and win over the fainthearted. When he arrived at Rastenburg's *Wolfsschanze*, or Wolf's Lair headquarters, he was given bad news. The Führer's briefing would be held in a wooden hut with open windows – not nearly as deadly in an explosion as the still-unfinished concrete bunkers. It was also to be held early, so Hitler could welcome his fellow dictator, Mussolini, who had recently been rescued by German troops from the mountains where the Italians had imprisoned him. So they had to move quickly. He and his adjutant went to 'freshen up' and carefully to assemble and prime the two bombs they had brought. This delicate task was made no easier by Stauffenberg's missing hand and fingers. They were suddenly interrupted and told they were late for the briefing, so duly decided that one bomb must suffice.

The colonel hurried to the conference, knowing that acid was eating away at a ten-minute fuse. He placed his briefcase under the wooden table only a yard from Hitler's feet, and awaited a pre-arranged 'urgent telephone call' which gave him the excuse to leave the room. Then something terrible happened that changed the course of history. Colonel Heinz Brandt, who was actually one of the conspirators but who knew nothing about the bomb plot, became irritated by the briefcase at his feet, and reached down and lifted it to the other side of the stout wooden table support.

Stauffenberg waited until the bomb exploded, blowing out the windows in clouds of smoke. He then bluffed his way through three checkpoints and caught his plane to Berlin.

What he did not know was that Hitler had, in fact, been saved from most of the blast by the thick oak support. He staggered out blackened and shaken, but he survived and was soon able to show Mussolini the wrecked room. 'Duce! I have just had the most enormous good fortune!' He did not know how good.

Stauffenberg, convinced he had killed Hitler, after a three-hour flight was appalled to find that nothing had been done in Berlin. Frantically, he arrested his wavering boss, General Fromm, and began to work the telephones. It was too late. Goebbels, the Propaganda Minister, had telephoned a key figure, Major Otto Remer, Berlin's Guards' commander, with Hitler at his side. 'Do you recognize my voice?' shouted the deafened Führer.

Major Remer did and unfortunately rose to the occasion himself, starting to arrest, not support, the Berlin conspirators.

The Wolf's Lair's teleprinters countermanded their well-planned orders. In Paris, the army had literally put out sandbags to prepare for the shooting of the SS and Gestapo. If it had happened, the war would have been over. Then came the final proof – Hitler's unmistakable voice on national radio. 'A minuscule clique of ambitious, unscrupulous officers of criminal stupidity have been plotting to get rid of me and to liquidate virtually the entire German command staff.'

The game was up. In Berlin, Fromm escaped, arrested Stauffenberg and his comrades and, to try to hide his own equivocal position, quickly had them shot in the courtyard. Stauffenberg's brave last words were 'Long live sacred Germany!' Fromm's cowardly action did him little good. Hitler's suspicions ran deep and wide, and his revenge was terrible. Fromm joined nearly 5,000 people, not just officers but civil servants, professionals and clerics, who were executed, some by slow strangulation hanging by piano wire, with Hitler gloatingly watching the filming each night.

Colonel Brandt, who had saved Hitler's life by mistake, died in hospital. At first, he was promoted by Hitler to general to increase the pension for his family, until fellow patients recalled him crying out in delirium, 'How callous of Stauffenberg to place the bomb at my feet, when I was one of the conspirators!'

Had Hitler died, it would have shortened the war by nearly a year, saving millions of lives and preventing Eastern Europe going behind a savage Iron Curtain.

What a terrible pity it was that, when at last a German officer had risen to the occasion, everything should be wrecked by such multiple bad luck.

EUGENE ESMONDE AND THE SIX SWORDFISH

'It's Gneisenau.'

'Yes, it's turned out nice here too.'

The muddled response of a poor young Wren manning the telephone at Dover Castle was typical of a whole plan that was falling apart, becoming the single most disgraceful incident for Britain in World War II.

There were a lot of people who did not rise to the occasion during the 'Channel Dash' of the battlecruisers *Gneisenau* and the *Scharnhorst* – all of them British.

There were three who did rise to the occasion; two were German and one was Irish.

Since the Norway campaign in 1940, when they had sunk the aircraft carrier *Furious*, and then in a successful commerce raid into the Atlantic, the two heavy battlecruisers had been trapped in the French port of Brest, offering a vague threat to shipping, but otherwise becoming increasingly vulnerable to British bombing. It was Adolf Hitler who realized that they should be moved to much more valuable work protecting Norway or threatening the Arctic convoys to Russia. He boldly followed one of his 'hunches', deciding that the ships could pass the Straits of Dover in daylight, because the British would be expecting them at night. Operation *Cerberus* was born. 'You will find that this operation will turn out to be our most spectacular naval success of the war.' The Führer's confidence was not misplaced.

The other German to rise to the occasion was Adolf Galland, the Luftwaffe ace who carefully masterminded a fighter umbrella using every Messerschmitt 109 and Focke-Wulf 190 in the west that he could lay his hands on – 280 of them.

The British had been planning for such an eventuality for a year, but Operation *Fuller* was judged so secret that hardly anyone knew about it, especially those who were meant to carry it out.

As so often happens in war, when the time came, multiple bad luck also intervened. In the early hours of 12 February 1942, the moment of sailing was hidden by a smokescreen provided by a bombing raid on Brest. The submarine watching the entrance had withdrawn to recharge its batteries. Three Hudson reconnaissance planes each developed mechanical problems and two Spitfires missed the ships under the clouds. The Germans had also progressively increased their jamming of the British radar. The armada, undetected, was on its way at 28 knots, with the two 32,000-ton battlecruisers supported by the heavy cruiser *Prinz Eugen* and 30 destroyers and E-boats. Every ship had added extra flak guns, supplementing an already formidable anti-aircraft threat.

After nearly 12 hours, the ships and their swarm of fighters were at last detected by radar and slowly the British began to stir. But there were no capital ships to oppose the Germans, the modern Beaufort torpedo bombers had to be brought in from Scotland and Cornwall and the plans for Operation *Fuller* were actually locked up at the fighter base at Biggin Hill. As the hours passed, the strange inactivity made the Germans ecstatic but nervous, as Helmut Backhaus in the *Scharnhorst* wrote:

A Focke-Wulf 190 closes in on Esmonde's stricken Swordfish, while *Scharnhorst* proceeds unscathed. ('Channel Dash' by Charles Thompson, GAvA, ASAA)

Yes, the first time, you know, we were very glad, and I tell you every seaman cried, 'Hooray, hooray, we're going back home', then half an hour later we were singing. But this was very dangerous because this is under the English coast. You know what might happen now. But we go for one hour and the second hour, nothing happened, and then nearly Dover…

Now virtually all that stood between the German fleet and safety was six Swordfish biplanes commanded by Lieutenant-Commander Eugene Esmonde, an Irish aristocrat who had been flying for the RAF and now Coastal Command for several years. He had been awarded the DSO for his torpedo attack from HMS *Victorious* that had helped to destroy the *Bismarck* in May 1941, and in that November had been able to fly his Swordfish off the sinking *Ark Royal* near Gibraltar.

The Fairey Swordfish, despite its antiquated appearance, was actually quite modern, entering service in 1936. Bizarrely, it was one of the most successful aircraft in the war, among many actions not only crippling the *Bismarck*, but sinking three Italian battleships at Taranto (and inspiring the Japanese attack on Pearl Harbor).

But the Swordfish, nicknamed 'the Stringbag', was very slow indeed. Loaded with a torpedo, it could scarcely manage 100mph. Once, in a strong headwind in the Mediterranean, an Italian fleet had actually sailed away from pursuing Swordfish.

So to use just six Swordfish in broad daylight was literally suicidal. Admiral Ramsey pleaded with Admiral Sir Dudley Pound, the First Sea Lord, not to use the Swordfish alone, but, now with a furious Churchill on his back, Pound merely said, 'The navy will attack the enemy whenever and wherever he is to be found.'

Esmonde was waiting at Manston for the vital protection of 60 Spitfires. In the confusion, only ten turned up. But as the ships steamed northwards, he could wait no longer. A fellow pilot noted his appearance with horror: 'Although his mouth twitched automatically into the semblance of a grin and his arm lifted in a vague salute, he barely recognized me. He knew what he was going into, but it was his duty. His face was tense and white. It was the face of a man already dead. It shocked me as nothing has ever done since.'

As the Swordfish lumbered slowly along, the ten much faster Spitfires had to weave just to keep in contact. Soon, they were all overwhelmed by the swarms of pouncing German fighters. Then a blizzard of flak of all calibres began to shred the surviving canvas-covered biplanes.

Esmonde's port wing was shattered, he staggered on, but 8,858ft from the target his plane burst into flames and he crashed into the sea. Captain Hoffman of the *Scharnhorst* exclaimed, 'Poor fellows, they are so very slow. It is nothing but suicide to fly against these big ships.'

Indeed. All six Swordfish were shot down. Out of 18 airmen, only five survived, only one of them unwounded. *Scharnhorst*'s navigator, Helmut Geissler, added his praise: 'Such bravery was devoted and incredible. One was privileged to witness it. Although they were shot down by our anti-aircraft fire before they could get into position to release their loads, they knowingly and ungrudgingly gave their all to their country and went to their doom without hesitation.'

Dover passed. Some destroyers and motor torpedo boats now tried to attack but were easily beaten off. The Germans were almost out of danger and the 270 aircraft that belatedly turned up scored no hits. Hitler's hunch had been vindicated.

The British, of course, added their praise for the Swordfish attack, and Eugene Esmonde was awarded a posthumous Victoria Cross, the citation concluding: 'His high courage and splendid resolution will live in the traditions of the Royal Navy, and remain for many generations a fine and stirring memory.'

However, the decorations and the public's focus on the bravery of his little group, and not on the incompetence of so many others, were reminiscent of the shower of VCs and the Victorian adulation for the defenders of Rorke's Drift, to mask the disgrace of Isandlwana (see page 231).

Many senior heads, perhaps, should have rolled. If not Churchill's, then Sir Dudley Pound's for the Royal Navy and Air Marshal Trafford Leigh Mallory's for the RAF.

But, of course, they didn't.

ALBERT JACKA AND HIS ONE VICTORIA CROSS

It was a unique tribute in the country's history. In the little town of St Kilda, a coffin was being carried by eight other Australian holders of the Victoria Cross, watched by tens of thousands. Australia's greatest war hero was being laid to rest. And, but for the conservative attitudes of the British Army of that time, they might have been watching something else unique – the burial of a holder of not one but three Victoria Crosses.

By chance, Albert Jacka was born in Victoria and was working for the Victoria State Forests Department when, 8,000 miles away in Sarajevo, a young Serbian killed an Austrian archduke. Great Britain found herself at war and, like all the volunteers of the Australian Imperial Forces, 'Bert' Jacka decided to fight for the 'Old Country' and the Empire.

Jacka was typical of Australia's troops, intensely independent, outspoken, even sometimes 'difficult'. But, as one historian put it, 'some of the best men in the trenches were those who had given most trouble in training'.

After nine months, Acting Lance-Corporal Albert Jacka, aged 22, was in Gallipoli, rocky and inhospitable, facing unremitting, brave and skilful resistance by the Turks (see page 95). Thanks to feeble British generalship, the Anzac forces had never broken out of their beachhead and were constantly being

Albert Jacka, Australian hero, whom many think should have been awarded three Victoria Crosses rather than one. (Australian War Memorial)

shelled or under attack. Losses were just as bad as they were on the Western Front, for which Gallipoli was meant to be an easier 'diversion'. At a vital point on the ridgeline, 'Courtney's Post', the two front lines were only yards apart and on the night of 19 May 1915 the Turks attacked.

While others withdrew, Jacka doggedly held his position and continued to fire. An officer, Lieutenant Hamilton, tried to help, but was instantly killed, shot through the head. Another, Lieutenant Crabbe, gathered volunteers to help Jacka, but the first man to move was wounded three times in seconds, such was the intensity of the machine gun fire. Stopping Crabbe and the others from suicidal exposure, Jacka decided to go it alone and, under diversionary fire, he charged the Turks, shooting five and bayoneting two. He held their trench until dawn and Crabbe found him surrounded by bodies, with an unlit cigarette in his mouth. 'Well, I got the beggars, Sir!' Jacka was the first Australian recipient of the Victoria Cross.

By the blazing heat of August, he was a company sergeant-major and his battalion suffered 600 casualties out of 800 at Chunuk Bair. Eventually, after 26,000 Australian casualties, the Allies withdrew in the cold of winter that December.

Now commissioned as a second lieutenant, Jacka then performed his second memorable feat. During the horrifying Somme offensive, the Australians had captured the shattered village of Pozières, losing thousands of men. Under intense shelling during the German counter-attack, a grenade rolled into Jacka's captured German dug-out, and he and the survivors of the blast staggered out to find themselves 200 yards behind the second wave of advancing Germans. What is more, the Germans nearest were escorting 42 Australian prisoners to their rear. Jacka, with just seven men, did not hesitate, but launched himself at the 60 Germans. Two of his comrades were killed, all the others were wounded and Jacka was wounded seven times, but picked himself up and personally killed 12 of the enemy. The Australian prisoners were freed, the Germans now surrendered and the ridge was retaken.

As a stretcher-bearer said, 'the bravest man in the Aussie Army is on that stretcher. It's Bert Jacka, and I wouldn't give a Gyppo piastre for him – he's knocked about dreadfully.'

Jacka survived, but sadly his own company commander had been hundreds of yards away and his battalion commander played down Jacka's action. So Jacka 'only' received a Military Cross, but C. E. W. Bean, the Australian Imperial Force historian, rightly described it as 'the most dramatic and effective act of individual audacity in the history of the AIF'.

After his long convalescence, Jacka refused to go back to Australia to help recruiting and he was soon back in action with his 14th Battalion, for long known as 'Jacka's mob'. At 'First Bullecourt', he crawled in darkness into No Man's Land, capturing two Germans. More important, he had also noted that the thick German barbed wire had not been cut by the British artillery. He desperately warned his brigadier that next day's Australian attack would be 'pure murder'. His advice was ignored and the Australians were indeed murdered. Once again, he was recommended for a VC by his own battalion commander, but the brigadier, perhaps guiltily, downgraded it to another MC.

What is more, the AIF's commander had secretly ordered 'that Jacka's report be expunged from the records of the AIF and that he was to be systematically ignored both in regard to decorations and promotions'. Which is why another brave action at Polygon Wood, where he became *de facto* commanding officer, was not rewarded even with the recommended DSO. Nor was he promoted beyond captain.

In the last year of the war, he was badly gassed and finally arrived back in Australia to a rapturous welcome. He became mayor of St Kilda but died, at 39 still a young man, of his war wounds, declaring to his father, 'I'm still fighting, Dad.'

On each 17 January, to this day, a service at St Kilda commemorates a remarkable Australian.

KING BRIAN BORU AND HIS BRIEF UNITED IRELAND

In the centuries after his death in 1014, the descendants of Brian Boru, the O'Briens (the author's family), have made sure that he was honoured as an Irish hero, 'who liberated Ireland from the Vikings'.

In reality, it was not *quite* like that – although nobody would deny that Brian Boru was one to rise to the occasion. However, Brian was not really in the simplistic mould of a Simon Bolivar, liberator of South America, or a Toussaint L'Ouverture in Haiti, or even glorious failures like Queen Boudicca and Vercingetorix trying to resist the Romans.

Rather, he was the winner of a civil war, albeit with foreign participants. We could, therefore, liken him more easily to Franco, Lenin, Augustus Caesar or (dare we even mention it in Ireland?) Oliver Cromwell. But he was, in ancient times, Ireland's last great hope of unification.

Just as they had along England's coasts, the marauding Vikings had

Brian Boru, High King of Ireland. (O'Brien family)

first arrived in Ireland in the 8th century. Within 100 years, their little fortified villages had become towns and Ireland's future cities – Cork, Wexford (Waesfjord), Limerick, Waterford (Vaderfjord) and, above all, Dubhlinn (Dublin). Within generations they had settled down, inter-married with the Irish and become Christians. They had not conquered Ireland, they had been assimilated. However, that did not eliminate endless tensions and warfare within Ireland.

Brian was the son of the King of Thomond. Their tribe, the Dalcassians, straddled the Shannon, Ireland's long and strategic river. Brian was dubbed 'Brian Boroimhe' (Brian of the tributes), originally because of the tolls he levied on the river crossings.

He became well used to conducting river-borne raids up the Shannon, and it gave him a life-long expertise in 'naval' or amphibious operations. Obvious rivals were the Hiberno-Norse inhabitants of Limerick at the mouth of the Shannon, and the Dalcassians both fought them and traded with them. In 976, Mahon, Brian's elder brother, was lured to a 'reconciliation meeting' and murdered. Brian, aged 35, now King of Thomond, took his revenge, killing personally the Viking King Ivar and Máel Muad, his Irish ally, but then shrewdly befriending his son Cian, giving him his daughter in marriage and making him an ally for life.

For the next 20 years, Brian, intelligent and educated, built up his power base, often in partnership with the Vikings, also using their weapons (developing from them the Dalcassian battleaxe) and their skills. This included his clever use of ships and soldiers working together, an early form of 'combined operation'.

In 1002, his greatest rival, King Malachy of Meath, bowed to the inevitable and allowed the ever more powerful and successful Brian to take his title of 'Ard Rí', or High King. Brian had no intention of allowing this to be a mere honorary title. He could see how vulnerable a small island with splintered interests could be, and was determined to unify the country to be able to resist foreign invasion. He continued his conquests throughout the whole of Ireland – eventually dubbed 'Emperor of the Irish'. He also rebuilt monasteries and roads, improving Ireland in many ways, especially financially.

But things started to unravel. Máel Mórda, ruler of Leinster, together with the Viking King of Dublin, Sihtric 'Silkenbeard', revolted. Brian besieged them in Dublin, but had to retreat due to the winter weather and lack of supplies.

Now Brian's rather enthusiastic love life intervened. Power, as they say, is an aphrodisiac and many women had played a role in Brian's life, including no fewer than four wives. His divorced third wife was Gormlaith, which had been a complicated relationship, because she was Máel Mórda's sister and Sihtric's mother and, moreover, had been married first to the King of Dublin, then to Malachy and finally to Brian!

This beautiful and dangerous woman, perhaps with 'the fury of a woman scorned', became Brian's nemesis. She urged her son Sihtric to obtain foreign help before Brian returned and they recruited, on the promise of plunder, Vikings from Scotland and the Isle of Man.

As expected, Brian returned in the spring, now quite an old man, but one who had lost none of his determination and resourcefulness.

His forces were somewhat weakened by his son Donough's contingent being away, fighting in the south. Moreover, not all the Irish would join Brian. Some would fight for him, some against. Some, like Malachy, on the pretext of a slight, would stand aside. Vikings would fight on both sides.

At dawn on Good Friday, 23 April 1014, the two armies began their massive battle to the north of the city, at Clontarf. The sea was full of Viking ships moored off the beach, but Brian carefully noted the state of the tide. He directed the battle while, for once, not participating.

Vicious hand-to-hand fighting raged all day. Brian's eldest son and heir, Murrough, and most of the leaders on both sides fell. The foreign Vikings finally broke and tried to make it through the surf to their ships. Few succeeded because the incoming tide meant that they were now in deep water half a mile out to sea.

Irish victory turned to tragedy. One Viking, King Brodir of Man, with a small group, found Brian Boru praying in his tent, unprotected by his bodyguard who had gone off to loot, and felled him. But the dying king, aged 73, struck back and killed Brodir, and their bodies were found together.

Although the power of the Vikings was indeed broken forever, Brian's unnecessary death removed the vital unifying force needed to resist foreign invasion. While the Irish fell back to squabbling, over the sea William the Conqueror was winning the battle of Hastings.

Less than a century later, the forceful, efficient Normans were to arrive in Ireland, which would then be ruled by outsiders for another 800 years.

JOSEF FRANTISEK AND HIS POLISH FRIENDS

In warfare's long history, very few young heroes have volunteered to fight for more than their own country. Josef Frantisek rose to the occasion for four nations, one after the other. And considering his lack of discipline, it was a miracle he served any of them.

He was born the son of a carpenter, growing up near Prostejov in Czechoslovakia, a country created after World War I, and one which was perilously close to a menacing Nazi Germany. Aged 20, he volunteered for the Czech Air Force and graduated as a pilot, at first on observation planes. His ill-disciplined approach, including lateness and drunken fights, nearly got him kicked out, but because he was an exceptional pilot, his superiors made him a fighter pilot instead.

Stationed near Prague in 1938, with Hitler threatening to invade, they waited to fight the Luftwaffe, but first the betrayal by France and Britain at Munich gave away half their country, and a year later Germany occupied the rest. Frantisek did not wait for internment but flew north to Poland, reportedly scattering a column of triumphant Germans on the way.

Hurricane airfield under attack at the height of the Battle of Britain. (Tony Cowland)

Josef Frantisek joined the Polish Air Force just in time for the German invasion on 1 September 1939 and watched the Luftwaffe reduce his base, Deblin, to rubble. Against all the odds, he and his comrades somehow kept flying but after three weeks of desperate fighting, the remaining aircraft, three piloted by Czechs, escaped to Romania. They were interned, but quickly escaped again. Frantisek now decided to head for France.

He managed to take a steamship to Beirut, then another to Marseilles. In France, he quickly joined his third air force, L'Armée de l'Air, and, partly because he had quarrelled with a Czech officer, he volunteered to fly once again with his friends the Poles. Like them, he had little reason to love the Germans, who once again in May 1940 invaded with the usual swarms of screaming dive-bombers and fighters. Frantisek is credited with shooting down 11 of them, but the records were lost and muddled, because he changed his name briefly to protect his family back home from the Gestapo. He certainly received the *Croix de Guerre* for his actions.

With France overwhelmed, in June 1940 Frantisek took a Polish ship from Bordeaux to Falmouth and by August was with 303 Squadron, a Polish unit based at Northolt. He was just in time to play his own legendary role in the Battle of Britain.

Now at last, the Luftwaffe pilots were to meet their match. The RAF's Spitfires and Hurricanes were modern, the whole integrated defence system well organized, with radar allowing the controllers to have their fighters in the right place at the right time. On 2 September, the Hurricanes of 303 Squadron were scrambled three times and Frantisek shot down a Messerschmitt Bf 109 fighter. He repeated the exploit the next day. Three days later it was a bomber and a fighter, just five minutes apart. The same again three days later.

It was desperate fighting against experienced enemies. Several of his Polish friends died. He was badly shot up in one fight with German fighters. With his wings, fuel tank and radiator full of holes and with a seized engine, he landed in a cloud of smoke and steam in a cabbage field in Kent. Like any other commuter, he caught the train from Brighton to London to go back to work.

As his score mounted, it became obvious that his strange ill-disciplined approach was successful. He would sometimes deliberately leave the squadron early and go off to hunt down German planes heading for home, with tired crews and low on fuel and ammunition. Once again his superior, Squadron Leader Witold Urbanowicz, himself an ace, was faced with a dilemma – to discipline him or have him transferred. Eventually he cleverly declared Frantisek a 'squadron guest' and, as a spare pilot, he was free to continue his *metoda Frantiszka*, or lone-wolf tactics.

His best day was 11 September 1940, with two fighters and a bomber to his credit. The Poles and their Czech guest were bringing a murderous determination to the battle, fuelled by a particular hatred for what the Germans were doing to their two countries and to their loved ones. It was to make them a deadly instrument of revenge. In spite of the fact that Fighter Command's Air Marshal Dowding cautiously released it late into the Battle of Britain, 303 Squadron, with 126 kills, was the most successful squadron in the battle. Frantisek was the highest-scoring pilot of any nationality during that September, with 17 confirmed victories and one probable.

And just after the battle, it all ended. After a routine and uneventful patrol on 9 October, Josef Frantisek was found dead in a field, his neck broken, near his crashed Hurricane. It was inexplicable. It may have been extreme fatigue or perhaps, once again, lack of discipline may have done it – he was suspected of flying an aerobatic stunt to impress a girlfriend.

But he had certainly risen to the occasion often enough to be a hero for any of the countries that he served.

5

WITHOUT FAME AND FANFARE

ALAN TURING AND HIS 'BOMBES'

Of course the policeman knew exactly who it was. But he still had to ask him to uncover his face before he could let him through the gate. Dr Alan Turing's habit of cycling to work wearing a gas mask 'to keep out pollen' was a little disconcerting, to say the least. But while he was probably the most eccentric of all the eccentrics at Bletchley Park, he was also the most brilliant of the brilliant.

Born of British middle-class, civil service parents, Alan Turing had been recognized by all his schoolteachers as quite out of the ordinary, ever since he was tiny. He grew up to be a shy, rather scruffy loner – but plainly a mathematical genius. He also happened to be homosexual, and at Sherborne School fell in love with a fellow pupil, whose accidental death from poisoning affected him deeply.

At King's College, Cambridge, he found himself in illustrious company – John Maynard Keynes, Bertrand Russell, Lytton Strachey and Ludwig Wittgenstein. In 1935, on the basis of a learned thesis on 'The Central Limit Theorum', he was made a Fellow, prompting a rhyme:

> Turing
> Must be alluring
> To be made a Don
> So early on.

The next year he published his paper on 'Computable Numbers with an Application to the Entscheidungs Problem', which did not create the stir among his peers that he expected. He crossed the Atlantic to study for two years at Princeton – a university then full of the many genius thinkers who had fled Europe, notably Albert Einstein.

With war clouds looming, Turing returned to England and, in August 1939, he joined a motley group of people who had arrived at a rather ugly Victorian country house called Bletchley Park. The group, disguised as 'Captain Ridley's shooting party', were the first of 10,000 to work on what was to be one of the most significant projects in British history. The site was now 'Station X', the Government Code and Cypher School – Britain's code-breaking centre. Their most important and immediate task was to tackle Enigma.

With their Enigma machines the Germans could be forgiven for thinking that they had created an unbreakable code system. It was a simple machine, first developed for keeping commercial secrets. It had movable rotors and a plug board, the settings of which were all changed every 24 hours. Before they were overwhelmed by the German *Blitzkrieg*, the Poles had been able to recreate an actual Enigma machine, which they passed to the British. But without the codebook that decided each day's settings, the odds of breaking the code were an incredible 158 million, million, million to one. No wonder the Germans were confident and had issued thousands of the machines to their armed forces. But they had not allowed for Bletchley Park, or Alan Turing.

The mansion of Bletchley Park, soon surrounded by huts with nearly 10,000 people, assembled to break the German codes. (Bletchley Park)

Bletchley Park was typically British and eccentric. The teams worked in crowded wooden huts, and comprised linguists, mathematicians, chess players, crossword champions and technologists – anyone with the lateral thinking to break codes – backed by an army of support staff. The overwhelming majority were women, both service and civilian. They lived in billets in the local countryside, often cycling, like Turing, many miles to arrive at their work – three shifts covering 24 hours a day.

Turing realized that traditional methods of code breaking would be far too slow to deal with the blizzard of Enigma messages that needed to be deciphered. Always non-conformist, Alan Turing and his colleagues wrote directly to Prime Minister Winston Churchill for help to improve their facilities. Churchill responded with the order, 'make sure they have all they want on extreme priority, and report to me that this has been done'.

Faced by a machine like Enigma, Turing also deduced that it could only be defeated by another, bigger, electro-mechanical machine. In fact,

Enigma, the code machine. The Germans thought that the odds against breaking its codes were 158 million, million, million to one. (Bletchley Park)

the Poles had created one, which they called a 'Bombe', but improvements to Enigma had defeated their limited pre-war resources. Now Turing designed and built his own version: 6.5ft wide, 7ft tall and weighing 1 ton. It had 90 rotors, and 10 miles of wiring, the equivalent of 30 Enigmas working at once. Eventually, there were to be 200 of the 'Bronze Goddesses' clattering away in the many huts now built round the old mansion at Bletchley Park. Turing was cleverly using weaknesses in not only the Enigma's original design but in the predictable and sometimes lazy way the Germans used it.

It worked, and the time necessary to decode, translate and act on Enigma messages came down from weeks to days and then to minutes. And all the while the Germans never suspected, partly because the British made great efforts to hide their success and to trick the enemy into thinking that the intelligence had come from other sources.

Churchill used the code name 'Ultra' for the increasingly vital intelligence coming from Bletchley Park. Outstanding examples of its successes were the Battle of Britain, the Atlantic U-boat war, Montgomery's victory at El Alamein, D-Day and the advance into Europe.

Information was freely shared with the Americans, who eventually had 300 staff at Bletchley Park, and who were able to convince their own leaders, like Eisenhower, of just how valuable the material was.

In spite of his ambition to create a real 'thinking computer', Turing was actually away in America when the team at Bletchley Park built 'Colossus', the world's first semi-programmable computer, to defeat 'Lorenz', the Germans' next generation of codes.

At the end of the war, which some people feel Bletchley Park may have shortened by two years, everything there was destroyed on Churchill's orders – the bombes, Colossus and all the paperwork. Since everyone who had ever worked at Bletchley Park was sworn to secrecy (Churchill's 'geese that laid the golden egg that never cackled'), it was 30 years before even the British knew what had gone on there – so perhaps the Germans can be excused for their overconfidence.

Alan Turing had been awarded an Order of the British Empire in 1945, but without any explanation, of course, as to why. But his life ended in tragedy. He was working on mathematics and computing at Manchester University when he was accused of 'gross indecency' with another man (homosexuality then being a criminal offence). To avoid going to jail, he accepted probation and oestrogen injections, a form of chemical castration, which made him grow breasts. His security clearance was removed, and he was no longer able to work for the government. He became very depressed.

On 8 June 1954, he was found dead, with an apple laced with cyanide beside him. His friends remembered sadly his fascination with the Disney film *Snow White and the Seven Dwarfs* and the lines he used to chant as he walked down the corridors of King's College 20 years before:

> Dip the apple in the brew,
> Let the sleeping death seep through …

Alan Turing was treated very badly by the country he did so much to save. He is now honoured in Cambridge, Manchester, Bletchley Park and, indeed, all over the world as one of the great founders of modern computing.

JEAN-BAPTISTE EBLÉ AND HIS BEREZINA BRIDGES

In 1805, Napoleon reflected, 'A man has his day in war, as in other things. I myself shall be good for it for another six years, after which even I shall have to stop.' Prophetic words.

It was exactly six years later that he planned his most ambitious adventure – the invasion of Russia. As Emperor of Europe and now with a son and heir, some would say this was a venture too far, although we now know that Napoleon had become justifiably suspicious of Tsar Nicholas' intentions.

In the high summer of 1812, Napoleon crossed the River Niemen in Poland with 530,000 men of 20 nations, 30,000 wagons and 170,000 horses. His huge army crossed on pontoon bridges built by General Jean-Baptiste Eblé and his well-drilled *pontonniers*. Eblé was soon, quite literally, to save Napoleon's skin by disobeying an order.

Eblé was a dedicated, austere and resourceful officer who had fought for his emperor, commanding artillery from Austerlitz to Spain. Now in charge of the pontoon bridge train, he had welded his *pontonniers* into an elite force with specialized equipment, including mobile wagon-mounted forges.

Unusually, Napoleon's supply system was creaking from the start, with the normal ruthless foraging in the impoverished countryside scarcely supplementing his own supplies. Thousands of troops and horses succumbed to the heat. None of his usual brilliant and decisive victories came, and the battle of Borodino drained Napoleon's forces further, claiming the lives of thousands of men and valuable officers, including 35 generals. He captured a deserted Moscow, becoming furious and frustrated that he had nobody to negotiate with, and the city then burned down.

At the end of October, with the dreaded Russian winter approaching, Napoleon reluctantly decided to retreat, but his initial decision to leave nothing behind meant that progress was painfully and fatally slow. The horses started failing, and when the snow and ice arrived days later, their fate, as they tried to eat bark off the trees, was finally sealed.

It is hard to appreciate the feats of Eblé and his men unless one first considers the weakened state into which the Grande Armée, now only 105,000 strong, rapidly descended in that terrible retreat. Hunger, illness and the extreme cold, -20°F, took a steady toll on even the finest officers and men. Napoleon himself, at his lowest ebb, seemed briefly to lose his grip on command. Too late, he ordered all the wagons to be destroyed – including Eblé's pontoons. Eblé begged at least to retain his workshop wagons, but Napoleon, who was burning his own papers as an example, refused. For once, Eblé then quietly disobeyed his emperor (something which would normally have sent him to the second part of this book).

It was, in fact, to be an inspired decision, because suddenly came the fearful news that the Borisov Bridge, the only route to safety across the raging ice-filled Berezina River, had been destroyed. The French seemed trapped by the huge Russian armies closing in. But a reasonably shallow spot 5 miles to the north was found and Eblé and his 400 men, urged on by a revitalized Napoleon, set to work, tearing down the local village for its timber. It was at this point that the saved wagons with their tools, mobile forges and precious charcoal came into their own. But the feverish construction on the banks was the easy part, because now the trestles had to be manhandled into the freezing water, with ice forming round shoulders, arms and legs, and chunks of floating ice hitting the struggling men. However, within hours, the first bridge for infantry and cavalry was ready and Napoleon's troops rushed across to confront the Russians gathering to block them. Three hours later, the artillery and wagon bridge was opened. The weight of traffic broke it that evening, and once more Eblé's shivering *pontonniers*, after his entreaties, plunged into the icy water – now in complete darkness. In the night it collapsed again. 'For God's sake, hurry!' begged General Lauriston. Eblé replied calmly, 'You can see what we are doing' and, at 54 years old, waded into the water with his younger men.

By such almost superhuman efforts, 50,000 men, the fighting elements of the army, crossed over. But thousands of stragglers – the wounded, deserters, camp followers, wives and children huddled on the eastern bank, oblivious of the Russians closing in. Eblé repeatedly warned them that he must burn the bridges at 7am on 28 November. The Russians approached and began to fire. With horror, Eblé watched one officer's widow, wounded by a bullet, kiss her four-year-old daughter and then strangle the child – two pathetic dead bodies disappearing under the snow.

Waiting in agony until 9am, Eblé finally burned his miraculous bridges, and the remnants of the Grande Armée continued their horrific retreat. The bridge heroes paid for their courage with their lives. Nearly all of Eblé's 400 men died of the cold and their exertions, and he himself survived only another three weeks.

His momentary but studied disobedience and his subsequent bravery proved to be acts of the most steadfast performance of duty.

CONSTANCE BABINGTON SMITH AND THE LITTLE PLANE

Wing Commander Douglas Kendall stood in the doorway. 'I hear you want to see me, Babs.'

'Yes, I do. I want you to look at something I've found at Peenemünde. Don't you think it *might* be a catapult for a pilotless aircraft?'

A long silence as Kendall studied the prints. 'That's it!'

'So, you think it *is* for launching pilotless aircraft?' asked Flight Officer Constance Babington Smith.

'I *know* it is!'

Minutes later, she turned to study the very latest photographs of Peenemünde, taken only hours before by a Mosquito. Now, she found something else she was looking for, 'a tiny cruciform shape on the lower end of inclined rails – a midget aircraft actually in position for launching'.

Thanks to her, the Allies now knew the purpose of the mysterious 'ski-site' buildings and curious ramps going up all over Northern France. The clear and present danger was not the German rockets but the flying bombs. And, just in time, something could be done about it.

Constance Babington Smith examining a photograph. (Medmenham Collection)

The photographic interpretation unit that Constance had joined as a young WAAF officer two years before was located in a large mock-Tudor house overlooking the Thames near Henley. It was called 'RAF Medmenham', named after the Abbey famous for the black magic 'Hell Fire Club' in the 18th century. Now it was a form of magic, black or otherwise, that was being performed there. Like another old house that helped to win the war, Bletchley Park (see page 123), it was soon surrounded by huge huts, in this case full of people poring over photographs.

It is a little-known fact that Britain led the world in photographic intelligence. While both sides had used it above the trenches of the Western Front, its modern use by Britain was pioneered by an Australian, and a civilian at that, Sidney Cotton. Backed by Secret Intelligence Services, he equipped a small Lockheed airliner with three hidden cameras and started 'business trips' to Germany, even flying some German generals around while secretly clicking away at the military preparations below. Even after the war begun, he photographed the German fleet while RAF Blenheims could get nowhere near it.

The Blenheims were far too slow and vulnerable and continued to be shot down. Then Air Chief Marshal Sir Hugh Dowding, head of Fighter Command, was persuaded to hand over two precious Spitfires. In January 1940, the Air Ministry was shown a telling chart. The RAF had photographed 2,500 square miles but had lost 40 Blenheims. The French had lost 60 aircraft, photographing 6,000 square miles. But one lone Spitfire had photographed 5,000 square miles – completely unscathed.

Now, the unarmed, long-range and very fast Spitfires began to show their worth. They photographed the battleship *Tirpitz*, as well as the build-up of planes and ships before the German invasion of France, and they plotted the build-up of barges when the invasion of Britain threatened.

They not only took high-level vertical pictures, but also swooped low, 'dicing' as it was called, taking oblique, detailed photographs of ships, aircraft and buildings. All results were methodically interpreted in a system of three phases, the first completed only three hours after the aircraft had landed.

Only Bomber Command, at first, did not welcome the photographs, because they proved that many bombing raids, triumphantly claimed as successes, had actually been miles off target. But with the firm intervention of Churchill, it did mean that sophisticated navigation aids were quickly developed: 'Gee', 'Oboe' and 'H$_2$S', which changed everything for night bombing.

With the Spitfires now joined by even faster twin-engined, two-seater Mosquitoes, photographic successes continued: the precise building progress of U-boat construction, the break-out of the *Bismarck*, leading to her sinking, the layout of the Italian fleet at Taranto before the famous Swordfish raid, the destruction of Rommel's supply lines.

After Pearl Harbor the Americans arrived. They had traditionally used photographic reconnaissance mainly as a form of map-making. After visiting Medmenham they left very impressed and became ambassadors of the system back in the United States. And while the second daughter of Winston Churchill, Sarah, became one of Constance's colleagues, the second son of the president, Lt Col Elliot Roosevelt, arrived in Europe with two squadrons of photographic Lightnings. Soon British and American photo-reconnaissance and interpretation were completely integrated.

The next success of the 'eyes in the sky' was the tracking, detection and bombing of the factories for German fighter production, now very cleverly dispersed and camouflaged. Thus Germany became critically short of planes in time for D-Day. And often the planes they did have then were short of fuel, thanks to photography exposing the synthetic oil plants for attack. The D-Day defences and all the countryside behind them were meticulously photographed and analysed by the huge integrated Allied team, models were built and plans made accordingly so that there were few surprises.

All this time, an obscure place called Peenemünde on the Baltic had been under suspicion ever since the 'Oslo Report', when a mysterious parcel was delivered to the British Embassy in Norway in 1939, which mentioned 'rockets' there. R. V. Jones, Britain's scientific intelligence expert, took it very seriously, especially when Enigma messages revealed Peenemünde was being given extra petrol rations and courageous Polish underground fighters recovered parts of rockets and smuggled them to London.

Continuous photographic missions to Peenemünde did reveal V2 supersonic rockets, together with their large concrete test areas. Constance, an expert on aircraft since before the war, had also detected the little Messerschmitt Me-163 rocket fighter and the runway scorch marks of a twin-jet, the fearsome Me-262. With the evidence of these multiple threats building up, the RAF plastered Peenemünde with bombs from 500 Lancasters, and set back the V2 programme by weeks.

Meanwhile, however, all over Northern France curious, ski-shaped constructions were being erected by the Germans. It was at this point that Constance's team not only found a strange, tiny aircraft at Peenemünde, but went on to detect a crane-like ramp pointing out to sea. That is what she showed to Kendall, together with, the very next day, an actual flying bomb on its ramp.

Now the connection was made, the race was on, and Allied bombers were diverted to flatten every mushrooming launch site in France detected by the round-the-clock photography.

On 13 June, now weeks later than the Germans had planned, the first V1 rumbled off its catapult ramp in France, and set off towards London at 400mph, its ramjet making a noise like an old motorbike. At a predetermined point, the fuel was cut off and, several frightening, silent seconds later, it plunged to earth and its 1-ton warhead exploded, capable of destroying a whole street. Two hundred of the terrifying, robotic 'doodlebugs' followed the next day. We now know that the Germans planned to launch at least 700 a day, which would have swamped any possible defence. But thanks to the vigilance of the photo-reconnaissance pilots and the eagle-eyed interpreters like Constance, the launches were reduced to a fraction of that number.

Of the 10,000 'buzz-bombs' that the Germans did manage to launch, only 20 per cent got past the fighters, balloons and anti-aircraft guns massed on Britain's cliffs. While the droning, menacing V1s did kill 6,000 people, it could have been so much worse.

None of the Axis countries created anything like the brilliant photographic organization of the Allies. Before the war, General von Fritsch, then the German commander in chief, had forecast 'the side with the best photographic reconnaissance will win the next war'.

He was proved right.

CAPTAIN HALL AND HIS 'ZIMMERMANN TELEGRAM'

It was to prove the most momentous and stupid telegram of all time. On 16 January 1917, Arthur Zimmermann, Germany's bluff and good-humoured foreign minister, sent a coded telegram to his embassy in Mexico City. It was to change the world. Zimmermann, a career diplomat, was Germany's first non-aristocratic foreign minister. Throughout his career, a certain naïvety was apparent. He was to be equally naïve over America's attitudes, and in his underestimation of Britain's ability to break German codes.

In London, near Charing Cross Station, an Admiralty cryptography department, NID25, better known as Room 40, cracked over 15,000 key messages during World War I. This allowed the British to track the position of every German ship throughout the war.

As with Bletchley Park 20 years later (see page 123), Room 40 was staffed with its share of British eccentrics. One of these was the rather unlikely grey-haired figure of the Reverend William Montgomery, who was an expert on German religious tracts. Studying Zimmermann's telegram, he immediately realized that, even partly decoded, it was crucially important. He took it to his chief, the legendary Captain Reginald William Hall, RN, whom America's London Ambassador, Walter Page, described to President Woodrow Wilson, as 'a clear case of genius. All other secret service men are amateurs by comparison.'

Hall had been made Director of Naval Intelligence, partly because of his health – he was even known as 'Blinker' Hall because of a chronic facial twitch. But he had risen to the occasion and built Room 40 into a highly efficient organization and, in great contrast to many others in the intelligence business in most countries, he was a model of collaboration with others.

One glance at the decoded fragments of the telegram told Hall that here were words hinting at something cataclysmic. Phrases jumped out, like 'unrestricted submarine warfare', 'war with the USA', 'propose an alliance'.

At that stage, both Britain and Germany were both weak and exhausted from three years of bloody trench warfare. A reluctant Zimmermann had been persuaded by the generals that an all-out U-boat war was Germany's only chance. Bizarrely, he then seemed to have persuaded himself that Mexico might actually then make war with Germany against the United States, her powerful neighbour to the north.

Room 40 struggled to recreate a perfectly complete telegram, because, while it had to convince the Americans, it was also vital that it should not be obvious that the British had deciphered it. It was the classic dilemma of all code breaking – how to keep your enemy from realizing that you have broken his codes, so that he does not change them, ruining the work of months.

An advantage was that, ever since Germany's transatlantic cables had been cut by the British, all her telegrams went indirectly. One route, curiously with permission from America, went through Washington. Two Zimmermann cables arrived at Room 40. Moreover, a British agent also obtained, by rather un-British burglary, a copy of the Western Union cable that reached Mexico via the German Embassy in Washington, complete with its different headings and serial number. Now the leak would look as if it had come from Mexico, not London.

Hall's decoding was soon complete, and revealed these words:

We intend to begin on the first of February unrestricted submarine warfare. We shall endeavor in spite of this to keep the United States of America neutral. In the event of this not succeeding, we make Mexico a proposal of alliance on the following basis:

Make war together, make peace together, generous financial support, and an understanding on our part that Mexico is to re-conquer the lost territory in Texas, New Mexico and Arizona. The settlement in detail is left to you.

You will inform the President of Mexico of the above most secretly, as soon as the outbreak of war with the United States of America is certain and add the suggestion that he should, on his own initiative, invite Japan to immediate adherence and at the same time mediate between Japan and ourselves

Please call the President's attention to the fact that the ruthless employment of our submarines now offers the prospect of compelling England in a few months to make peace.

Zimmermann

The British knew that they had pulled off a devastating propaganda coup. Its revelations would infuriate even the most isolationist American. But would they need to use it? The Americans had broken diplomatic links with Germany, but had gone no further. After all, a reluctant President Wilson had been re-elected on the slogan: 'He kept us out of the war'. Finally, after many anxious days of waiting, on 22 February the British considered that they could delay no longer. Arthur Balfour, Secretary of State for Foreign Affairs, handed the telegram to the astounded Ambassador Walter Page in 'as dramatic a moment as I remember'.

President Wilson, despite his reluctance to get involved in a European war, now decided to act. The Press Association was secretly given the story and on 1 March it broke in every US newspaper. A few suggested that the

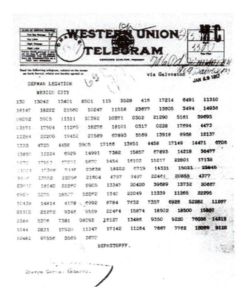

The Zimmermann telegram as it came through Western Union in Mexico City. The British had already decoded two other copies before they stole this one to protect their code breakers. Its revelations brought America into World War I.

telegram seemed so stupid and naïve that it must be a 'British forgery', and the Mexicans, Japanese and Germans quickly denied it all. But then Zimmerman compounded his folly. He defiantly confirmed it, and even defended his actions. Now, American public opinion really swung. Texans imagined another Alamo, with German and Mexican troops marching in to take away their state. The West Coast envisaged a Japanese invasion.

On 2 April, President Wilson went to Congress to ask for war, citing the now infamous cable. Soon, fresh American troops would pour into Europe to tip the scales against Germany and lead the US into becoming a world power.

In recognition of his momentous contribution, Hall was knighted in 1918, retired the next year as a rear-admiral and became an MP. Between the wars, he constantly lectured in the United States on intelligence issues and when World War II broke out, now too old to serve in the Royal Navy, Admiral Sir William Hall, a truly admirable officer, joined the Home Guard at 70 years of age.

RICHARD SORGE AND HIS VITAL MESSAGE

He was always likely to be a split personality. Richard Sorge had a German father and a Russian mother. He was born in Baku, part of Imperial Russia, and then educated in Germany. He fought for Germany in World War I, was wounded, fell for his nurse and was influenced by her Marxist father. His Communist leanings lost him his job, so he went to Moscow and became a Soviet spy – and he was probably to be the most influential spy in world history.

In 1929, he was in England, carefully instructed to lie low and 'not to be involved in politics'. He then returned to Germany and joined the Nazi Party as a cover and started a career as a journalist – also as a cover. As he later said, 'I believe all members of spy rings should have occupations such as newspaper correspondents or business representatives.'

Under the guise of writing for the *Frankfurter Zeitung*, he moved to Shanghai and began to construct his spy ring. He was always attractive to women. Agnes Smedley, a well-known left-wing journalist, was obviously smitten when she wrote to a friend: 'I am just "sort of" married you know, but he's a he-man. Never have I known such good days, never have I known such a healthy life, mentally, physically and psychically.' One suspects she was not referring to the gym! Agnes introduced Sorge to Hotsumi Ozaki, writing for the Japanese *Asahi Shimbun*, who agreed to join his spy ring.

In May 1933, his Moscow masters decided he should form a spy ring in Japan, after a stint in Germany to reinforce his Nazi credentials. With Germany itself so dangerous for spies, it proved a clever move to spy on German planning in Japan.

There his network included Ozaki, two other Comintern agents, and Max Clausen, who operated a successful business. Together they cultivated many military and political contacts, Ozaki especially with Prime Minister Fumimaro Konoye.

Sorge himself, professing to be an ardent Nazi, cosied up to the German Embassy in Tokyo, to Ambassador Herbert von Dirksen and to the Military Attaché, Eugen Ott – and, even more, to his wife. Eugen Ott became ambassador in 1938 and trustingly allowed Sorge access to secret information and cables.

The spy ring was run on a friendly basis with Sorge making suggestions. 'How about such-and-such a course?' One of his spies said it was 'like a Marxist club', but it worked.

The only threat was Sorge's heavy drinking, caused by the continuous strain he was under. An old friend from Germany, Hede Massing, wrote later about how shocked she was by his appearance in 1935. 'He had become a violent man, a strong drinker. Little was left of the charm of the romantic idealist student, although he was still extraordinarily good looking. But his cold blue, slightly slanting eyes, with their heavy eyebrows, had retained their capacity for self-mockery. But he had changed completely.'

Moscow became very clear about its requirements. 'We are anxious to have detailed information concerning changes in Japanese foreign policy. Reports which follow events are not enough. We must have advance information.'

He proceeded to give advance information of fantastic value, including prior knowledge of the Anti-Comintern Pact in 1936, the German–Japanese Pact of 1940 and even, a year later, the Japanese attack on Pearl Harbor, which, after all, eventually meant that America became an unlikely, but vital, ally of the Soviet Union.

Having provided such reliable and valuable material, Sorge must have expected that his next coup would be welcomed and acted upon. He now revealed the precise date, 22 June 1941, of Operation *Barbarossa*, Hitler's treacherous attack on his 'ally'.

Moscow thanked him, but Sorge was not to know that Stalin had sneered, 'There's this bastard who's set up factories and brothels in Japan and even deigned to report the date of the German attack as 22 June. Are you suggesting I should believe him too?'

Sorge was also not to know that Stalin was ignoring veritable mountains of such evidence. Some were from other spies. At the beginning of 1941, Harro Schulze-Boysen of the 'Red Orchestra' spy ring sent the Centre precise information on the operation being planned. Weeks later his colleague Leopold Trepper sent a detailed despatch giving the exact number of divisions withdrawn from France and Belgium, and sent to the east. In May, he also sent the proposed plan of attack, and the original date, 15 May, then the revised, and the final date. On 12 May, Sorge warned Moscow that 150 German divisions were massed along the frontier.

Spies from the Soviet intelligence services were not the only ones. On 11 March 1941, Roosevelt gave the Russian Ambassador the plans gathered by American agents. On 10 June, the British, thanks to the code-breaking at Bletchley Park, sent similar information. Soviet agents working in the frontier zone in Poland and Romania gave detailed reports on the concentration of troops.

A belated award, Richard Sorge was commemorated on a Soviet postage stamp years after Stalin abandoned his master spy to his death.

On 22 June, precisely as predicted, the Germans duly launched three million men, 3,600 tanks and 2,500 aircraft. As one Russian general put it later, 'As soon as I heard the explosions, I knew we were in for a classic Russian exercise – running with suitcases across broken ground.'

Sadly, it was more serious than that. Stalin's refusal to listen to Sorge, or any one else, resulted in catastrophe. Three thousand Soviet planes were destroyed in the first three days and three million men were soon encircled. While the front collapsed, so did Stalin, sure that the group of ministers who arrived at his dacha were there to execute him. But he revived, and gradually the Russian weather and the stubborn bravery of the Russian soldiers wore down the Germans as they advanced.

On 14 September Sorge sent another vital message, revealing that the Japanese were unlikely to attack the Soviet Union unless Moscow was captured. Two weeks later he confirmed that it was now definite that no attack was imminent. Now Stalin did believe his master spy and 400,000 winter-prepared, fresh troops and 1,000 tanks were rushed by rail to Moscow, which the Germans were now approaching.

As they rolled westwards, Ozaki was pounced on by the Japanese secret police. Sorge was warned, but foolishly threw the warning note away instead of destroying it. It was picked up by a secret policeman who was tailing him and he was arrested at his girlfriend's house. As he was being questioned, 5,000 miles away, the freezing, exhausted Germans were stalled, in sight of their prize, Moscow. In December, General Zhukov unleashed the troops that Sorge's message had released, to hurl the Germans back 200 miles. The Soviet Union and its ungrateful leader had been saved.

At first, Sorge managed to convince the Japanese police that he was a German Abwehr agent. And Ott and his other friends at the Embassy had no idea of his spying or of its effect, reporting to Berlin: 'As stated in the attached telegram, the arrest could be explained by the influence of Anglophile groups who are angered by the fall of the Konoye Cabinet, and attribute it, among other things, to German influence. An approach to Prime Minister Tojo, who as Minister of the Interior controls the police, should clear up the affair as soon as possible.' The affair was not 'cleared up' and Sorge stayed in jail for three years until he was executed.

After the war, Leopold Trepper talked to General Tominaga, who had been Japan's Vice-Minister of Defence: "'Why was Sorge sentenced to death at the end of 1941, and not executed until 7 November 1944? Why didn't you propose that he be exchanged? Japan and the USSR were not at war." He cut me off energetically. "Three times we proposed to the Soviet Embassy in Tokyo that Sorge be exchanged for a Japanese prisoner. Three times we got the same answer: The man called Richard Sorge is unknown to us.'"

So, because of Stalin's guilty conscience, Richard Sorge died, unknown and unrecognized until years after the monstrous dictator's death. Only in 1964 was his story revealed. He was made a 'Hero of the Soviet Union' and his sardonic face put on a 4 kopek stamp.

Not really much of a tribute to the man who stopped Hitler ruling the world.

ANTOINE DE SAINT EXUPÉRY AND HIS LAST FLIGHT

If you are not French, you may never have heard of Antoine de Saint Exupéry. But, on the other hand, if you were one of the millions of children all over the world born after 1945, a smile might pass your lips when *The Little Prince* is mentioned. It is a charming book about a crashed pilot marooned in the Sahara Desert who is rescued and entranced by a little boy from a tiny asteroid – a story rooted in the author's very real experiences.

Airline passengers landing at Lyons, France's second largest city, may notice that its airport is now called Saint Exupéry International, commemorating this very French hero who was born in the city in 1900, the son of a provincial aristocrat.

Young Antoine first studied architecture, but during his military service he decided to train as a pilot. Flying became his life and he was destined to be the finest writer in the world to describe this passion.

But then, for three miserable years, he abandoned flying because of the wishes of his fiancée's parents. Luckily for the rest of us, he abandoned both the fiancée and his boring office job and was soon back in the air, becoming one of the pioneers of flying rickety biplanes to deliver the mail – like Charles Lindbergh in America (see page 225). He flew mail planes both between France and Africa, and also in South America. He was proud of the challenge of such frail, primitive aircraft, complaining only a few years later that 'modern' 1930s planes made pilots 'like accountants'. Flying inspired several books; *Courrier Sud* (Southern Mail), about a crashed pilot crucified by nomads and, in 1931, *Vol de Nuit* (Night Flight), about a crash in the Andes.

Four years later, crashing an aircraft in a remote place became a terrifying reality. He attempted to win a 150,000-franc prize for flying in record time from Paris to Saigon. He and his navigator crashed in the Libyan Sahara, uninjured but lost and with food and drink for scarcely a day. After three days, they were so dehydrated that they ceased to sweat but began to hallucinate. Near death, they were rescued on the fourth day by a Bedouin on a camel. *The Little Prince* was inspired by this extraordinary experience in the unforgiving desert.

When World War II broke out, Saint Exupéry, already 39, volunteered for the French Air Force. He was soon flying a Potez 63.11 three-seater, twin-engined reconnaissance plane. In 1940, in their desperate efforts to help France's armies who were being ravaged by the German Panzers and Luftwaffe, his brave group, GR11/33, saw 17 of their 23 planes shot down in a few days. His *Flight to Arras* is a devastating description of those desperate days. Their lumbering planes were 100mph slower than the German fighters and proved as vulnerable as the British Blenheims, in marked contrast to the fast and unscathed Spitfires that Air Marshal Hugh Dowding had just given Britain's photo-reconnaissance arm (see page 129).

Saint Exupéry bitterly described the reckless and useless sacrifice of his friends as 'glasses of water thrown into a forest fire.' He survived this terrible losing battle but, unlike many French pilots, refused to join the RAF because he disagreed with Charles de Gaulle. Instead, he went to live in New York, becoming friendly with other exiles – artists like Jean Miró, Salvador Dali, Yves Tanguy and Max Ernst.

He also renewed his friendship with Anne and Charles Lindbergh, the first man to have flown the Atlantic. Anne Lindbergh regarded him as a literary muse and also plainly found the hard-drinking, womanizing Frenchman very attractive and a rather welcome contrast to her earnest, ascetic husband.

He received the National Book Award for his desert memoir, *Wind, Sand and Stars*, and settled down to write *The Little Prince*, soon to be a bestseller. He could have remained in America as a rich, middle-aged literary celebrity.

But soon he could no longer bear to be on the sidelines with France still suffering under the German occupation. He rose once more to the occasion and, now a rather plump and balding 42, rejoined his old unit which was based in North Africa, 'Risking flesh to prove good faith'.

At least this time he had a reasonably fast plane from which to take his

A middle-aged Saint Exupéry squeezes into the P-38 Lightning in which he would be killed over the sea, ironically by a German pilot who had always admired the author's writings.

photographs – an American P-38 twin-boom Lightning. But even that did not save him because on 31 July 1944, just before his birthplace in the Rhône Valley was to be liberated, he was sent off to photograph German troop movements there. Tragically, a familiar, prowling Messerschmitt 109 shot him down into the Mediterranean.

Ironically, it was piloted by Horst Rippert, who later claimed with regret that Saint Exupéry had always been his favourite author.

NOOR, ODETTE, VIOLETTE: SPIES BEHIND THE LINES

Licking the wounds from defeat in France, and with bombs raining down on London, it seemed there was little that could be done to hit back against the Germans. Winston Churchill chose Britain's 'darkest hour' to launch the Special Operations Executive (SOE), which would soon employ 13,000 men and women.

The British have never liked secret organizations, not just because they were considered 'ungentlemanly' but because they were also thought unnecessary in a democracy. But by 1940, such niceties had to be abandoned. The mission of the SOE was to encourage espionage and sabotage behind enemy lines and to serve as the core of a resistance movement. The SOE was sometimes referred to as the 'Baker Street Irregulars' after Sherlock Holmes' fictional group of helpers, because its HQ was 64 Baker Street, or as 'Churchill's Secret Army', or 'The Ministry of Ungentlemanly Warfare'. It was also a joke that SOE stood for 'Stately 'Omes of England' after the large number of country houses and estates it commandeered and used for training. However, whatever the various definitions, Churchill wanted the SOE to 'set Europe ablaze'.

Churchill's rhetoric was rather grandiose and somewhat over-optimistic. The fact was that, after her swift and humiliating defeat, the morale of France was in the dust. So supine was the mood that it took just 35,000 Germans to rule a country of 40 million. Frenchmen did all the Germans' dirty work for them, looting the country of her riches, denouncing other Frenchmen and shipping Jews to their doom. Two million French prisoners of war remained illegally held in Germany as hostages. It was 18 months before the first German was even harmed. French resistance was initially non-existent.

But gradually the mood was changing. The French General Maxime Weygand had predicted that 'Britain will have her neck wrung like a chicken'. Churchill had retorted, 'Some chicken, some neck!' The successful Battle of Britain showed Britain's resilience, and Britain's bombers droning their way to Germany reminded the French of it every night. Pearl Harbor meant that one day the Americans would surely come back to France. Above all, the German attack on the Soviet Union and their huge defeat at Stalingrad persuaded France's Communists to resist the German attempts to augment their depleted workforce by trying to ship thousands of Frenchmen to work in their factories.

So now 39 women of the SOE could play a very special role, as French-speaking spies and radio operators working with the Resistance. It was incredibly dangerous and would, in some cases, prove fatal.

Flown in the dark to a field by a Lysander was Noor Inayat Khan, half Indian and half American. 'Quiet, shy, sensitive and dreamy', she studied child psychology and classical music in Paris until the German attack in 1940. Overcoming the pacifist religious traditions of her family, she trained as a wireless operator in the WAAF, but then volunteered for 'less boring work' at SOE. Soon after she landed in France, all her colleagues in the 'Physician' network were quickly caught by the alert and efficient Germans. She refused an offer to return to Britain, and sent back valuable information for four months before being betrayed by a jealous Frenchwoman. This 'gentle, sensitive' girl now actually scared her *Sicherheitsdienst* and Gestapo interrogators, who regarded her as 'really dangerous'. She escaped twice and eventually was sent to Dachau concentration camp, where she was shot at once with three other women agents. Her last word was 'Liberté'. She was awarded the George Cross, Britain's highest civilian decoration, posthumously in 1949.

A much more famous GC recipient was Odette Sansom. Born in Amiens, she had married a British hotelier and moved to England. After Dunkirk, she responded to a War Office broadcast appealing for photographs of France. Asked to bring in more snapshots, she was recruited into the SOE. Her desire to redeem France's honour was backed by her intelligence, vivacity and a steely determination.

She was landed by boat and joined Captain Peter Churchill's 'Spindle' network, which was providing vital intelligence and building up the Resistance before the future Allied landings.

For over a year, Odette evaded capture by the vigilant German radio detectors, only to be betrayed by 'Colonel Henri', in reality a double agent, Sergeant Bleicher of the Abwehr. Taken to Fresnes Prison in Paris, she was brutally tortured, her toenails torn out and her spine branded. She managed to get through 14 interrogations by pretending that she, not Peter Churchill (with whom she had fallen in love), was the network leader, that she was married to him and that he was the nephew of Winston Churchill. Both her captors at Fresnes and later the commandant at Ravensbruck thought the pair might be useful as high-profile hostages, so both survived.

Odette received the George Cross, but modestly regarded it as a tribute to all her brave colleagues. A major film, *Odette*, starring Anna Neagle, was made about her exploits. Half a century later, aged 81, she said, 'They are all our mothers and sisters, you would not be able to either learn or play in freedom today, yes, you may not even have been born, if such women had not stood their soft, slender bodies before you and your future like protective steel shields throughout the Fascist terrors.'

Odette Sansom with her future husband, Peter Churchill. (Getty Images)

Modest and self-effacing as she was, Odette called Violette Szabo 'the bravest of us all'.

Violette was the daughter of a Frenchwoman. A strikingly beautiful girl, she had met Etienne Szabo, a French Foreign Legion officer, at a Bastille Day parade in London in 1940. Just five weeks later they were married. But Etienne was killed at El Alamein, leaving Violette with a baby daughter. She turned up at SOE with a personal desire for revenge: 'My husband was killed by the Germans – and I am going to get my own back.'

Her second parachute mission was near Limoges, and she was given orders to sabotage the road and rail connections to the landing areas in Normandy. This was a great success, with many of the German formations forced off the disrupted railways and compelled to move slowly up the road system. It was a distinctly unhealthy place to operate. The SS Division 'Das Reich' had just taken revenge for a brave but premature Resistance attack on Tulle by hanging 99 of its innocent menfolk from lamp posts (they ran out of rope before achieving their target, so they deported 101 to make up the numbers). They had also paused in their advance towards

Normandy to butcher 642 men, women and children at Oradour-sur-Glane. So the area was very 'hot', and Violette was caught by a chance roadblock. She allowed her Resistance comrades to escape by grabbing a Sten gun and ammunition, opening fire and retreating to a house. Moving from room to room, she had the satisfaction of revenge, killing and wounding several of her enemies before, after several hours, dropping from exhaustion. Captured, she was tortured time and again but revealed nothing. She was executed at Ravensbruck in February 1945, aged just 23. Like Odette, she received the George Cross and, also like her, a film was made, *Carve Her Name with Pride*, with Virginia McKenna playing the lead.

Because of the films, the stories of these two brave women are quite well known. It is only recently that the secrets of the American equivalent to SOE, the 'Office of Strategic Services', have been revealed. Once again, its inception was reluctant. 'Gentlemen don't read each others' mail' had been the reason for closing down its predecessor in 1929. But soon after Pearl Harbor, OSS, with British advice, grew and grew, employing many women. One of the most successful and colourful was Virginia Hall. Having lost a leg in a hunting accident, she used a wooden one that she called 'Cuthbert'. After working in SOE, she joined OSS. She and 'Cuthbert' were landed by sea and she trained hundreds of Resistance fighters. She was awarded the DSO, the only woman civilian to receive the decoration.

There was no German, Japanese or Italian equivalent of these brave women volunteers behind the lines. Only the Allies used them so successfully.

BARON LARREY AND HIS FLYING AMBULANCES

Since the dawn of time, to be wounded in battle was all too often a sentence of death – by shock, infection, disease and primitive surgery. Luckily for those unfortunate enough to have to fight, there would eventually be several pioneers who would rise to the occasion in what many military men would regard as an unromantic, inglorious and often hidden aspect of warfare.

'If ever the soldiers erect a statue, it should be to the Baron Larrey, the most virtuous man I have ever known.' Thus spoke Napoleon of his legendary chief surgeon.

Although born poor, Dominique-Jean Larrey was a nephew of a surgeon and had then trained under the famous surgeon Pierre-Joseph Dessault in Paris. Enlisting first in the navy, he suffered from chronic seasickness. Only a year after transferring to the army in 1792, the 26-year-old Larrey realized that the battlefield was a terrible place for a wounded man if he was to have any chance of survival. He created the *Ambulance Volante* or 'flying ambulance' service of light, horse-drawn wagons with a team of a medical officer, a quartermaster, an NCO, a drummer boy (carrying the bandages) and 24 men. His ambulances could evacuate the wounded back to proper hospitals within minutes. Soon the whole French Army followed his lead, as did foreign armies.

No mere administrator, Larrey was personally a calm and brilliant surgeon, working so fast, to minimize the shock of no anaesthetic, that he completed 200 amputations in 24 hours after Borodino, and no fewer than 300 at the crossing of the Berezina River, where he had been passed to safety over the heads of the soldiers, who revered him.

While serving his emperor in more than 60 battles, he found time to pioneer new techniques and write books on military surgery, which were translated into several languages. He also adopted the then unusual principle of tending *with equal care* both friend and enemy, increasing the universal respect in which he was held.

At the height of the battle of Waterloo, the Duke of Wellington peered through the smoke and suddenly asked, 'Who is that bold fellow?'

'It's Larrey', someone answered.

'Tell them not to fire in that direction; at least let us give the brave man time to gather up the wounded.' He then doffed his hat.

'Who are you saluting?' enquired the Duke of Cambridge.

'I salute the courage and devotion of an age that is no longer ours,' replied Wellington, pointing at Larrey with his sword.

Only a few hours later, his lifetime of helping enemy wounded was to save Larrey's own life. Captured by the Prussians, he was to be executed. But a German doctor intervened – a former student of Larrey – and pointed out to Marshal Blücher that Larrey had recently saved the life of Blücher's own son.

So Larrey was released, and went on to become the most popular surgeon in France, boosted by the 100,000 francs left to him by Napoleon in his will, because 'he is the worthiest man I ever met'.

Larrey was followed by others who contributed to the welfare and survival of the wounded. The first was a woman, Florence Nightingale. But for all her famous nursing skills in the Crimean War, she later realized with horror and remorse that she had not understood the greatest threat to wounded men once they had been extracted from the battlefield. Britain's James Simpson, the Austrian Semmelweis and Louis Pasteur had begun to identify secondary infection as the real killer. Joseph Lister in Edinburgh pioneered the sterilization of wounds and the mortality rate in his wards dropped from 50 per cent to 15 per cent.

He even helpfully produced a pamphlet for the French in their war against Prussia. Either it did not reach them or they ignored it, because losses were horrendous. The mortality rate after amputations performed by French military surgeons hovered at 75 per cent or more. The official and appalling tally was 10,006 deaths among 13,173 soldiers, many of whom had just minor amputations, such as fingers and toes.

Luckily for the wounded in the intervening years, three lessons – removing them from battlefields quickly, looking after them in sanitary conditions and cutting down infection – have vastly improved their chances of survival.

Of those wounded in World War I, 45 per cent then died, in World War II it was 30 per cent, in Korea, Vietnam and the Falklands 24 per cent and today in Afghanistan and Iraq it is only 10 per cent.

M.A.S.H. may have been a humorous film and television series, but it portrayed a real success story. Those medivac helicopters were the direct descendants of Larrey's flying ambulances.

'WEARY' DUNLOP AND HIS PATIENTS

They even took a grand piano. In April 1943, 7,000 British and Australian prisoners were told by their Japanese guards at Changi Prison in Singapore that they were 'to go up country to a nice place in the mountains' where their 2,000 wounded could recover. They were cruelly deceived.

After a long train journey in open sugar wagons, they abandoned their piano and even their medical supplies as they faced an appalling 200-mile march over 17 nights. They arrived at a filthy camp site in the jungle to start work the next day.

The Japanese had rampaged through Asia and the Pacific, defeating their overconfident enemies – the British, the Americans and the Dutch. In Singapore they had unexpectedly captured over 130,000 British and Australian prisoners and, against every rule of warfare, they intended to put them to work, especially on one vital project, the Thailand–Burma Railway – what we now call the notorious 'Kwai Railway'.

In spite of their earlier victories, the Japanese had lost control of the sea off Burma, and so were forced to build a railway through the rugged jungles from Bangkok to Burma to supply their armies which were trying to break into India at Kohima and Imphal. In peacetime, this would take five years, but they calculated that they could do it in one year if they used their thousands of prisoners of war as slave labourers.

Among those who arrived from Changi was a man who would become a legend in Australia, Lieutenant-Colonel Edward 'Weary' Dunlop. Born on a sheep farm, Dunlop had studied to be a surgeon, and at university had been called 'weary' because of the word association beloved of Australians ('Dunlop saves you wear and tear').

At 6ft 4in., he played rugby fearlessly for Australia, beating the mighty New Zealand All Blacks for the first time, and his height made him stoop over the operating table, reinforcing his nickname.

He had joined up as a reservist officer in the Royal Australian Army Medical Corps and was in England when war broke out. He enlisted at once: 'I couldn't get into the army quick enough'. He served in Palestine, Greece, Crete and Tobruk and then returned with Australian forces to try to guard against the Japanese threat. His troopship was diverted to Java to try to help the Dutch and he found himself running a hospital in Bandung. He could have escaped capture by the Japanese but could not bring himself to leave his wounded patients.

What 'Weary' found in the railway construction camp was appalling. The prisoners were suffering from illness, brutality, and lack of food and medicine which soon reduced fit young men to human wrecks. The Japanese were frantic. 'Speedo, speedo', they kept repeating to the sick, hollow-eyed skeletons staggering in the jungle dressed in loincloths, threatening, 'It will be built even if it is over the dead bodies of each and every one of you.' The brutality of the Japanese should have come as no surprise – they treated each other just as brutally, and also their Korean allies. So polite at home, they had already committed major acts of bestiality abroad – with 200,000 civilians slaughtered during 'The Rape of Nanking' in 1938, and 6,000 Chinese slain in Singapore. Gang rape was regarded as soldierly bonding, as was bayonet practice on prisoners. Only 4 per cent of Allied prisoners died in German camps, but in Japanese camps the figure was 29 per cent, and for the Australians POWs an appalling 36 per cent. Half the Australians who perished in the war against Japan died as helpless prisoners.

But on the Thailand–Burma Railway it was even worse. 12,000 Allied prisoners were to die, 29 per cent of the British and no less than 69 per cent of the Australians – of cholera, beri-beri and malaria, but mostly of malnutrition and starvation (as they were given only two cups of rice a day) which made the prisoners fatally susceptible to typhus, dysentery, scabies, and tropical ulcers. The Japanese also shipped in innumerable *romusha*, conscripted Asians. By the end there was a dead body for every railway sleeper – 55,000 corpses.

As a lieutenant-colonel, 'Weary' Dunlop found himself acting not only as a surgeon but commanding officer of 'Dunlop's Thousand' men. When operating, in terrible conditions, he improvised, making needles and artificial limbs from bamboo, but he also stood up to the Japanese to save his men ('You will have to put those bayonets through me first!') and was often tortured. One prisoner wrote, 'When despair and death reached us, Weary Dunlop stood fast. He was a lighthouse of sanity in a universe of madness and suffering'. He became an inspiration in the camps, raising the morale of the desperate Australian prisoners and trying to make them survive.

While Weary Dunlop was rising to the occasion, the Japanese were not. What is truly extraordinary about the 'Death Railway' is the sheer stupidity of the cruelty and neglect. Because, given enough food and medicine, the prisoners would have built it so much faster. But with their workforce sick and dying, the schedule fell months behind.

When the lines from Thailand and Burma finally and belatedly met, the Japanese made a propaganda film of the 'last spike' ceremony for what they plainly thought was

The moving statue to 'Weary' Dunlop, created in his honour in his hometown of Benalla. (Benalla Museum)

an engineering triumph. The film crew were appalled by the appearance of the naked, emaciated men and quickly gave them costumes – which they snatched back when the filming was over.

The idiocy of the brutal behaviour was one of the greatest blunders of the war. Because it was built so late, the railway never achieved its purpose of supply. At Kohima, after 64 days of knife-edge battle, General Sato signalled to his superiors in despair, 'Since leaving the Chindwin, we have not received one bullet from you, nor a grain of rice', and he ordered withdrawal, which became a horrific and unheard-of retreat, and the greatest disaster in Japanese military history.

The indomitable 'Weary' Dunlop survived and returned to Australia where he married the fiancée he had met five years before.

He became one of the world's leading surgeons and an international authority on medicine. He also helped prisoners of war and even fostered reconciliation with the Japanese. There is a moving statue of him at his home town of Benalla, he was awarded innumerable international honours, his face appeared on the 50 cent coin and in 1992 he was knighted. He died the next year, and 10,000 mourners attended his funeral.

Sir Edward Dunlop, AC, CMG, OBE, KstJ, was undoubtedly a great man.

THE KRUPP FAMILY AND ITS WEAPONS OF WAR

A few days into World War I, the watching people of Liège were amazed at the sight. Two hundred of the invading Germans, in special protective clothing, were swarming over a massive, squat, black gun dragged into the Boulevard Avroy. 'What on earth is it?' asked a Belgian onlooker. '*Dicke Bertha*' ('Big Bertha'), smirked an invader proudly, then blocked his ears. The next moment a huge explosion shook the earth, every window shattered. A yard-long shell left the gaping muzzle and after a whole minute of flight utterly destroyed the last of Liège's 'impregnable' forts. The monstrous guns had been rushed from Essen in the Ruhr by Krupp, their resourceful builder, to solve the crisis caused by the obstinate Belgian forts. So the German Army could resume its Schlieffen-planned invasion of 'neutral' Belgium.

In reality, Bertha Krupp was anything but *dicke*, big or fat. She was a slim and pretty young woman. Eight years earlier, at 16, she had inherited, as sole proprietor, the huge company of Friedrich Krupp of Essen, and was the richest person in the world. What is more, no industrial family has ever wielded influence on such a scale, with such effect and for so long. For good or evil, and Germany's opponents would certainly call them evil, the Krupps would rise to the occasion only too often.

It was Bertha's great-grandfather, Friedrich Krupp, who had first dreamed of harnessing the Ruhr's huge coal deposits to the making of 'English' steel. His teenage son, Alfred, took over his dream with a tiny workforce of seven and graduated from knives and forks to railway wheels and rails for world markets. Then, fatefully, he made his first rifle, and from then on it was for cannons that the name Krupp became famous.

Alfred Krupp, against huge army opposition, persuaded Kaiser Wilhelm I of Prussia to abandon traditional bronze cannons, reminiscent of Napoleonic fighting of 50 years before, and adopt modern, steel breech-loading rifled guns. In 1870, Prussia, desperate to unite the myriad Germanic states into 'Grossdeutchland', tricked the overconfident French into declaring war. It was Krupp's terrible guns that overwhelmed the French at long distance and brought swift and unexpected victory to Prussia.

The resulting unholy alliance between Kaiser Wilhelm I, Bismarck and their Essen gunmaker would soon propel provincial Prussia and then Germany into a world power. To the fury of many, Krupp became so important that he could bully the Kaiser's army and navy into *only* buying Krupp guns and armour-plate, while getting away with selling to dozens of other nations, some of which might, and indeed did, become enemies.

Overlooked by the brooding and colossal Krupp family castle, Essen became the ultimate 'company town', with its streets named after family members. In 1906,

For generations, Krupp of Essen supplied his masters with munitions, starting with the breech-loading steel cannon that won the Franco-Prussian war in 1870, right up to this colossal World War II railway gun requiring about 3,000 men in all to work and protect it.

the incumbent *Konzernherr* Fritz Krupp committed suicide after damning and spectacular publicity about his orgies with young men on the island of Capri. So, without a male heir, his daughter Bertha had to be married. A starchy little diplomat was duly found, Gustav von Bohlen und Halbach. The aggressive new Kaiser, Wilhelm II, even came to Essen to bless the marriage and ordained that Gustav was 'now a Krupp'. And Gustav reciprocated by creating for his bombastic 'All Highest' the ultimate in arms races. To Britain's growing concern, Krupp guns armed Krupp-steel Dreadnoughts. Then Krupp built U-boats and new diesel engines. Millions of bullets and shells, thousands of rifles, machine guns and, above all, artillery pieces poured out of hundreds of Krupp factories. Never before or since has one family, indeed one man, created an arms race which led to a world war.

When the Kaiser got his war, Krupp would play out his end of the deal. And, in an ultimate irony, German troops were killed every day for four years by British Vickers shells fitted, under an 1896 contract, with Krupp fuses. After the war, Vickers, Krupp's British arch-rival, amazingly even sent a large cheque!

Germany's bitter defeat brought occupation of the Ruhr by French troops. For a brief moment, Essen's skies were clear of factory smoke. But Krupp's days of influence were far from over. In 1933, Gustav Krupp and his fellow 'smokestack barons' listened to the desperate pleas for money from Adolf Hitler and his ambitious but financially struggling Nazi Party. Sure enough, it was Gustav who literally 'rose to the occasion', leaping to his feet with the first pledge of money. In the Führer, he had found his next partner, and was to be well rewarded as Germany frantically rearmed. A quarter of a million *Kruppianer* once again churned out their weapons of death – guns, shells and tanks, as well as whole production lines of U-boats and even great ships like *Tirpitz* and *Bismarck*.

At the Nuremberg War Crime Trials, Alfred Krupp was sentenced, rather leniently, to 12 years in prison for employing slave labour. However, he did not even serve that. With the Russians blockading Berlin and the invasion of Korea, the West became frightened of Communism. Krupp was needed again, and Alfred was released early – once again the richest man in Europe.

But when he died, something dreadful happened to the Krupp dynasty. His son Arndt refused to take over as planned – and became a playboy instead. Faced by a financial crisis in 1968, Krupp became an ordinary joint-stock company with an ordinary board of directors.

And Bertha? She lived to a ripe old age. In spite of the fact that she legally owned the sprawling empire, she had behaved like a good German *Hausfrau* and never intervened in Krupp's operations. Instead, she had become famous for her charity and good works.

Which is more than could be said of the terrible, fat, black guns that once bore her name.

PART 2

... AND THOSE WHO DIDN'T

1

TOO CONFIDENT BY HALF

JOHN F. KENNEDY AND THE BAY OF PIGS

It was the climax of one of the most incompetent and arguably immoral foreign policy actions in which the United States has ever become involved. In the darkness of the night on 16 April 1961, 1,500 armed men waded ashore at two beaches in a bay on Cuba's south-west coast, called 'Bahia de los Cóchinos'.

By the end of the 1950s, America had become obsessed with Communism. The vicious and unrestrained anti-Communist witch hunts by Senator Joe McCarthy and his Un-American Activities Committee had only just ended, J. Edgar Hoover was devoting an inordinate amount of FBI time to domestic Communism, and the Central Intelligence Agency was certainly not going to be outdone in such paranoia.

Imagine the horror of the United States and its government when, in 1959, Communist Fidel Castro overthrew the corrupt Mafia-linked Batista regime in Cuba. While the Mafia and its casinos were kicked out of Cuba, Communism was now on America's doorstep, just 90 miles away.

With the approval of President Eisenhower, in 1960 the CIA started to plan a way to discredit Castro. Ludicrous plans included spraying LSD into a TV studio or making Castro's beard fall out. More seriously, the CIA was working with the Mafia on actual, if hardly more credible, murder plots.

John F. Kennedy. He showed inexperience over the Bay of Pigs, but later rose to the occasion with the Cuban Missile Crisis. (Ted Spiegel / Corbis)

During the presidential campaign of 1960, young Senator John Kennedy repeatedly and cynically accused Eisenhower of 'not doing enough about Cuba', knowing perfectly well that the Republican administration of Eisenhower and Nixon was indeed hatching a coup against Castro, but could not reveal it. Eisenhower had in fact approved a CIA plan and a budget to attack and overthrow Castro, using US-trained and armed Cubans, recruited from the thousands of anti-Castro exiles who now lived in Miami and Florida. Eisenhower had been a top military man and he knew that in warfare half-heartedness never wins. By contrast, Kennedy was a young politician on the make, and rather too impressed with James Bond-like action.

Just 19 days after his election, Kennedy met round his Florida swimming pool with CIA director Allen Dulles and his deputy Richard Bissell to review Bissell's plan for an amphibious invasion. They also hoped that their various plans to murder Castro might make it easier or unnecessary.

Kennedy then made the first of several mistakes. Obsessed with 'plausible deniability' to disguise American involvement, he changed the landing site. Instead of the port of Trinidad, an anti-Castro city close to the Escambray Mountains where fighting was already going on, it was moved to the 'quieter' Bay of Pigs. Now, if anything went wrong, the invaders could not take to the mountains – they would be trapped on a beach. Tragically, loose talk among the Cuban exiles in Miami and in the US media meant that Castro was only too alert; he arrested 100,000 Cubans, and many anti-Castro leaders were shot before the invasion occurred – eliminating any potential support. There would now be no 'opposition' for the tiny invasion force to link up with.

Not surprisingly, there was honourable and justified opposition to the whole idea by many politicians. On 29 March, Senator Fulbright wrote to Kennedy 'to give this activity even covert support is of a piece with the hypocrisy and cynicism for which the United States is constantly denouncing the Soviet Union in the United Nations and elsewhere. This point will not be lost on the rest of the world – nor on our own consciences.'

Kennedy and his team, buoyed up by infectious optimism and over-confidence in their own luck, ignored such opposition. Arthur Schlesinger was told firmly by Robert Kennedy, 'Once the President has made up his mind, we support him and we keep our mouths shut.' The invasion went ahead. It was a disaster.

Aviation proved the key and, once again, Kennedy had compromised on the original plans. Sixteen elderly B-26 light bombers were to destroy the Cuban Air Force and to support the landings. But Kennedy was worried and limited it to six planes, saying 'It sounds like D-Day. You have to reduce the noise level of this thing'.

Then, when nearly all Castro's planes had been destroyed, Kennedy suddenly cancelled most of the further air strikes. So one of the surviving Cuban Sea Furies was able to sink the *Houston* supply ship. The invaders *were* indeed now trapped on the beach, short of ammunition, fighting 15,000 Cuban troops and militia armed with Russian tanks. The lack of support appalled one CIA man, who said, 'It was like finding out that Superman is a fairy.'

The Cuban people did not rise to join the invaders. The Cuban defenders proved well organized and competent, and Castro himself displayed calm and impressive leadership. Soon the exiles were begging for help. Their commander, Pepe San Roman, radioed to the CIA, 'I am taking to the swamps. I can't wait for you. And you, sir, are a son of a bitch.' The last radio message from Brigade 2506 said, 'We have nothing left to fight with. How can you people do this to us, our people, our country?' A good question.

Out of the 1,500 men who landed, about 200 were killed and 1,197 captured, later to be ransomed, privately, for $53 million's worth of food and medicine.

While publicly taking responsibility, Kennedy made the CIA the scapegoats. As he said to Richard Bissell, 'If this were the British parliamentary government, I would resign and you, being a civil servant would remain. But in our government, you and Dulles have to go and I have to remain.'

Three months later Che Guevara, during an economic conference, sent a note to Kennedy. 'Thanks for Playa Girón. Before the invasion the Revolution was weak. Now it's stronger than ever.' It probably did not improve the President's mood.

Neither the Kennedys nor the CIA learned their lessons well enough. The Kennedys, with their exaggerated competitiveness and feeling that they had lost just a round in a game, authorized Operation *Mongoose*, a whole series of illegal and sometimes ridiculous attempts by the CIA to eliminate Castro, including poison pens, exploding cigars and contaminated wet suits. Moreover, the Kennedys became involved in an unholy alliance with the Mafia. One of the go-between tasks of Jack Kennedy's mistress, Judith Exner, was the very dangerous job of asking her other boyfriend Sam Giancana (the head of the Mafia) for help over Cuba!

More important than this decidedly grubby and hidden side of 'Camelot' and the glamorous young Kennedys, was another result of the fiasco – Castro's request for defensive help from the Soviet Union. Nikita Khrushchev responded by placing nuclear missiles in Cuba, capable of obliterating any American city. Faced by Communism *really* being on the doorstep, a calm and brave John Kennedy now did rise to the occasion in a nuclear confrontation which terrified the world, 'The Cuban Missile Crisis'. The Soviets 'blinked first', backed down and, to Castro's fury, withdrew their missiles.

We now know that one reason for Kennedy's improved performance was medical. Medication for his secret health problems, including Addison's disease, had gone wrong during both 'Bay of Pigs' and his Vienna summit with Khrushchev, who thus underestimated him. During the 'Missile Crisis', he was able to rise to the occasion because, in health terms, he was a different man.

While Castro has survived no fewer than ten United States presidents, Cuba destroyed Khrushchev. The Soviet Praesidium dismissed him a year later, quoting his 'harebrained scheming, hasty conclusions, rash decisions and his actions based on wishful thinking'.

But Cuba may also have destroyed Kennedy. The bitterness of the Bay of Pigs failure, together with feelings of multiple betrayal, ensured that when he was assassinated in Dallas two years later, the many candidates for suspicion included pro-Castro Cubans, anti-Castro Cubans, the CIA *and* the Mafia.

KING GUY OF JERUSALEM AND HATTIN

On 20 September 2001, in one of his first public speeches after the horrors of the 9/11 attacks, President George W. Bush said, 'This crusade, this war on terrorism is going to take a while.' Embarrassed and more worldly officials realized his mistake, and he never used the word 'crusade' again.

In the Western world, a 'crusader' is an honourable and even romantic title. One talks of crusaders for justice, for green issues, for civil rights, for feminism. In the Muslim world, however, it has a very different meaning – outsiders who invade to kill, steal or debase. The outrage of 9/11 was directed against 'the crusaders', as is resistance in Iraq and Afghanistan.

The Crusades themselves were an extraordinary military anomaly. The Byzantine Emperor, Alexius I Comnenus, had appealed to Pope Urban II for mercenaries to help him resist Muslim attacks on his empire. The Pope went much further and, in 1095, he announced an expedition that would to travel 2,500 miles from where he preached in France, to seize Jerusalem. His racist attitude was only too obvious and would set the tone for the First Crusade. 'Hasten to exterminate this vile race from the lands of your eastern brethren.'

The subsequent Crusades make the Falklands Task Force look like a simple affair. For the First Crusade, perhaps 100,000, many of them aristocratic knights, would leave their wives and lands to fulfil this religious purpose. Their reward would be the 'indulgence' of entering the Kingdom of Heaven. This was, indeed a 'Holy War'.

The motives were not, of course, entirely high-minded and religious. Many saw that the break-up of the Seljuk Turkish empire could bring riches.

The First Crusade was, apparently, a success – albeit an appallingly bloody one. Against powerful forces, the Crusaders did indeed capture Jerusalem. Seventy thousand Muslims were butchered there – men, women and children – and the Jews who had helped them to resist, together with any Eastern Christians who got in the way. In the mosques and synagogues, the Crusaders boasted that the blood was ankle-deep. In other cities, Edessa, Antioch and Tripoli, Latin colonies were soon established. However, faced with such a brutal outside threat, a quiescent Islamic spirit was wakened.

The Crusaders quarrelled with Byzantium, so no further forces could arrive by land, and the flow of settlers and pilgrims had to come by sea. Repeated Crusades became a part of medieval life.

From a technical military point of view, Europeans had to adapt. First, a secure supply of water would always be critical. Then, the Turks used masses of light cavalry and horse archers, so it was essential to protect the Crusaders' cavalry with a screen of infantry, crossbowmen and pikemen. Only then could the concerted heavy cavalry charge win the day. It required strict discipline and intelligent leadership – not always a forgone conclusion.

A century after the First Crusade, the Christians were now facing a new and formidable foe, Saladin. A Kurd, he was born in Iraq in the town of Tikrit – later to spawn a far less attractive figure, Saddam Hussein. Saladin became Sultan of Egypt, whose economy he revitalized, and he united the Muslim states of Syria, Northern Iraq, Palestine and Egypt. He was a strict Sunni Muslim, and as a rule did not maim, kill or harm his prisoners. His reputation for chivalry was later enhanced by his hospitality, bordering on kindness, to his enemy, King Richard 'The Lionheart'.

After a series of battles with the Crusaders, an uneasy truce was declared. Saladin was now faced with Guy de Lusignan. Born in Poitou, Guy was a rather unsavoury and controversial figure. He had murdered the Earl of Salisbury on his return from a pilgrimage and had been banished from Aquitaine by Richard. As part of a political struggle, he was married rather suddenly to Sybylla, becoming Count of Jaffa and Bailiff of Jerusalem. Later, Sybylla became Queen of Jerusalem and was forced to annul her marriage to Guy, but she insisted 'on a free choice of her next husband'. She then promptly remarried him! This caused fury among the other rulers, notably the powerful Raymond III of Tripoli. The Christians, facing a united Muslim world under Saladin, were now bitterly divided.

Relations with Saladin were strained to breaking point by one of Guy's ardent supporters, Raynald de Châtillon. One of the free-booting newcomers to the region, he did not see the need to compromise and he harassed Muslim trading and pilgrimage routes, threatened to attack Mecca and Medina, and looted a huge caravan of pilgrims. Saladin decided to act. He besieged Tiberias, where Raymond of Tripoli's wife held out in the citadel. Saladin wanted to lure the Crusaders away from their water supply at Saffuriya. At the war council, Raymond himself insisted that his wife could hold Tiberias and very nearly convinced Guy that such a dangerous move was exactly what Saladin wanted. But Raynald accused him of cowardice, Guy was easily persuaded, and the fatal decision was made.

The army, 1,200 knights, 15,000 infantry and 500 mercenaries in three divisions, marched out, constantly attacked by Turkish horse-archers.

Heroic statue of Saladin in Jordan.

It paused for water at Turan, still 9 miles from Tiberias. Once again, Guy made a fatal mistake and decided to push on. Saladin surrounded him, blocking retreat to the water at Turan. Guy was now forced to camp without water.

Raymond understood all too well and was heard to exclaim in despair, 'Alas, Lord God! The war is ended, we are all delivered over to death, and the realm is ruined.'

In the morning, the thirsty Crusaders were blinded by smoke from fires lit by Saladin's men and had to endure a steady barrage of arrows. They tried to reach the springs at Hattin, but the infantry suddenly deserted to the high ground known as the 'Horns of Hattin'. Raymond of Tripoli valiantly charged several times with his cavalry and eventually broke through, but this merely removed him from the battle. Maddened by thirst, and exhausted by fighting, Guy's remaining army was forced to surrender.

When Guy was brought to Saladin's tent, he was offered a goblet of water as a sign of Saladin's generosity. But when Guy passed it to Raynald, Saladin struck it to the ground, accusing the one man he actually hated of being an oath-breaker. Raynald contemptuously replied, 'kings have always acted thus'. An enraged Saladin personally beheaded him. Guy fell to his knees, but Saladin told him to rise, saying, 'Real kings do not kill each other.'

Saladin soon recaptured most of the Kingdom of Jerusalem, including the city itself. The shock of the news is said to have killed Pope Urban III, and his successor, Gregory VIII, announced a Third Crusade financed by a 'Saladin tithe'. It was led by England's King Richard I, 'the Lionheart'. Although they never met, he and Saladin built up a relationship of mutual respect.

Hattin marked the turning point of Christian control of the Holy Land. Other Crusades would follow. The Fourth, disgracefully, was diverted to loot Constantinople; another went to the Baltic; yet another, the Albigensian Crusade, was against France's own citizens.

But the original crusading purpose, to regain and hold Jerusalem, was never achieved, and Guy and Hattin can be blamed for that.

REINHARD HEYDRICH AND HIS COMMUTING ROUTINE

Of all the unpleasant Nazis under Hitler, the icy, blonde Reinhard Heydrich was arguably the most evil and dangerous, and also one of the most physically brave.

Heydrich was born into a comfortable and highly musical family; indeed his (violently anti-Semitic) father, Bruno, founded the Halle Conservatory of Music. However, a musical career was not for the young Heydrich. When his family's wealth was ruined by Germany's inflation, he joined the navy. A serial seducer, he slept with the daughter of the shipyard director. When he spurned her, because he had fallen for his future wife, Linda von Osten, the furious director ensured that he was cashiered out of the navy.

It was Linda who then persuaded him to approach the fledgling Nazi Party and her husband soon became the right arm of Heinrich Himmler. Hitler and Himmler used the inaccurate rumour that Heydrich had a Jewish grandmother to try to keep this dangerous character under control. Most people, including senior Nazis, were simply terrified of him, seeing him as 'a young, evil god of death'. They had good reason. It was the ruthless Heydrich who helped to destroy Ernst Röhm and the *Sturmabteilung* 'Brownshirts' in 'The Night of the Long Knives'. He also unleashed *Kristallnacht*, the first public attack on the Jews, and engineered the fictitious assault on Gleiwitz radio station – the excuse to attack Poland – that started World War II.

Even more significantly, it was Heydrich who decided that the 'Jewish Question' was far too disorganized, and that the SS should now be in charge. He convened and ran the notorious lakeside 'Wannsee Conference' that planned the 'Final Solution' for no fewer than 11 million Jews. Heydrich then directly commanded the Gestapo's 'Jewish expert', Adolph Eichmann, who succeeded in killing six million.

At this stage most British and Americans had never even heard of him, but by 1942 Heydrich had created an extraordinary and unique power base. He was second in command of the SS, and head of both the *Sicherheitsdienst* (SD) and of the *Reichssicherheitshauptamt* (RSHA), the overall security umbrella of the Reich. But this coldly complex man also had a brave, reckless streak. As a captain on the Luftwaffe reserve, he went off and flew combat missions in

One of the most efficient and brutal men of the Nazi Party, Reinhard Heydrich. (Imperial War Museum)

the Polish, French and Russian campaigns, and was once forced down behind Russian lines. When Hitler discovered this, he quickly forbade any more such dangerous escapades.

It was Germany's desperate need for the manufacturing strength and the arms industries of Czechoslovakia that had created the Munich Crisis of 1938. One-third of the tanks that invaded Poland a year later were Czech. Now in 1942 Heydrich was given yet another job and was sent to Prague to boost production, as 'Reich Protector of Bohemia and Moravia', as Czechoslovakia was now called. He cleverly started to use his 'sugar and whip' method – combining harshness with rewards – and vital Czech production started to rise. It was in response to this that the British backed a Free Czech attempt to kill the 'Hangman of Prague'.

Heydrich's contempt for the Czechs, coupled with his arrogance and disdainful bravery was to spell his doom.

The most hated man in the country made the classic mistake of taking exactly the same route every day from his villa to his office in the centre of Prague. What is more, he had no escorting bodyguards and drove in an open, sports Mercedes.

IN THE HEAT OF BATTLE

One morning he saw a figure trying to shoot at him (the cheap British Sten gun had jammed). Instead of driving ahead, he instinctively tried to rise to the occasion and ordered his driver to stop. But that was when a grenade was thrown, which drove car debris deep into his body. He managed to chase his assassin but collapsed after a few yards. Within days his wounds were to turn septic and, despite the efforts of the finest doctors rushed from Berlin, he died in agony.

While publicly praising 'the man with an Iron Heart', in private Hitler was devastated and furious that his possible successor had died through his own fault, writing, 'Such heroic gestures as driving in an open, unarmoured vehicle are just damned stupidity, which serves the country not one whit. That a man as irreplaceable as Heydrich should expose himself to unnecessary danger, I can only condemn as stupid and idiotic.'

The Nazis took a terrible revenge for the death of a favourite son. In an innocent Czech village called Lidice, all 173 men and boys were shot, 196 women and children sent to concentration camps, the houses torn down and the rubble shipped away on a specially built light railway. Finally, the place was ploughed flat. All this, the Germans gloatingly photographed and filmed, thus ensuring that Lidice and Heydrich's overconfidence would become famous forever.

There are many who think that had he lived, Heydrich would have been the one to ruthlessly push forward the new weapons, including the atomic bomb. Knowing him, he would have used it.

LIEUTENANT-COLONEL CHARLES PIROTH AND HIS GUNS

In 1954, the French Army thought it had created a trap at Dien Bien Phu. They were partly right.

After the defeat of the Japanese in 1945, the French returned to their colonies in Indo-china to find things had changed. Having seen Asiatics beat Europeans, the peoples of the East were no longer prepared to be colonial subjects. Laos and Cambodia reluctantly accepted independence within the French Union. In Vietnam, formal elections were held and the Viet Minh won, and elected Ho Chi Minh president.

166

Negotiations for independence broke down in 1946, the Viet Minh moved north to Hanoi, while the people of South Vietnam seemed resigned to being ruled by the French.

A French poster, deploring the sacrifice at Dien Bien Phu.

From 1946 to 1953, the French fought the Viet Minh to a stalemate. But when the Korean War ended, the Chinese were able to provide the Viet Minh with huge quantities of heavy equipment, including field and anti-aircraft guns. That happened to coincide with General Navarre's decision to launch his trap, Operation *Castor*. In 1954, he parachuted French troops into a small valley with a tiny and unknown village – Dien Bien Phu.

It was completely isolated, and everything had to be flown in to its airstrip. The engineers warned that they needed 35,000 tons of stores. It was all over-ambitious, because it would have required 2,000 flights. In the event, they received only 4,000 tons, of which 3,000 were barbed wire.

As the 'fortress', a series of defensive forts quixotically called after girls' names, settled down, many planes flew in, loaded not with vital supplies but with distinguished visitors, including American Vice-President Richard Nixon.

Eventually, 15,000 French Foreign Legionnaires and parachutists and 12 tanks, built up from kits, waited for an unknown enemy.

The trouble was that it *was* an unknown enemy, and one which the French were seriously underestimating. They had, above all, not learned a recent lesson from Korea, where the United States Air Force, much bigger than the French, had failed to interdict the Chinese movement of troops and supplies.

Artillery was going to be the key, and Colonel Piroth, the French artillery chief, was certainly experienced, popular and brave. He had fought in Italy in World War II and had served three tours in Indochina. He had also been badly wounded, with his arm amputated without anaesthetic.

To fight the battle, he had four big 155mm howitzers, 24 105mm guns and 18 heavy mortars. He placed them in positions without top cover, to give them the flexibility to fire in all directions. He even gave a confident demonstration to the distinguished visitors, fatally allowing himself to boast that 'any gun that the enemy *might* bring up will be destroyed after just three shots'.

What the visitors and their French hosts did not realize, in their complacency, was that General Vo Nguyen Giap had surrounded the place with five well-trained divisions, all secretly supplied by 1,200 trucks and then by thousands of peasants with mules and bicycles, each of which could carry 200lb on their handle bars. Even more shocking would have been the realization that the French faced twice as many enemy guns, all brought up in pieces, reassembled and then dug into caves on the surrounding hills. Completely hidden, with only their muzzles projecting, their crews could see everything that moved in the valley below and could plot their targets, especially the command posts with their forests of radio aerials and the vulnerable open gun pits. Nor would the French had been heartened to learn that the Viet Minh were being advised by Chinese and Soviet officers, masters of the use of artillery. So, the French were not springing a trap – a trap was being sprung for them.

On 3 February, the first day of the Tet festival, an avalanche of shells suddenly howled in, plastering Dien Bien Phu. Within minutes, the guns on 'Beatrice' were knocked out and the outpost's commander killed. In six hours, it had fallen, losing 75 per cent of its men. The airport was closed by Viet Minh artillery and the French had to start rationing precious ammunition. 'Gabrielle' fell next, after bitter fighting. Back at headquarters, Navarre heard with incredulity that within 48 hours two key outposts had fallen.

Piroth tried to respond, but his enemy's guns were hidden, while his own were all too visible. The Viet Minh shells pulverized the skimpy French trenches and obliterated bunkers, command posts and gun pits. Colonel Christian de Castries, the garrison's commander, rounded on Piroth and publicly upbraided him for the failure of his artillery. It was too much for Charles Piroth. He walked around the camp to say goodbye to his friends, muttering 'I am completely dishonoured'. He had, in fact, more accurately, been completely outwitted. The poor man, a brave and honourable officer, then went to his bunker and killed himself with a grenade. They tried to cover up his death, but there was a leak, and newspapers dropped in by air revealed the news, doing little to enhance morale.

In the days to come, 'Anne Marie' fell. 'Dominique', 'Eliane' and 'Huguette' were lost and retaken – but all at the cost of men and ammunition, which the Viet Minh could afford but the French could not. Eventually, after 56 days of brutal hand-to-hand fighting, 7,000 French surrendered, with 2,000 killed and 6,000 wounded or missing.

Forced by public opinion 'on the streets of Paris', the French quit Indochina within weeks, a sad beginning of the end of their imperial history.

BYRHTNOTH AND THE VIKINGS

The greatest poems are often inspired by the most dismal defeats – this is well known. That they are often inspired by events seemingly trivial in the great trajectory of war is less so. The serious Greek historians make no mention of the siege of Troy in Asia Minor commemorated so vividly by the poet Homer in the *Iliad*. Similarly, the *Anglo-Saxon Chronicle* refers only briefly, and in passing, to the death of 'Ealdorman Byrhtnoth' at Maldon.

Lust for glory, as opposed to simple arrogance, has often been the downfall of military leaders. The Greeks had the word 'hubris', the Anglo-Saxons spoke of *ofermöde*, literally 'over-mood': a spirit of confidence so lofty that it flies above fear for oneself, concern for others and even common sense. Byrhtnoth, the Ealdorman of Essex, whose extraordinary decision to sacrifice himself and his army rather than compromise honour, had this

At Maldon, a statue of Bryhtnoth threatens defiance across the water towards Northey Island, whence came the Vikings. (Alec Wilson)

169

spirit in abundance – as his followers, led to their deaths before an overwhelming force of Vikings, were to discover.

Tenth-century England was ruled by King Aethelred the 'Unready', so called not because he was unprepared but because his book-learning was not of the best. Now, though, he is remembered chiefly for his shameful espousal of 'Danegeld', the practice of paying what we would now call protection money to the wild raiders of Scandinavia, the Vikings. Some historians have sought to exonerate him, claiming that he was only following well-established and not dishonourable precedents. However that may be, the great achievements of King Alfred, the subduer of the Norsemen, had been forgotten: once again, the fierce warriors of Denmark and Norway were allowed to range unchecked across the coasts of England. As ever, there were some who thought pragmatism meant appeasement, and others, seeing further perhaps, who determined upon resistance. Byrhtnoth of Essex, an Ealdorman, a respected landowner and levier of troops, was of the latter persuasion.

Norse invaders were of two different types. Some had settled and intermarried – as at Yorvick in England or Dubhlinn (Dublin) and other towns in Ireland. Others were still intent on opportunistic raiding, *í Víking* in old Norse.

In August 991, one such large expedition, perhaps as large as 4,000 fighting men, had profitably attacked Ipswich and then, under the command of Olaf Tryggvason, sailed 40 miles south and up the Blackwater River. They disembarked at Northey Island, 2 miles from Maeldun, the 'Hill with the Cross'.

Hearing of their threatening presence, Byrhtnoth gathered his forces. Except for his household guard, they were not soldiers but local householders and peasants. According to religious legend, Byrhtnoth was 'neither shaken by the small number of his men, nor fearful of the multitude of the enemy'. Perhaps *ofermöde* was kicking in. But he did have one sound reason for such confidence. Northey Island is separated from the mainland by a narrow causeway, flooded at high tide and at low tide bordered with the black, sticky ooze of the Essex mud flats – impassable for fighting men. The causeway would thus be defended by a tiny force, much as Horatius had defended his Roman gate (see page 39). Faced by this barrier, Olaf Tryggvason shouted across the water that if he was paid off in gold and silver he would sail away.

Byrhtnoth refused, the tide ebbed, the Vikings tried to attack across the causeway and were indeed beaten back by a handful of Byrhtnoth's best fighting men. The raid, it must have seemed, was over.

Then something extraordinary and almost unique in the history of warfare occurred. A deputation from the Vikings' leader, Olaf, made a remarkable request. They asked that the Saxons retire from the causeway – rather like a sportsman asking for a 'level playing field'. One can imagine the feelings of Byrhtnoth's retainers as he considered this. Were they to throw away their one advantage? Yet, amazingly, Byrhtnoth agreed with the deputation. It was a fair demand, he argued. Perhaps he hoped, piously, that right would prevail over might. The Vikings advanced across the causeway and the Saxons formed their famous defence – the ring of shields, which had faced down the native Britons and conquered England.

What followed is preserved in one of the greatest poems in Old English literature, *The Battle of Maldon*. It tells of how warrior after warrior 'shook his shield' and rampaged through the enemy. But each such story ends the same way, in silence. The poet recounts the glories of the heroes of Maldon only to end them in a brief, terse phrase. The manuscript of the poem has no formal ending, but the trajectory is clear and the result unmistakable. When faithless Godric fled the field riding Byrhtnoth's horse, the Saxons thought it was their leader Byrhtnoth fleeing and panic spread. Far from it, he had died fighting and his headless body was found among the Saxon dead.

Sadly, they had all died in vain. The bishops of Essex timorously decided to pay Danegeld, the first payment of no less than 10,000 pounds, a vast sum. Other counties followed suit. Soon, King Aethelred would pay each year 5 tons of silver to try to keep the peace.

If Byrhtnoth had defeated the Vikings at Maldon, a more confident Anglo-Saxon England might have resisted the Norsemen, much as Ireland did under Brian Boru (see page 117). Seventy-five years later, it might even have resisted their descendant, William the Conqueror, changing the history of the world. Who knows?

Byrhtnoth led his warriors to ruin, through a misplaced sense of justice. Yet the poem that commemorates him remembers this spirit and dignifies it too. The English have been known, reviled, and praised for many attributes: justice, geniality, hypocrisy, snobbery – and fairness. *The Battle of Maldon* is the epic of 'Fair Play', and

Byrhtnoth its first exemplar. 'Madness', some would say on reading of his decision; 'honour', others would cry. Byrhtnoth both rose to the occasion and failed to. He fell at the head of his troops, as, perhaps a leader should, especially one who has led his men to their deaths.

We must wonder, though, what his men thought of him. The anonymous, probably monkish, poet tells us what at least one of his men felt. After Byrhtnoth has fallen, an old servant and friend, Brythwold, shakes his spear and says:

> Courage must be the harder, heart the keener,
> Spirit must be the greater, the more our strength diminishes.
> Here lies our lord, all hacked and hewn.
> Do all of you what you will, but I will stand and die
> By the side of the lord I loved so much.

HERMANN GOERING AND HIS UNIFORMS

To a casual outsider, Goering seemed the most attractive of the Nazis. Handsome and dashing, he had indeed been a fighter ace with 22 victories, winning Germany's equivalent of the Victoria Cross, the *Pour le Mérite* or 'Blue Max'.

In July 1918, after the death of the 'Red Baron', Goering had taken command of Manfred von Richthofen's famous 'Flying Circus', and with brilliant leadership and by disciplining its star pilots to work as a team, he had made it ever more deadly. When the Armistice came that December, before surrendering amid bitter talk of 'betrayal', they deliberately wrecked their Fokker D-8s. But they could grimly console themselves that their *Geschwader* had shot down 644 enemy planes for the loss of only 56 of their own pilots.

Gripped by revolution, Germany was no place for a brave young pilot. But, as a genuine war hero, Goering was a wonderful recruit for Adolf Hitler's tiny Nazi Party. In 1923, he followed Hitler into the ill-fated Munich Beer Hall Putsch and, marching with him, was shot down by the police. The agonizing pain of his leg wound later caused his drug addiction and his obesity.

Exiled to Stockholm with his Swedish wife Carin, he was confined to an asylum, where his psychiatrist described him as a 'sentimentalist lacking in basic moral courage'. Indeed, time and again Goering would try to rise to the occasion, but this character flaw would usually make him back down, or simply fail.

When the Nazis, who many regarded as little more than gangsters, came to power, Goering appeared to be the respectable, bluff and jovial one. But in fact he was just as ruthless as the others. As Prussia's Interior Minister, he soon made the police a tool of the Nazis. It was he who exploited or, some say, organized the Reichstag fire that allowed Hitler to consolidate his dictatorial power with both the feared Gestapo secret police and the first concentration camps, before handing them over to Himmler.

Hermann Goering always loved his uniforms, which he changed several times a day, but he was to let down Germany at critical moments. (Imperial War Museum)

He also played a leading role in the brutal massacre of Ernst Röhm and the SA 'Brownshirts' in the 'Night of the Long Knives', adding several old enemies to the death lists. Asked later how he could murder an old friend, he said with a smile, 'But he was in the way!'

Contrary to myth, it was not him, but Hess, who actually said, 'When I hear the word culture, I release the safety catch of my Browning.' Goering loved culture. Why else did he become one of the world's greatest art thieves?

He also had a rather ambivalent attitude to the Jews. His beloved godfather and mentor, Hermann Epenstein, was of Jewish descent, and Goering was always getting into trouble with other Nazis for helping the Jewish friends of his second wife, Emmy. But that did not stop him looting Jewish art works, and it was his signature on the written order to Reinhard Heydrich to carry out the 'Final Solution of the Jewish Question.'

Goering was now the undisputed second man of Germany and Hitler's official deputy. But the seeds of his decline had been sown. He had built Germany's Air Force from nothing, but it had disorganized leadership and weak technical support. In his ever more grandiose uniforms, which he changed five times a day, he gradually became a faintly ridiculous and out-of-touch figure, ignoring the detailed work required for modern airpower. Indulging his hobbies, *Der Dicke*, 'the fat one', made himself Reichsminister for Hunting. A passionate hunter himself, he decorated his East Prussian homes, with stags' heads and big-game trophies.

It gave rise to a curious and little-known incident. John Guille Millais, the son of the great Pre-Raphaelite artist, was an intrepid explorer, leading naturalist and well-known big-game hunter. At the International Big Game Exhibition in Berlin, his heads and trophies had won 12 gold medals. But Goering had purloined six of them for himself, a bizarre act of greed. So, in a fury, Millais packed his favourite Mannlicher-Schönauer .275, and set off to shoot the greedy and bulky Nazi, an easy enough target for such an excellent shot with a classic Austrian hunting rifle. Unluckily for him, but luckily for the world, Millais suddenly died of peritonitis on the train.

The world was indeed lucky, because Goering was to prove the most incompetent leader of his air force. If he had been replaced by someone more realistic and efficient, history might have been very different.

One thing Goering was realistic about was the dangers of Germany's going to war early – or even at all. He played a leading role in trying to create a behind-the-scenes accommodation with Britain and France. But, once again, his moral cowardice meant that he could not hold Hitler back. 'I always make up my mind to tell Hitler things, but the minute I enter his office my courage deserts me.'

When war came, the Luftwaffe at first appeared unbeatable, destroying Polish, Norwegian, Belgian, Dutch and French air forces on the ground, and its screaming Stuka dive-bombers acting as flying artillery for the Panzers in their successful *Blitzkrieg*. But all this disguised the fact that the Luftwaffe was a tactical air force built on the cheap.

Goering was not only vainglorious, but arrogantly ran the Luftwaffe as his personal fiefdom, constantly ignoring bad news or good advice. His errors of judgement were catastrophic. In 1937 he cancelled the advanced plans for the

Uralbomber, a fast long-distance strategic bomber that could have ravaged all of Britain and much of Russia. Then, in 1939, he slowed the development of vital experimental aircraft. Germany's lead in jets and rockets was fatally postponed. At Dunkirk, he insisted, 'This is a special job for the Luftwaffe!' So the Panzers were halted for three days and his planes tried to do their worst. But now they got a shock, because well-organized Spitfires and Hurricanes blunted their attacks. So 338,000 trapped British and French troops duly escaped to fight another day.

During the Battle of Britain, he underestimated the British radar stations, and then cut his aircraft production so that 'The Few' fighters of the RAF actually began to outnumber his Luftwaffe's fighters. He even allowed Hitler, in a fit of pique, to turn at the critical moment from the battered RAF stations to bomb London. The battle was lost for Germany. His frivolous, overconfident words, 'If a bomb ever falls on Germany, you can call me Meyer', were to haunt him, as Germany was soon battered day and night from the air. Berlin's air raid sirens became cynically known as 'Meyer's Hunting Horns'.

Goering failed to stop Hitler's attack on the Soviet Union, proposing his own campaign through Spain to the Mediterranean. In Russia, the familiar early successes disguised the fact that the Luftwaffe was far too over-stretched to handle such a vast and gruelling campaign, while also fighting in the Mediterranean and trying to resist the ever more devastating British and American bombing of the homeland. Hitler literally screamed at Goering after the 1,000-bomber raid on Cologne.

His mistakes continued as he tried to regain his lost prestige and Hitler's favour. The worst and most tragic was Stalingrad. Against the advice of his own appalled commanders, he intervened to boast that his weakened Luftwaffe, in dreadful weather, could supply the 270,000 encircled, starving, freezing troops at Stalingrad. It was bound to fail. Three months later the Russian steppes were littered with the smashed, snow-covered remains of 1,200 precious transports and bombers. And on 12 January 1943, the very day the last 90,000 pathetic German survivors of the battle were being marched east by the Russians, Goering was out hunting as usual and receiving as a birthday present from some businessmen a magnificent 2,400-piece Sèvres china dinner set, enough for 150 close friends, which he certainly no longer had.

Now scarcely on speaking terms with his Führer, the bombastic one-time 'Iron Knight' of Nazi Germany, dispirited and disillusioned, retreated most of the time to

Carinhall, dressed in bizarre, effeminate clothing and playing with his model railway, while his faithful Luftwaffe, short of planes, pilots and fuel, fought to the death. When the Russians approached Carinhall, trainloads of looted paintings and priceless treasures were sent south.

With Hitler trapped in the Berlin bunker, Goering, as his deputy, tried to assume power to negotiate with the Allies. Hitler's last radio messages ordered him to be arrested for treason and shot by the SS. But it was all too late for the last of the Führer's hysterics.

Goering surrendered to the Americans and, after a spirited legal defence, was condemned to death at Nuremberg for 'crimes against humanity'. When he was refused the 'soldier's death' of the firing squad, he assured his wife 'They will never hang me'. He was right. Just two hours before his appointment with the hangman, he killed himself with cleverly concealed cyanide.

As he saw it, he had, at last, risen to the occasion.

WILLIAM FETTERMAN AND HIS 'MASSACRE'

As with other military disasters, there were many who could be blamed for the so-called 'Fetterman Massacre'.

The Indian tribes had been faced by almost continuous duplicity by the United States government, which was itself the victim of the inexorable and almost inevitable encroachment westwards by the American white population and its railroads.

In June 1866, a 'pow-wow' or peace conference was called at Fort Laramie under no less than the Civil War hero General William T. Sherman. Tribal leaders Red Cloud, Dull Knife and Spotted Tail were requested to allow emigrants to cross land only recently granted to the Sioux and the Cheyenne. Moreover, Sherman announced that they planned to build three forts along the Bozeman Trail towards the mines in Montana. When a column of troops arrived outside and their colonel, Henry Carrington, entered the conference tent, Red Cloud leapt up and declared that he saw through the deception of sending presents 'to buy a road', while sending 'eagles' (referring to Carrington's silver badges of rank) to steal it. Leading the angry chiefs out, he vowed, 'I would rather die fighting than by starvation.'

Ignoring such warnings, the government foolishly decided to build the forts anyway. Carrington set off with 226 wagons, loaded with the usual powder, shot and rations, but also doors, windows, locks, chains, musical instruments, vegetable seeds, mowing machines and a steam saw mill. Anticipating a long stay, light wagons carried army wives and children. His men had obsolete muzzle-loading single-shot Springfield rifles and, bizarrely, only his bandsmen had Spencer repeaters.

Crazy Horse, who was to be the nemesis of William Fetterman and, a few years later, the more famous George Custer.

Henry Carrington was a good choice to build a fort – if not to defend one. A Yale graduate, he was a good draughtsman and engineer and he read the Bible each day in Greek or Hebrew. But, during the Civil War, he had been kept on the staff and had not served with the 18th Infantry Regiment that he had helped to raise, a fact soon to be used by his fellow officers who were veterans of the regiment's fighting.

As Fort Phil Kearny was under construction, it came under increasing pressure from the surrounding hostile tribes, who were picking off the men and harassing the wood-gathering parties. Carrington begged for reinforcements from a penny-pinching army, who had even told him to get rid of his scout to save money. He received 95 'green' infantrymen and 65 cavalry recruits who could scarcely ride a horse. When finished, the fort was besieged and the Bozeman Trail virtually closed by Red Cloud's large, allied, well-organized and well-provisioned force of Indians.

Now Carrington came under pressure from his own side. The frustrating situation was too much for his right-hand man, Captain William Fetterman. An outstanding and brave young officer in the Civil War, he had not enjoyed the lucky breaks that had propelled George Custer to become a brigadier-general at 24, and was itching for a fight that would make his reputation. He despised the Indians for their hit-and-run tactics, and had boasted, 'Give me 80 good troopers and I will ride right through the Sioux nation!' He fumed at Carrington's patient approach, even plotting and speaking viciously against him behind his back. Red Cloud's waiting warriors had just the right enemy and just the right leader to deal with him – Crazy Horse, an experienced young leader at the height of his powers.

The 'Achilles Heel' of the fort was its need for timber – the wood-cutting parties were constantly being attacked. On 21 December 1866, the last wood-cutting party of the winter was planned, and Carrington ordered a steady officer, Captain James Powell, with 79 men, to relieve the wood-cutters.

But Fetterman thought that he should be the one to rise to the occasion. He grabbed Carrington by the arm and demanded, as the next senior officer, to be given the command. After weeks of harassment by his brash young deputy, Carrington weakly acquiesced, but gave him a written order ending 'Under no circumstances pursue beyond Lodge Trail Ridge'. As he loudly repeated the order twice, Fetterman's cocky friend Captain Fred Brown, vowing to 'bring back Red Cloud's scalp', galloped up and joined the party. Fetterman now had exactly 80 men with him.

Crazy Horse and a small group lured Fetterman on, using the oldest trick in Plains warfare, the classic Indian decoy game. Keeping just out of range, Crazy Horse rode slowly, pretended his horse was lame, dismounted several times and even appeared to give up, building a small fire and letting the other decoys 'abandon him'. At the last minute, he mounted and rode after his braves. It was all so realistic that Fetterman fell for it and steadily pursued, against orders, over Lodge Trail Ridge out of sight – and to his doom.

At a signal from Crazy Horse, 2,000 Sioux, Cheyenne and Arapaho rose from where they had been quietly hiding in the grass along the flanks of Peno Creek and charged the tiny force. In 20 minutes all the infantry were dead. Only a few more minutes saw the end of the cavalry further up in the rocks. Almost all were killed by the 40,000 arrows that rained down. Before the end, Fetterman and Brown stood up, counted to three, and shot each other to avoid torture and death. A total of 81 soldiers lay dead at the meagre cost of ten Sioux, two Cheyenne and one Arapaho.

With most of his fighting men gone, Carrington was fearful for the fort and that the wives and children would fall into the hands of the Indians. Calmly, he prepared the magazine to explode and to kill them all. Luckily, a freezing blizzard started and the Indians moved away to shelter from the driving snow.

The 'Fetterman Massacre' shook the army and the nation. The Bozeman Trail was closed down, but the cynical wars to oust the tribes from their homelands continued. The 'blame game' ruined Carrington, although he was later exonerated. Fetterman, who had plainly brought disaster on himself and his unfortunate men with his rash and stupid disobedience, was briefly fêted as a hero, and a year later a new fort in Dakota Territory was even named after him.

Nine years later, that other firebrand, George Custer, was given command of the 7th Cavalry. He was to show that he had learned nothing from Fetterman's fate.

SADDAM HUSSEIN AND HIS DELUSIONS

For a man from a small country who would throw the whole world into turmoil three times, Saddam Hussein's ability to rise effectively to the occasion was hampered by two problems.

First, terrified subordinates tend not to tell ruthless and brutal dictators the whole truth. The inevitable result is that leaders begin to delude themselves and then make serious and disastrous miscalculations. Even in such exalted company as Stalin and Hitler, Saddam Hussein stands out as an arch miscalculator.

Secondly, Saddam shared another weakness with them. None of them had ever visited the countries they were to confront, so they had little real idea how their enemies would react, behave or perform. Hitler, for instance, had no concept of the colossal output of America's industry once it turned to building ships, tanks and planes. Stalin was thwarted by the technological skills and determination of the Americans and British during the Berlin Air Lift.

For Saddam Hussein, being able to watch CNN was no real substitute for proper intelligence.

Saddam Hussein was born into a family of shepherds in 1937. Ironically, the name his mother gave him, Saddam, means in Arabic 'one who confronts'. Seldom has a name been so apt. After years of ruthless intrigue within the Ba'ath Party, Saddam became President of Iraq in 1979, and surrounded himself with sycophantic advisors from his hometown of Tikrit, a move hardly likely to enhance his grip on world affairs. Then, after only a year in power, he tried to gain leadership in the Middle East by opportunistically attacking the much larger Iran, now ruled by Ayatollah Khomeini. The Americans, fresh from their setback in the region – losing their ally the Shah, and the humiliation of President Jimmy Carter over the Iranian Embassy hostage crisis – now regarded Saddam as the lesser of two evils and supplied him with arms.

But Saddam had underestimated the largest nation in the region and committed his country to a murderous slogging match for eight years, the longest continuous war in the 20th century. He had amassed the fourth largest army in the world, but in the meantime had bankrupted Iraq – his expenditure was twice his oil revenue.

The world and the Americans were now waking up to Saddam's true nature, especially when, in 1988, he killed 5,000 Kurds in the town of Halabja with poison gas. The pictures of contorted women and children did fatal damage to his reputation.

Driven by pride to solve his economic problems, Saddam decided to use force and take over oil-rich Kuwait. His dilemma was how to gauge the possible reaction of the United States. Now, his propensity to miscalculate was helped by April Glaspie, the US Ambassador, who did not, as she should have done, bluntly warn him against a move on Kuwait. Instead, after urging peaceful restraint, she casually said, 'We have no opinion on the Arab–Arab conflict, like your border dispute with Kuwait. Kuwait is not an issue for America.' Understandably, perhaps, Saddam took this as a green light and a week later on 2 August 1990 invaded Kuwait. Glaspie later said, 'We did not realize he was stupid.'

Saddam now seemed mightily surprised to find himself facing a United Nations coalition of 32 countries with 700,000 troops. Then, given the option of withdrawing, he fooled himself again. He thought his own huge, but old-fashioned army with its 7,000 tanks and 3,000 artillery pieces could successfully resist. He simply had no idea of the technological advantages stacked against him, especially from the air. Many of his tanks were clinically destroyed without any warning by missiles launched from invisible aircraft miles away.

In spite of setting fire to Kuwait's oil wells (another public-relations disaster), his forces were overwhelmed in just 100 hours, losing 100,000 men to just 274 Allied deaths.

Unfortunately, President George Bush was now without Margaret Thatcher as Prime Minister of Great Britain to stop him 'wobbling'. Shocked by graphic photographs of dead Iraqis killed fleeing Kuwait City, Bush failed to rise to the occasion himself and, against the advice of his commanders, halted the battle 44 hours early. Saddam survived, together with his Republican Guards – who were brutally able to put down US-inspired, but not supported, revolts by the Kurds and the marshland Shiite Arabs.

After his failure in Kuwait, his regime was ever more ruthless. His two sons, Uday and Qusay, became powerful and terrifying versions of their father. Having promised forgiveness to his two sons-in-law for defecting to Jordan, Saddam had them divorced from his daughters within hours of their return and then killed. Lesser enemies filled his jails and torture chambers or ended up in mass graves in the desert.

By now, one would have thought that Saddam might have learned some lessons – but no. With his country subjected to crippling sanctions and no-fly zones, Saddam was not finished with his intransigence. Over the next few years, he allowed the world to think he was developing 'weapons of mass destruction'. He also convinced himself that he could block inspections and that America would not attack, perhaps confining itself to a bombing campaign. He was deluding himself about the United States. If he had been up against Bill Clinton, he might have been right, but he was now facing a belligerent George W. Bush, who not only seemed determined to complete his father's unfinished business, but was also going to lash out at what he considered to be any available Muslim terrorist target after the Al Qaeda attacks of 9/11. (The fact that Saddam was actually an enemy of Al Qaeda was ignored.)

Once again, Saddam brought a war that he could not win onto his long-suffering people and, once again, Iraq's forces were obliterated by American and British technology. Despite the laughably unrealistic announcements of his Information

Minister, 'Comical Ali' (see below), the Iraqi government collapsed and fled. Saddam Hussein, bearded and dirty, was dragged by an American soldier from a hole in the ground in Tikrit. He had lost his sons, his country, his power, his dignity and finally would lose his life.

THE SAYINGS OF 'COMICAL ALI' (MOHAMMED SAEED AL-SAHHAF), MARCH–APRIL 2003

- The Cruise missiles do not frighten anyone. We are catching them like fish in a river. Over the past two days, we managed to shoot down 196 missiles.
- They are trapped in Umm Qasr. They are trapped near Basra. They are trapped everywhere.
- As our leader Saddam Hussein said, 'God is grilling their stomachs in hell'.
- I can say, and I am responsible for what I am saying, that they have started to commit suicide under the walls of Baghdad.
- Britain is not worth an old shoe.
- They are not even 100 miles from Baghdad. They are not anywhere. They are like a snake moving in the desert.
- They are sick in their minds. There is no presence of American infidels in the city of Baghdad at all.
- We surrounded their forces with our special Republican Guards and we are finishing them off.
- The Americans are going to surrender or be burned in their tanks. They will surrender.
- These cowards have no morals. They have no shame about lying.

2

FATAL INATTENTION

ADMIRAL GENSOUL AND HIS MISSING CLAUSE

'A hateful decision, the most unnatural and painful in which I have ever been involved'. Winston Churchill sat down in the House of Commons with tears streaming down his cheeks. He had just finished explaining 'a Greek tragedy' which had occurred at Mers-el-Kebir on 3 July 1940.

Britain had her back to the wall. Above London, her pilots were battling the Luftwaffe, many of her ships had been sunk off Norway and then Dunkirk, invasion was expected in days and France had capitulated. A vital part of the French fleet, the fourth largest navy in the world, was moored in the harbour of Mers-el-Kebir, a port near Oran in French Algeria.

It was crucial that this fleet should not fall into the hands of the Germans. If it had, Britain might have lost control of the Mediterranean, the Middle East oilfields and perhaps even the war.

'Force H' arrived off Mers-el-Kebir, commanded by a reluctant Vice-Admiral Sir James Somerville. He had one aircraft carrier, two battleships, one battle cruiser, two cruisers and 11 destroyers.

Somerville had been ordered to deliver a carefully worded ultimatum to the commander of the French Fleet, Admiral Marcel-Bruno Gensoul. It was to be firm, but friendly and polite.

It is impossible for us, your comrades up to now, to allow your fine ships to fall into the power of the German enemy. We are determined to fight on until the end, and if we win, as we think we shall, we shall never forget that France was our Ally, that our interests are the same as hers, and that our common enemy is Germany. Should we conquer we solemnly declare that we shall restore the greatness and territory of France. For this purpose we must make sure that the best ships of the French Navy are not used against us by the common foe. In these circumstances, His Majesty's Government have instructed me to demand that the French Fleet now at Mers el Kebir and Oran shall act in accordance with one of the following alternatives:

(a) Sail with us and continue the fight until victory against the Germans.

(b) Sail with reduced crews under our control to a British port. The reduced crews would be repatriated at the earliest moment.

If either of these courses is adopted by you we will restore your ships to France at the conclusion of the war or pay full compensation if they are damaged meanwhile.

(c) Alternatively if you feel bound to stipulate that your ships should not be used against the Germans unless they break the Armistice, then sail them with us with reduced crews to some French port in the West Indies — Martinique for instance — where they can be demilitarized to our satisfaction, or perhaps be entrusted to the United States and remain safe until the end of the war, the crews being repatriated.

If you refuse these fair offers, I must with profound regret, require you to sink your ships within 6 hours.

Finally, failing the above, I have the orders from His Majesty's Government to use whatever force may be necessary to prevent your ships from falling into German hands.

Somerville decided not to present these terms in person, but rather to send Captain Cedric 'Hooky' Holland, commanding the aircraft carrier *Ark Royal*, in to negotiate with Admiral Gensoul. The negotiations should have succeeded because Holland was very pro-French, spoke the language excellently – having been naval attaché in Paris – and was even involved with a French woman.

However, things were to go very wrong. First, the French in general were not as keen on their erstwhile ally as the British thought they were. Dunkirk, for the British a miraculous deliverance, was for many French a cowardly retreat and betrayal. Secondly, several misunderstandings and mistranslations had dogged

After the botched signal, the British battleships were forced into the agonizing decision to open fire on their former allies. (Corbis)

negotiations between Britain and France since her defeat. There was an atmosphere of touchy mistrust.

Now Gallic pride played a fatal part. When Somerville did not appear in person to present his options, Gensoul huffily refused to attend the negotiations with someone junior to him, sending his deputy to meet Captain Holland.

When Holland reiterated that he was obliged to deliver the terms in person, Gensoul signalled that he should re-board his ship and leave the harbour.

Eventually, Gensoul relented and Holland set off in his launch across the harbour to Gensoul's flagship, the *Dunkerque*, and was at last admitted to Gensoul's cabin.

There, in the stifling heat of the battened-down ship, they negotiated for two hours. But, unknown to Holland, Gensoul had made a terrible and fateful error. Inexplicably, even though it was close to one of the options the French had been considering, the most attractive option, c), *allowing the French to sail to the United States*, was never sent to Gensoul's rather anti-British Marine Minister, Admiral Darlan. Years later Gensoul was to say, 'I still cannot explain why I did not do it or why my officers did not draw it to my attention. I think it was the obsession that haunted me that I was being offered two alternatives, either to sink my ships or see them sunk by the British.'

Whatever the reasons for the fatal omission, it had the effect of Darlan ordering French ships to rally to Gensoul – a signal immediately intercepted by the British. Churchill became impatient.

When he was shown the signal, Captain Holland knew his efforts had been in vain. He saluted, with tears in his eyes, as he left the *Dunkerque*, because he 'could not believe this was happening'.

At 5.15pm, Somerville was forced to give a 15-minutes ultimatum: 'Accept, or I must sink your ships'. At 5.54pm, HMS *Hood*, *Valiant* and *Resolution* opened fire with huge 15in. shells. In ten minutes, several of the French ships were sunk in the harbour, with 1,300 Frenchmen dead, 977 of them on the *Bretagne*, whose magazine blew up, in as severe a tragedy as the *Arizona* at Pearl Harbor. The battle cruiser *Strasbourg* and five destroyers escaped to France where, ironically, in 1942, the Germans tried to seize them, and the Vichy government kept its promise and scuttled them.

This one-sided and murderous battle between two friends and former allies horrified all but the Germans, who exploited its propaganda value to the full. The British officers involved were grief-stricken. Somerville wrote to his wife: 'And so that filthy job is over at last. An absolutely bloody business, the biggest blunder in modern times.' Captain Holland asked to be relieved of command of *Ark Royal*, ending his naval ambitions.

The Free French leader, General Charles de Gaulle, in his broadcast to the French people, called the action 'deplorable and detestable', but added that it was better the ships be sunk rather than join the enemy. However, it hardly helped his efforts to recruit Frenchmen to fight with him alongside the British.

The most important effect was actually in America. The very ruthlessness of the decision against the fleet of a former ally and friend convinced Roosevelt and his government of Britain's absolute determination, and strengthened their desire to help.

In France, on the other hand, it is only understandable that the tragedy of Mers-el-Kebir continued to feed those with anti-British leanings, and convinced them that it was merely typical of 'Albion Perfide', the 'traditional enemy'.

If only Admiral Gensoul had made sure that he had received the whole of Sommerville's message.

VICE-ADMIRAL SIR GEORGE TRYON AND HIS SIGNAL

By all accounts, Vice-Admiral Sir George Tryon was a formidable and difficult personality. He was regarded by the Royal Navy as its premier expert on navigation and fleet handling. He regularly expected the captains under his command to execute complicated movements suddenly and without warning.

Tryon was also a martinet, and rather taciturn, seldom sharing his intentions with his colleagues so that, theoretically, they could take the unpredictable in their stride. He definitely did not suffer fools gladly. This generated mixed opinions in the navy. 'Most people felt it was no use arguing with George Tryon, and that it was better to acquiesce quietly,' revealed one admiral. Another said that 'he was regarded by his subordinates with a professional confidence almost equal to the Deity'.

On the hot afternoon of 22 June 1893, the Mediterranean Fleet was set to anchor in formation off Tripoli. The Fleet was a magnificent sight, with ten battleships organized in two divisions. Leading one was Tryon's flagship, HMS *Victoria*, a ship with two enormous guns in one forward turret, a strange design accepted by the Board of Admiralty on the confident basis that 'no British battleship would ever be called to fire astern'. Rear-Admiral Albert Markham led the second division in HMS *Camperdown*. Even at his rank Markham was justifiably nervous because Tryon had publicly humiliated him on manoeuvres five years before.

Tryon had decided to create a truly magnificent spectacle by turning his two columns 180 degrees towards each other, forming a narrower column and then anchoring all together. His staff pointed out that 1,600 yards was required for safety, not the 1,200 that the Admiral was about to signal. Tryon curtly insisted on 1,200. The signals were sent and were acknowledged by all but one battleship – that of Markham. He had seen the danger of the ships coming far too close at once and did not acknowledge the flag signal, and was about to send

Admiral Tryon, who so frightened his fellow navy officers that no one dared question his decisions.

HMS *Victoria* sinking swiftly after her collision.

a semaphore message saying that he did not understand (or agree with) Tryon's signal. But before his query could be sent, Tryon rudely asked by semaphore, 'WHAT ARE YOU WAITING FOR?'

Markham had no intention of being humiliated again. He assumed that his chief had something up his sleeve and knew what he was doing. So he now acknowledged the signal and ordered *Camperdown* to turn to starboard. *Victoria* turned to port and, steaming at 8.8 knots, they swung inexorably towards each other. Soon enough, it became perfectly obvious to everyone that the leading ships, *Victoria* and *Camperdown*, were going to collide. Captain Burke of the *Victoria* three times asked for permission to reverse his propellers before Tryon would allow it.

Camperdown's great armoured prow struck *Victoria* below the water line near the bow, and she began to flood rapidly. Many of the crew rushed up on deck, but the engine room teams stayed below to keep the pumps and machinery running. Quite suddenly, after only 13 minutes, perhaps caused by the weight of her two huge guns, *Victoria*'s bow plunged below the surface and the ship went down, her propellers still turning. A total of 358 were lost, including Tryon who was heard to say, 'It's all my fault'. Indeed it was, and the Court of Inquiry found him guilty of causing the worst accident in the Royal Navy's history.

Despite much debate, we will never know what was going on in Tryon's mind. It was not as if he did not know the dangers. What is really ironic is that he had recently issued a 'Memorandum' ordering his captains that, if in doubt, they should use their own initiative, and that safety was paramount (see below).

So it is a huge reflection on his extraordinary, dominant personality that ten captains and one rear-admiral did not rise to the occasion and refuse to obey his suicidal order.

ADMIRAL TRYON'S MEMORANDUM

While an order should be implicitly obeyed, still circumstances may change and conditions may vary widely from those known or even from those that presented themselves at the time orders were issued. In such cases the officer receiving orders, guided by the object he knows his chief has in view, must act on his own responsibility.

a) Orders directing the movement of ships, collectively or singly, are invariably accompanied, as a matter of course, with the paramount understood condition - 'With due regard to the safety of HM [Her Majesty's] ship'.

b) When the literal obedience to any order, however given, would entail a collision with a friend, or endanger a ship by running on shore, or in any other way, paramount orders direct that the danger is to be avoided, while the object of the order should be attained if possible.

An admiral leading a fleet relies with confidence that while the order of the fleet is maintained, each ship will be handled and piloted with all the care and attention that is exercised in the guidance of the leading ship.

Risks that are not only justifiable, but are demanded during war, are not justifiable during peace.

GENERAL JAMES LEDLIE AND THE CRATER

It was a good plan and, unlike most military plans, it came up from the ranks.

Four years into the Civil War, Confederate forces had for months been holding off the Union troops in the trenches around Petersburg, only 23 miles from the Confederate capital, Richmond, which was vital for its supply and communications. Some former coal miners in the Union's 48th Pennsylvania Regiment had noticed that their lines were just 140 yards from a key Confederate fort. Why not dig a mine right under it and blow it up, punching a hole right through the line? Their colonel, Henry Pleasants, took the plan to his corps commander, General Ambrose Burnside, the man whose moustache gave us the term 'side-burns'. General Meade, Burnside's boss, gave the project grudging support, but did little to help.

However, the miners completed their task in under a month, carving a 5ft tunnel 520ft long, and with 40ft tunnels spreading out sideways under the enemy fort in which to plant tons of explosives.

When it was detonated, troops were meant to rush the defences on either side of the resulting crater, advance on an unfortified ridge behind and then into Petersburg. 50,000 men stood ready to overwhelm 15,000 Confederates. So much for the plan, which then quickly fell apart.

Burnside had correctly decided to use his largest and freshest division to lead the assault. This was General Ferrero's 4th Division, the first with African-American troops. They had trained diligently for the operation for 11 days and were eager to prove themselves. Suddenly, Meade suffered a bout of 'political correctness'. If it failed, would they be blamed for sacrificing their first all-black division? Burnside was ordered to use another assault force. Discouraged, he did not rise to the occasion and logically use his next strongest division. Instead, he simply let his commanders draw lots. And the weakest division and the weakest commander, General James Ledlie, drew the 'short straw'.

It is important to realize that the US Army had been tiny before the Civil War. What is more, unlike in most European countries, the people of the United States had always had deep suspicions of 'standing armies' and of a professional 'officer corps'. They smacked far too much of the old Europe, colonialism, elitism and royalty.

The remains of the massive crater at Petersburg, the scene of the worst missed opportunity of the American Civil War. (Petersburg National Battlefield)

Thus the Military Academy at West Point had been, started up only reluctantly under the pretext that it would turn out engineers to build not only forts but civilian projects like harbours, canals and railroads. With West Point's handful of former cadets now occupying the top positions on both sides, the huge new armies needed thousands of other officers who had, unfortunately, little military training. Ledlie was one of these.

A civil engineer by profession, he had been steadily promoted beyond his capacity and had done little more warlike activity than supervise some coastal guns. With this weak leader, his hapless troops, with no training or even briefing, now waited to lead the key attack.

On 30 July 1864, the fuse was lit and a gigantic explosion hurled earth, guns and bodies 200ft into the air, destroying two Confederate regiments and stunning and terrifying the rest. Complete surprise had been achieved.

But instead of the rapid, violent, planned advance to the right and left of the massive, smoking crater, Ledlie's men wandered down into it, almost out of curiosity. As one rebel soldier described it, 'They halted, peeped and gaped into the pit, and then, with the stupidity of sheep, followed their bell-wethers into the crater, where huddled together, all semblance of organization vanished.'

And where was their commander? Ledlie was not rising to the occasion by vigorously leading his men. He was not even with them. He was hundreds of yards in the rear, in a bunker – and with a bottle of rum.

An indecisive hour passed and, also at a distance, Burnside ordered some more troops forward. Most of them, now including Ferrero's black troops in spite of their training, also plunged into the deep crater, where there was soon standing room only. Why? General Ferrero was also nowhere to be seen. He was back in the bunker, sharing Ledlie's rum.

The Confederates recovered, advanced and poured mortar and rifle fire into the crowded pit, a slaughterhouse from which there was no easy escape. There were no ladders, but why should there be? Nobody was meant to be down in the crater.

Eventually, after suffering constant firing and eight hours of thirst in the July heat, those who had not been killed surrendered. For some, even that was not easy. 'Take the white man, kill the nigger!' shouted the enraged Confederates.

Union losses were 4,500. No advance was made, Petersburg was not taken and the stalemate continued. General Grant, the overall commander of the Union Army, described the disaster as 'the saddest affair I ever witnessed'.

Among those who had not risen to the occasion was Burnside, who had not properly supervised or supported the attack. He was quietly retired. Ledlie was dismissed. Later, as a civilian, he became a very competent railroad engineer. Ferrero, mysteriously, escaped censure.

But one nagging thought remains. Regardless of the obvious failures of the senior commanders, where were the resourceful more junior officers and NCOs who might have risen to the occasion? One cannot believe that a Sergeant York, an Audie Murphy, a Patrick Kenneally or an Erwin Rommel would have gone into a hole and waited there to be shot.

CHARLES D'ALBRET AND HIS NOBLES

As he faced the little English Army at Agincourt, Charles d'Albret, the Constable of France, had two factors to contend with – the longbow and the pride and arrogance of his own aristocracy. The extraordinary thing is that this was to be the third time in 100 years that this combination would prove fatal for France.

Since time immemorial, from the Greek phalanx or the Roman legion, via Shaka's Zulu impis and right up to today, successful military leaders have needed three things. First, a good understanding of the strengths, weaknesses and even the position of the enemy; meaning intelligence gathering and reconnaissance. Second, training and well-drilled practice at working together. And finally, a cohesive battle plan, with contingency plans if things change. All these seem to have passed the French by during the Hundred Years' War. Three times they gathered great armies of their finest nobility, who then with arrogance and overconfidence had only one thought in mind – to get to grips with their social equals on the other side, the equivalent of mass jousting. Their leaders had no chance of controlling what were little more than aristocratic rabbles. Many had never fought a battle before – and never together. It was like trying to win the Boat Race by asking some well-born onlookers on the riverbank to step into the boat.

Then there was the English longbow, a formidable weapon, carefully created from a stave of yew, its heartwood compressing and its sapwood tensing. An experienced archer could fire 15 steel-tipped arrows a minute, capable of penetrating armour at 350 yards. The 110lb draw required great strength, and yeoman archers were required to train regularly (golf was even banned for a while as a distraction from archery practice). A disciplined body of English archers could fill the sky with lethal arrows.

The first time this happened was at Crécy in 1346. The chronicler Froissart recorded the deadly effect. 'And ever still, the Englishmen shot where they saw the thickest press. The sharp arrows pierced the knights and the horses, and many fell, both horse and man. And when they were down they could not rise again, the press was so thick that one overthrew another.'

Lawrence Olivier acted Henry V in the film version of Shakespeare's play, released during World War II to boost national morale. (John Springer / Corbis)

He was describing the 15 futile charges, under the feeble leadership of King Philip, all of which resulted in slaughter from the sky, perhaps 60,000 arrows a minute. Among the bodies of less exalted dead lay no fewer than 1,542 of the cream of French chivalry, including the blind King of Bohemia who had quixotically charged into battle, his bridle roped to the two flanking knights who lay dead beside him.

Only ten years later, there was similar carnage at Poitiers. Decades passed and now King Henry V of England, with a tiny force of 6,000 men, many weakened by disease, was facing more than 25,000 Frenchmen, some of them the grandchildren of the nobles at Crécy and Poitiers, near the little village of Agincourt near Calais. Five thousand of the English were archers.

This time the French were not even led by their king. Charles VI was weak and mentally ill. Charles d'Albret, the Constable of France, and Boucicault, the Marshal, were experienced soldiers but they had no chance of rising to the occasion, because their rank of nobility was not high enough for their orders to be obeyed.

The French then proceeded with the only kind of a plan of attack they understood – to march straight towards King Henry and to attack him and his 1,000 men-at-arms. They ignored the longbow archers as not worthy of attention. After all, if they could snobbishly disregard their own commanders, why would they pay any attention to a crowd of scruffy Englishmen and Welshmen in leather jerkins?

Squeezed in a narrowing valley between two woods, their massed dismounted men-at-arms were the first to receive the English arrow storm, which had the intended effect of goading the French cavalry into charging. Under a shower of 40,000 arrows, most of the horses never even reached the lines of sharpened stakes protecting the archers. Maddened and wounded horses smashed back through the waiting men-at-arms. These then advanced, but were so densely pressed they could hardly raise their weapons. And all the time, the deadly arrows struck.

The second wave of French had to climb a wall of dead and dying men and horses before they too were struck down by arrows.

When the confusion was at its worst, the archers laid down their bows, waded into the collapsing charge, and attacked the French, many lying helpless in the mud, with swords, and even the mallets they used for hammering stakes into the ground. The French army collapsed into total chaos and retreat.

Once again a whole generation was crippled. The French commander, Charles d'Albret, and 500 members of France's noble elite were killed, along with 7,000 other French knights. Hardly a French noble family did not lose someone, and many family lines simply ended.

Only the advent of Joan of Arc would restore French fortunes.

ROMANUS DIOGENES AND MANZIKERT

It was a battle neither side had wished for. It came about through a broken treaty and broken alliances, and it changed the nature and even the shape of Europe forever.

The Byzantine Empire had lain on the borders of the Islamic world for almost 400 years. After numerous attempts to conquer it, the Muslim powers had learned to accept the presence of the obstinately unconquerable successor to the Roman state and to respect its impregnable capital, Constantinople. The two cultures had much in common, and had much to share. Then the Turks came.

They could not have come at a worse time for the empire. The historian Michael Psellus records no fewer than 11 Byzantine emperors between Basil II (976–1025) and Michael VI Doukas (1071–78). During this time the throne had become the plaything of two aged spinsters and any number of adventurers. The army, once the terror of the eastern Mediterranean, was demoralized, the peasantry disenfranchised. A self-serving civil aristocracy, having decided that it could run the empire more effectively than a self-aggrandizing rural aristocracy, had seized the reins of power and was determined to keep them.

But, as is so often the case, the ruling class was in danger of crushing its own crib. Their policies had made the empire unfit for effective resistance to the incoming Turks. By 1060, these had ceased to be a nuisance and had become a real threat. Their raids were penetrating deeper and deeper into Byzantine territory in Asia Minor. When the news broke that Caesarea in Cappadocia had fallen, it became clear that a new and firm hand was needed. The Empress Eudocia settled on the handsome, sullen Romanus Diogenes for a husband, in defiance of the ruling Doukas clan. He had proved himself a capable if somewhat wilful commander in various campaigns – but his loyalty to the ruling house had been questioned on several occasions. The Doukas submitted with bad grace but kept their malice warm. Their day would come again. Romanus Diogenes became co-emperor with two men who hated him.

Romanus had inherited a troublesome legacy. The historian John Scylitzes had this to say about the state of the army:

Instead of swords and other weapons they held … only pikes and scythes. And this was not even in time of peace… Their very standards rang dully when struck, and looked dirty as if blackened by smoke, and there were few to care for them. All this caused great sadness in the hearts of those who saw them, when they thought upon the condition from which the Roman armies had come, and that to which they had fallen.

Undeterred, Romanus decided to turn these forlorn and neglected men into soldiers. He would need them. For the Turkish sultan had been lax in observing treaties, and, in the opinion of Romanus IV Diogenes, it was time for him to be taught a lesson. Three Byzantine victories pushed the Turks beyond the Euphrates River. It must have seemed to many that the Turkish threat would prove transitory. The Persians, the Arabs, the Slavs, the Bulgars, the Avars, the Pechenegs, even the mighty Russians, had all been humbled or neutered – why not the Turks?

Alp Arslan himself, the Seljuq Turkish sultan, had no designs – as such – on Byzantium. If anything, his busy mind was exercised more over Fatimid Egypt. However, his predecessor, Turghul Bey, had repeatedly invaded Armenia, and the new sultan could not ignore his interests there. His capture of the Armenian capital of Ani in 1068 gave Romanus the excuse he needed. Moreover, the sultan appeared unwilling or unable to control the bands of Turcomans that roamed unchecked across the fields of Asia Minor.

The army assembled in the summer of 1071 by the emperor was immense – nearly 70,000 strong. It was composed of native Greeks, Armenians, Pechenegs, and, unusually, Varangians from Scandinavia. The presence of mercenaries was a new and ominous token of the Byzantine military decline.

More ominous still was a command deeply and fatally divided. Romanus was a capable captain, but in many ways a dismal general. He had entrusted his reserve to Andronikos Doukas, a member of the very family that sought his ruin and his direct rival. He then made a classic military blunder. He split his command, sending Joseph Tarchaniotes with 30,000 men to Khelat. His whole campaign then unravelled. Half of the army disappeared – there is no other word for it – with Tarchaniotes at Khelat. What happened there is still debated; perhaps he fled, perhaps he was defeated. Scouts sent to engage what appeared to be skirmishers found themselves ambushed by a vast force of Turks. On the eve of the 26 August, the mighty force that had set out across Asia Minor to defeat the Seljuq threat was no longer overwhelming – and was now matched in numbers by the Turks.

The field of Manzikert is low and flat – ideal country for the Turkish mounted archers. The emperor, having received an offer of truce from Alp Arslan, who had marched in haste down from Armenia and replenished his army with 10,000 Kurds, rejected it. It was a hubristic decision. He had lost half his army, although he did not realize it, and had been harried by Turkish archers for days. Yet he trusted his judgement, and his generals.

But he inspired no loyalty in those officers and little in his troops. Attaliates, the soldier who chronicled the battle, speaks of how Romanus increasingly distanced himself from his army, keeping a luxurious baggage train and behaving with mounting hauteur to those around him. This was not what Byzantine soldiers expected of their emperors, and morale suffered.

On Friday 26 August, the emperor's reduced and harassed army marched out in formation to meet the enemy. Alp Arslan, whose system of reconnaissance was clearly very much better than Romanus', knew all about the emperor's movements and had decided to take his time, and space. The imperial army captured the Turkish camp at Manzikert with little opposition, but – where was the Turkish Army? It was circling, biding its time.

Dusk advanced. The Turkish Army had spread itself into a soft, yielding crescent in the face of the hard, square lines of the legions, refusing to give battle but endlessly attacking the flanks with arrows, withdrawing when challenged in classic steppe hit-and-run tactics.

No more could be achieved that day; Romanus decided that the army must withdraw and encamp. The traditional signal for this was that the standards be reversed. Yet it seems that not all understood the signal; and from this misunderstanding, with outright treachery playing its familiar part as well, disaster fell.

The mercenaries were the first to break, and then the panic spread. The eagles had been reversed – that must mean retreat. The reserve under his enemy Andronikos Doukas, instead of covering the withdrawal, simply peeled away. The Cuman Turks defected. The emperor and his guard were left denuded before the horde that suddenly swept down on them.

Attaliates brings home the horror and confusion of the battle with still resonant vividness:

Some maintained that the emperor was still fighting with what was left of the army, and that the barbarians had been put to flight; others claimed that he had been killed or captured. Everyone had something different to report…

It was like an earthquake: the shouting, the sweat, the swift rushes of fear, the clouds of dust, and not least the hordes of Turks riding all around us. Depending on his speed, resolution and strength, each man sought safety in flight… What indeed could be more pitiable than to see the entire imperial army in flight, defeated and pursued by cruel and inhuman barbarians … the whole Roman state overturned, and knowing that the Empire itself was on the verge of collapse?

These last words were prescient indeed.

On the eve of battle, it is said, the sultan had arrayed himself in white, the traditional colour for one who expects to become a *shahid*, or martyr. Incompetently led and laughably ill-informed the Byzantines may have been, but their reputation was still a force in the Middle East. One did not lightly take on the empire, and the sultan understood fully, and perhaps fearfully, the magnitude of what he was attempting.

In defeat, Romanus was brave to the last, rallying his last retainers, fighting till, wounded, he could no longer hold his sword, and so surrendered it. In victory, all agree, Alp Arslan was magnanimous. Having overcome his astonishment at the ragged and pitiable shape of the emperor, he ceremoniously placed his foot on the neck of his defeated foe and then proceeded to treat him with a courtesy bordering on the surreal. A remarkable exchange followed:

'And what,' said the Sultan, 'would you have done to me had fortune granted you victory?'

Romanus, never a diplomat, answered with his customary bluntness.

'I would have had you flogged with chains.'

'So I imagined,' answered Alp Arslan. 'But I have heard that your prophet, Christ, preached mercy. And mercy I will show to you.'

He was as good as his word. His terms were severe, but not, in the circumstances, unreasonable. The emperor was obliged to give up his claims to Armenia and to surrender Antioch. A large annuity was also proposed, but when the emperor said that he could not give so much, Alp Arslan graciously reduced it. The emperor was then freed. That should have concluded the matter. The empire had suffered a shattering loss of prestige, to be sure, but the catastrophe that followed need not have happened, and would not have happened but for the malice of the Doukas family and the hungry intentions of the Turcoman tribes.

Romanus attempted to reassure the capital that something could be salvaged from this appalling debacle, but the Doukas-dominated court had seen its chance and took it. In three successive battles, Romanus was defeated by Doukas forces – his fatal inability to inspire loyalty undermined his undoubted military gifts. Captured, he was cruelly blinded and exiled to an island. Michael Psellus, perhaps the greatest of Byzantine scholars and the disgraced emperor's most inveterate and malicious enemy, sent him a letter of congratulation 'on having attained martyrdom'. History does not record the emperor's response, but his feelings may be guessed. Soon he died from an infection.

With Michael Doukas now emperor, the collapse of Byzantine power in Asia Minor was thereafter swift and complete. In 1073 the Turcoman tribes poured into the empire's military and economic heartland, often at the invitation of contending factions within the imperial court. The Black Day of Manzikert (as it has been called) led to the dissolution of the Byzantine Empire, the rise of the Ottoman Empire and the eventual eclipse of south-eastern Europe. All because an earnest, erring general could not unite those whom he led.

Romanus IV Diogenes tried to rise to the occasion, as none of his immediate predecessors had. But he failed, betrayed by his inattention to his own political weakness, and by a self-regarding clan that refused to recognize that their behaviour was creating the most terrible threat to the empire they sought so greedily to rule.

3

FLAWS AND OBSESSIONS

DOUGLAS MACARTHUR AND THE CHINESE

On a quiet Sunday morning, 25 June 1950, in a place that most people could not find on a map, the 'Cold War' between Communism and the West suddenly lurched towards something much more dangerous.

Tanks and infantry of Kim Il-Sung's Communist North Korea poured across the border at the 38th Parallel. South Korea's inexperienced forces reeled back. The intervention of her ally, the United States, was hardly more propitious. The American Army in Korea and Japan was a half-trained garrison – many had simply enlisted for the educational opportunities. It found itself fleeing from the Soviet- and Chinese-trained North Koreans just as fast, as far, and as ignominiously as its South Korean allies. Its few feeble anti-tank weapons bounced off the vintage T-34s spearheading the North Koreans' advance. Only American airpower saved a desperate situation and slowed the retreat to the south.

The man who now had to rise to the occasion was General of the Army Douglas MacArthur. He was an extraordinary figure and had enjoyed an extraordinary career. His father had been the army's senior general and had won the Medal of Honor in the Civil War. His mother, from a leading Virginian family, had pushed her son to pursue excellence. There was, however, always something strange in the young man's make-up. At West Point, his fellow cadets called him 'Sarah Bernhardt', either because

His great moment of triumph: MacArthur wades ashore when, as promised, he returned to liberate the Philippines. (Imperial War Museum)

of his theatrical histrionics or due to a rather feminine side to his character. There is little doubt that there were some latent personality flaws that would emerge, especially in times of stress. Certainly, the description 'prima donna' would always be appropriate.

He was certainly brave, as his exploits as a young officer in World War I demonstrate. He was also an innovative Superintendent of West Point. As army chief of staff, he had disobeyed President Hoover's orders and attacked the 'Bonus marchers', with a very embarrassed Major Dwight Eisenhower by his side. It would not be the last time he would defy a US president. Roosevelt thought him 'one of the two most dangerous men in America', and was happy to have him out of the country in the Far East.

MacArthur's defence of the Philippines in December 1941 was an abject failure, partly because he overestimated his own abilities and underestimated the Japanese. A full nine hours after Japan's daring and successful aerial attack on Pearl Harbor, his aircraft were still lined up neatly, ready to be destroyed on the ground by the amazed Japanese flyers. Weeks later 76,000 defeated Filipinos and Americans on Bataan surrendered to the Japanese.

MacArthur, who had only visited his men twice in 77 days, was on the fortified island of the 'Rock of Corregidor' in Manila Bay. He boasted, 'They may have the bottle, but I have the cork.' But soon the Rock, too, was doomed by artillery and unopposed airpower and Roosevelt ordered MacArthur to escape by torpedo boat. He announced, 'I shall return!' Note, he did not say, 'We shall return.' The Rock surrendered, and its ragged defenders joined the men on the 'Bataan Death March', some still cursing 'Dugout Doug'.

He did indeed return, but it took three years of agony for the Filipinos and 56 amphibious landings on Pacific islands. But back home to an unsuspecting public, supplied by news from his self-serving press releases, he became an American hero. He was brilliant, brave, handsome, self-publicizing, arrogant and aloof. Even his wife called him 'General'. But he was also something of a fraud, and paranoid.

The other Allied commander who would display such strange personality flaws was Britain's prickly, ascetic and irritating Bernard Montgomery. Like MacArthur, he had no sense of humour and no ability to examine himself. The big difference was that MacArthur could display real charm and was worshipped by his close subordinates.

It was MacArthur who finally accepted the surrender of the Japanese in 1945 on the battleship USS *Missouri*. He then became their ruler, a regal and revered *shogun*, working closely with their emperor and bringing democracy to that country for the first time. It is certainly his most lasting and important legacy, and an extraordinary, unique position for an American soldier.

Having been in the Far East for years without returning to the United States, MacArthur had also built up an image as an 'expert on Asia'. In fact, it was a phoney image. His obsession was the notion that Americans or Europeans were basically superior to Asians. He had underestimated the Japanese, and now he would do the same with the North Koreans and the Chinese.

When the shocking news of the North Korean invasion first came in, he appeared, self-centeredly, pleased to be given 'Mars' last gift to an old warrior'. He also betrayed his usual feelings about an Asian foe. 'If Washington doesn't hobble me, I can handle them with one hand tied behind my back.' But when, even with American intervention, the North Korean advance inexorably continued, he began to panic and talked of abandoning Korea. Such dangerous mood swings, between elation and dejection, were going to punctuate his last memorable year of service.

Within weeks of the invasion, a comparatively primitive North Korean Army equipped with some tanks but hardly any artillery and no airpower, had managed to push the Allies, comprising 14 nations, into the very south-eastern tip of Korea in a defensive perimeter around the port of Pusan. It really did look as if they might be forced ignominiously 'into the sea'.

But MacArthur, aged 70, then very much rose to the occasion. He planned a masterstroke, a bold amphibious attack at Inchon, a port outside Seoul, halfway up the country. Against all advice, it went ahead and succeeded brilliantly, its very unexpectedness ensuring its success. The North Koreans were soon in full retreat back up the peninsula, trying to escape his trap.

After this unexpected triumph, it was not surprising that even President Harry Truman was in awe of MacArthur. Everybody else was. For his military superiors and for politicians, he was becoming as difficult to control as some proud and distant Roman general.

With the intention of unifying Korea, the Allies swept northwards, capturing the North Korean capital, Pyongyang, and headed towards the Chinese border on the Yalu River.

But the British and Allied troops were worried about the Americans. They never covered their flanks by moving into the hills, instead keeping to the roads in the valleys, while firing off unlimited amounts of ammunition at targets they could not see – 'prophylactic fire'. Above all, they never seemed to dig trenches to protect themselves in case trouble came.

The British were not the only people worried. President Harry Truman and his administration were too. In early October, he asked MacArthur to come to Washington to discuss the future of the war. MacArthur said that he was 'too busy', and thus forced his president to fly to meet him, almost cap in hand, at Wake Island. Truman said resentfully, 'Tomorrow I have to talk to God's right-hand man.' MacArthur did not even salute his president as Truman descended the aircraft steps.

Truman described how alarmed the Chinese seemed to be and how they appeared to be warning the United States. A few days before, on 30 September, Premier Zhou Enlai had declared, 'The Chinese people absolutely will not tolerate foreign aggression, nor will they supinely tolerate seeing their neighbours being savagely invaded by the imperialists.' Three days later, the Indian ambassador had been asked to brief the Allies urgently that China would definitely intervene if UN forces continued their advance. The Chinese Foreign Ministry repeated the warning.

At Wake, MacArthur confidently reassured Truman that the Chinese were bluffing and were 'no problem', and he flew back to continue his advance.

The Chinese were indeed very worried. For them, this might be a prelude to an attack on China itself, including an assault from Nationalist China in Taiwan. They decided to warn MacArthur more forcibly. They secretly infiltrated 130,000 troops across the Yalu. On 1 November they struck, chopping up several South Korean regiments. Six days later they broke off their action and disappeared into the snow. What more warnings could they give?

MacArthur seemed quite unfazed by this huge new development. 'I have plenty of troops to deal adequately with the Chinese and even the Russians.' He continued to prepare for his 'win the war by Christmas' offensive, but also provided his troops with some traditional luxuries. On Thanksgiving Day, 23 November, the British and other Allies were both amazed and envious, as American troops in the front line were treated to flown-in turkeys and 'all the trimmings'. Sadly, it was to be the last time they would be envious of the Americans, who started their offensive the next day.

On the 25th, the Chinese, now with 360,000 men, attacked with devastating force from where they had carefully hidden in the snowy mountains. The shock was complete. Briefly, there was contemptuous and ridiculous talk of 'not being afraid of Chinese laundrymen', ignoring the fact that most Chinese troops had been fighting all their lives. In the west, the Allied armies collapsed. Just as the British had feared, they were constantly outflanked by Chinese, armed only with small arms and mortars, who skilfully infiltrated from the hills and blocked the roads behind them. In panic, 'bug-out fever' took hold.

One American colonel said to his executive officer, 'Look around here. This is a sight that hasn't been seen for hundreds of years: the men of the whole United States Army fleeing from the battlefield, abandoning their wounded, running for their lives.'

Repairing US military honour in the east, the US Marines, with British Royal Marines fighting with them, conducted a valiant, orderly, if murderous and freezing retreat. When they reached the coast, they were forced to blow up the port of Hungnan, together with millions of dollars' worth of their stores as they left.

The harsh fact was that they were all back 300 miles, below the 38th Parallel once more. The ill-judged decision to ignore the Chinese anxieties and warnings and not to conclude a negotiated truce proved catastrophic for all concerned.

A shaken but unrepentant MacArthur now bombarded Washington with querulous signals and then did something worse. Trying, as usual, to use the media to get what he wanted, he talked publicly of extending the war into China, making the 'Chinese Commander surrender personally to me', and even of using atomic bombs, 26 of them. His tantrums showed he had lost all perspective. After consulting his military advisers, at last Truman sacked him.

A towering figure, Douglas MacArthur returned to an ecstatic ticker-tape parade from a public who had no idea of the whole truth, made a tear-jerking speech to Congress, promised to 'fade away', and did.

NAPOLEON AND HIS RUSSIAN CAMPAIGN

Whether they approve of him or not, most people would agree that Napoleon is one of the great figures of history – as an administrator, as a politician and, above all, as a soldier.

Born on the island of Corsica in 1769 and trained for military service in France, Napoleon was in the right place and at the right time to benefit from the French Revolution, helping to beat off the vengeful monarchies of Europe, and after a series of victories, he became emperor in 1804.

Napoleon was an organizational and military genius, and battles like Ulm, Austerlitz, Friedland and Wagram ensured that his continental enemies, Prussia, Austria and Russia, were subdued. Only Nelson's naval victories at the Nile and Trafalgar, and Wellington's successes in far-off Spain cast a shadow on his aura of invincibility and success.

By 1811 he was at the pinnacle of his career. He had abandoned his beloved Josephine because he was desperate for a male child, which she could not have. But now at last he had a son and heir, 'The King of Rome', by his wife Marie-Louise, daughter of his reluctant ally the Emperor of Austria. If he had, at this point, sat back and rested on his achievements, he might well have lived to a ripe old age as he contented emperor of the most powerful nation on earth.

But he was far too ambitious to rest on his laurels, and he joins the list of military men who were ruined by rising once too often to the occasion. He was obsessed with Britain which,

Napoleon, whose obsession over rivalry with England trapped him into his disaster in Russia. (Corbis)

secure as an island and protected by the Royal Navy, had never left his thoughts. Having failed to invade because of Trafalgar, Napoleon now tried to strangle her economically with his 'Continental System', a trade embargo which actually hurt France and her allies more than Britain. When Tsar Alexander, whom Napoleon had once regarded as his young protégé, opened Russia's ports to neutral (in reality British) shipping, Napoleon was furious and decided to punish him. Such an angry quest for revenge was to be a fatal and, in some ways, an inexplicable mistake.

Napoleon's attack on Russia was, on the face of it, well prepared and organized. His *Grande Armée* was 530,000 strong, comprising 20 nations, with 1,000 guns, 30,000 wagons and 170,000 horses. Furthermore, in splendid French style, his massive baggage trains and depots contained 28 million bottles of wine and two million fortifying bottles of brandy. But his Russian campaign began slowly to unravel.

First of all, his supply system was usually supplemented by systematic foraging, or 'living off the land'. Teams of soldiers would spread out and steal everything they could. In the primitive conditions they now encountered in Poland and Russia there was little to steal, and his normally efficient supply system broke down, so his advancing troops and horses actually starved.

There had been a drought the previous year and the peasants they encountered were themselves eating acorns and birch bark and feeding their precious thatched roofs to the animals. A Bavarian officer, seeing the trail of devastation and dead horses, wrote home, 'One felt one was following a fleeing rather than an advancing army.'

Amazingly, during the advance, Napoleon lost as many to illness, starvation and the heat as he was to lose to the cold on the way back. 'I am looking forward to being killed,' wrote one young soldier, 'for I am dying as I march.' Near Vilna, an appalling storm resulted in the deaths of thousands of horses and sapped the men's morale – many of whom fell sick. Shots rang out in the woods. Suicides were beginning to occur. At the battle of Smolensk, Napoleon lost many seasoned troops and was plainly confused and disheartened. He knew he must press on, and he continued through countryside blackened and deserted by the Russian 'scorched earth' policy.

The Russians decided to stand and fight before Moscow at Borodino. It was a brutal head-on battle, very unlike Napoleon's usual style, using enormously costly frontal assaults where he would normally have side-stepped and flanked his enemy. It was the bloodiest battle until Verdun or the Somme. The Russians lost 45,000 casualties including 29 generals, the French 28,000 and 48 generals dead or wounded. Many of the French losses were completely unnecessary. Inexplicably, Napoleon had forced his men and horses to stand and endure lethal artillery fire for hours, many falling when not even taking part in the battle.

The battle was also a strategic failure because the Russians were not destroyed and Napoleon lost far too many men and horses as well as good officers. Worse, he then captured a deserted Moscow to find no city officials, let alone the tsar with whom to negotiate, and much of the city then suddenly burned down, with the French Army losing control in an orgy of looting and worse. Meanwhile, the notorious Russian winter approached.

For weeks, Napoleon tried to negotiate with Alexander, who was in St Petersburg. He urged his emissaries, 'I want peace, I need peace, I must have peace. Just save my honour.' He received no reply and waited, tricked by the unusually fine weather at the beginning of October. But the first smattering of snow fell suddenly on the 13th and now, exasperated, he decided to withdraw. His army, laden with booty, was accompanied by as many 50,000 civilians. Like the soldiers, many would not survive the journey.

Napoleon made another mistake. Instead of travelling light, his initial decision was to leave nothing behind. This exhausted the horses, which had but one week's feed. Worse, Napoleon had ignored advice to give them winter horseshoes to grip on the ice. On 2 November the real, heavy snow came and the struggling army, now 105,000 strong and harassed by Cossacks, began to lose guns, wagons, horses and men in the freezing conditions.

Several Russian armies closed in and, in spite of courageous improvisation by General Eblé (see page 127) in bridge building which enabled the pathetic remnants of the *Grande Armée* to escape back across the Berezina River, 400,000 in all perished. Napoleon, faced by a political crisis in Paris, was forced to leave his men to their fate. 'From the sublime to the ridiculous, there is but one step,' he commented bitterly. It was part of a posture that blamed everyone but himself for the cataclysm. He was far from rising to the occasion.

Napoleon never really recovered from the disastrous loss of veteran soldiers, vital horses and prestige. From then on, he was on a slippery slope. He used all his old resourcefulness and military skill in a series of battles, but the one at Leipzig in 1814, 'The Battle of the Nations', was to lead to the invasion of France and Napoleon's eventual abdication and incarceration on Elba.

His comeback – the 'Hundred Days' that culminated at his defeat at Waterloo – was all part of a process that started with his vengeful and foolhardy decision to attack Russia.

In 1811, he should have suppressed his obsession about Britain and left well alone.

RUDOLF HESS AND HIS FLIGHT OF FANCY

Rudolf Hess really thought he was rising to the occasion for his beloved Führer. All alone, he would do something brave and dramatic which would help Adolf Hitler win the war. And it would scare off all those new people crowding round him.

Hess was born in Egypt and the family moved to Germany in 1908. During World War I, he fought in the infantry, was wounded and became a pilot, an expertise that would later make him famous.

After the war, he moved to Munich where he joined the veterans' Freikorps and enrolled at Munich University. But in May 1920, he first heard Adolf Hitler speak. His whole world changed as he became completely enthralled. Involved in the Beer Hall Putsch in 1923, he was jailed with Hitler in Landsberg Prison, where he helped to write *Mein Kampf*. He became Hitler's closest Nazi Party confidant as he first gained power. 'Hitler ist Deutschland und Deutschland ist Hitler!' he had shouted at Nuremberg rallies. But since the war had started, Hess had grown a trifle irrelevant and plainly felt it, showing distinct jealousy towards the war leaders and generals who now crowded round his beloved Führer. But he would show them all who was the really devoted one.

Quite late into the evening of 10 May 1941, a bulky package was delivered to the Führer in his study at the Berghof, high above Bertchesgaden, with its magnificent views over the Bavarian Alps. Adolf Hitler was very busy with his preparations for Operation *Barbarossa*, his attack on Russia, so he pushed it aside. It was, no doubt, nothing but another of Rudolf's long-winded, boring memoranda.

At almost exactly the same time that evening, Wing Commander the Duke of Hamilton and his staff at RAF Turnhouse near Edinburgh were puzzling over a lone Messerschmitt 110 which had entered their fighter sector's airspace. Where on earth had it come from, and why? A few minutes later, its pilot shut off its two engines, rolled the aircraft on to its back to avoid hitting its tail and parachuted into the darkness.

Next day, Prime Minister Winston Churchill was at Ditchley in Sussex, restlessly alternating between watching a Marx Brothers film and going outside to gaze at the heavy bombing of London. Suddenly the telephone rang. The caller was a personal friend, the Duke of Hamilton, who had almost incredible news of 'cabinet importance': Hitler's deputy had managed to fly all the way from Augsburg to land just 10 miles from the duke's house in Renfrewshire, and was demanding to meet him to discuss 'peace proposals between Germany and Britain'.

Back in Germany, with the package still sitting on his desk, Hitler was interrupted by an adjutant of Hess who handed him a slim envelope. Hitler glanced at the two pages and then slumped into a chair, bellowing, 'Oh My God, My God! He has flown to Britain!' Hysteria and speculation gripped the Berghof. Perhaps Hess had crashed? Or, much worse, the British had him and he might reveal Hitler's plans for Russia? Goering, who had been brusquely ordered to report in, thought – together with his Luftwaffe chiefs – that Hess could not have managed the audacious flight. Hitler thought otherwise. And he was right. Hess had prepared well for what was actually his fourth attempt, persuading Willy Messerschmitt into lending him the long-distance fighter, using the 'Y-beams' system that guided German bombers, and arranging for two radio stations to make a broadcast to fix his position. After an amazing solo flight of 850 miles, he landed in the dark almost within walking distance of the duke's Dungavel House.

After flying 850 miles alone, Rudolf Hess feathered his propellers, rolled his Me-110 and parachuted to meet the Duke of Hamilton – to no avail. (*The Fall of the Deputy Führer* by Charles Thompson GAvA, ASAA)

With silence from Britain, the Germans became frantic with worry, and, after ten drafts, issued a communiqué stating that this star of National Socialism had become 'a deluded, deranged and muddled idealist, riddled with hallucinations traceable to war injuries'.

While the planning and execution of the flight was a brilliant feat, its purpose was an appalling miscalculation. Hess was sincere, but ridiculously naïve. He assumed that the Duke of Hamilton, whom he had met casually at the 1936 Berlin Olympics, was some kind of leader of an 'opposition party'. As Lord Steward, he 'presumably dined with the king every night and could persuade him to make peace in spite of Churchill's war-mongering clique'. (In fact, the duke was one of four brothers gallantly serving as pilots in the RAF.) Hess did not even seem to know the names of any 'opposition leaders', nor realize that after two years under attack, Britain was united in her hatred and defiance towards Hitler's Nazis.

To the duke and to other questioners, Hess insisted he was 'on a mission of humanity', that 'Hitler admired Britain and only wanted a free hand in Europe' in exchange for Britain's 'free hand in its Empire', that Germany was bound to win the war anyway and that, by the way, Hitler would not negotiate with 'Churchill and his clique who had planned the war since 1936'.

Of course, he did not reveal his strongest motive, which was, with the imminent attack on Russia, to avoid a two-front war. His captors merely began to feel he was half mad. He must have been shocked and amazed when he did not meet the king nor the 'opposition party', and was quietly locked up by Churchill in the Tower of London for the duration of the war.

For his part, Hitler ordered that his old friend should be shot if he ever returned, and went back to planning his treacherous attack on Stalin – who was to be forever suspicious that Hess and Churchill had been plotting against him.

Hess was to meet many of his colleagues again in Nuremberg, scene of so many past rallies and triumphs alongside Hitler.

In the dock, he sometimes appeared so unstable that Goering, for one, asked not to sit next to him. But he rallied for his final, defiant speech, continuing to extol Hitler:

> It was granted to me for many years to live and work under the greatest son whom my nation has brought forth in the thousand years of its history. Even if I could, I would not expunge this period from my existence. I regret nothing. If I were standing once more at the beginning, I should act once again as I did then, even if I knew that at the end I should be burnt at the stake.

Of course he was not burnt at the stake, but sentenced to prison for 'crimes against peace'. In Spandau, he served 41 years, remaining there long after all the other war criminals had been released.

Winston Churchill wrote regretfully, 'Reflecting upon the whole of the story, I am glad not to be responsible for the way in which Hess has been and is being treated. Whatever may be the moral guilt of a German who stood near to Hitler, Hess had, in my view, atoned for this by his completely devoted and frantic deed of lunatic benevolence. He came to us of his own free will and, though without authority, had something of the quality of an envoy. He was a medical and not a criminal case, and should be so regarded.'

Faced by the Soviets' implacable refusal to release him, in 1987, aged 92, Hess appeared to hang himself with an electric cable. Some, including his son, thought he was murdered. Whatever the truth, it was a sad end for an idealistic man who, in one scatterbrained slip of judgement, sought to eclipse his political enemies and finally impress his Führer with his devotion.

SHAKA AND HIS MOTHER

Africa, the birthplace of mankind, has in its long history produced only one great military leader, Shaka the Zulu. And he was to prove a leader with a fatal flaw.

Everything that this ferocious ruler did in his spectacular and bloody reign was influenced by his mother. It was a baleful influence which would doom many in Africa, and then doom Shaka himself.

Shaka was born in 1787, the illegitimate son of Chief Senzangakhona and a young girl called Nandi from the nearby Langeni tribe. The union having broken many tribal rules, the boy was cruelly called 'Shaka', literally an unwanted intestinal beetle. Mother and son were both thrown out of Senzangakhona's family when Shaka, aged just six, could not prevent a dog killing one of his father's sheep. When Nandi tried to return to her own tribe at a time of famine, the unwelcoming Langeni banished both her and Shaka into destitution – for which the tribe would later pay dearly. Shaka's burning resentment and his anger on behalf of his mother grew and grew.

Befriended by another tribe, Shaka grew up strong and fearless and was soon invited to join the army of King Dingiswayo. There, after several years' service, he changed forever the way the Zulus were to fight.

He supplemented the traditional throwing assegais with a fearsome close-combat weapon, a long-bladed stabbing spear called the *iXwa* (the noise of the spear being withdrawn), he re-designed his shields to hook an enemy's shield to expose the body

Shaka, who created the most disciplined and fearsome army in Africa's history. (TopFoto)

and he trained his men to run 50 miles a day barefoot. Anyone who wanted to retain his sandals was executed.

Soon it was time to try out his new methods. One afternoon, the Buthelezi tribe faced Shaka for the traditional *giya*, by convention a bloodless confrontation of display and abuse. Shaka and his warriors killed all of them in moments. Soon in command of an army of 50,000, with well-drilled, ruthless discipline, Shaka perfected the fast-moving battlefield tactics which would rule Africa for 50 years, the *Impondo Zankhomo*, with the 'head of the buffalo' supported by the 'loins', with encircling 'horns'. There was simply nothing like it in Africa, and any tribes that did not succumb to Shaka's diplomatic methods of patronage and reward were destroyed in the field by a well-tried 'battle drill', of which any army would have been proud.

The *infecane* or 'crushing' of the other tribes of Africa probably resulted in an appalling two million deaths in a decade, let alone the huge displacement of populations trying to get out of harm's way.

Shaka brought his beloved mother, Nandi, to Bulawayo, 'the place of killing' (now Zimbabwe's second city), where she was set up in a magnificent kraal. Shaka ruled a huge area of Africa, threatened by no one, not even the British with whom he was friendly because one of them had saved his life, providing him with medical treatment after a battle. All seemed well with Shaka and the Zulu nation.

But suddenly in 1827 disaster struck. His beloved mother died. Shaka did not rise to the occasion in a controlled and dignified way, as befits a great leader. He appeared to go mad, literally becoming demented with grief. He ordered the killing of nearly 7,000 of his own followers for 'not showing enough respect' for his mother. And he did it in a perverse way. Young men were clubbed to death on the parade ground when they had visibly become aroused by beautiful girls ordered to dance provocatively in front of them. Milk, the basis of the Zulu diet, was not allowed to be drunk, no crops were to be planted and nobody should become pregnant – on pain of death for both wife and husband. Cows were even slaughtered so that their calves should know how it felt to lose a mother.

In spite of the iron discipline he had imposed, such obsessive, erratic behaviour went too far. When his army was away, his half-brothers Dingane and Mhlangana assassinated him and dumped him in an ignominious unmarked grave.

Shaka's driving force in life had been his obsessive love for his mother. The same love condemned him to an early death at the height of his power.

Shaka's military methods lived on after his death. In spite of the long-distance firepower of invading Europeans, if the Zulus could get close enough, their speed of movement and assegais could overwhelm their enemies. Their ultimate triumph was at Isandlwana (see page 231), where they totally destroyed a British force armed with rifles, rockets and artillery.

Shaka would have been proud of them.

BERNARD MONTGOMERY AND THE AMERICANS

The tanks of the 2nd Battalion Irish Guards were beginning their advance to 'The Island', the narrow road raised above the Dutch fields between Nijmegen and the bridge at Arnhem. Suddenly, there was a clang, and a Sherman tank's sprocket wheel came flying over the trees. 'I knew we were in big trouble,' said a young officer as eight more tanks exploded. It was not just the Irish Guards that were in trouble. So was the whole British Army.

The Guards Armoured Division were trying to play their part in Field Marshal Bernard Montgomery's Operation *Market Garden*, a bold attempt to punch a corridor into Germany's industrial heartland and 'win the war in 44'.

For months the Allied commanders had debated, often heatedly, about the best way to beat the Germans in the west. Britain's difficult and opinionated 'Monty' advocated a dagger-like thrust through Holland into the industrial Ruhr. The Americans favoured a broad push on all fronts. Indeed, if there were to be any thrusts, they would far prefer Montgomery's bitter rival, American General George Patton, to attack from the south.

After the D-Day landings, the Allies were bogged down for weeks, but now Paris and Brussels were liberated and the Germans seemed disorganized and close to defeat. Montgomery's idea, Operation *Market Garden*, was audacious. Thirty thousand British, American and Polish airborne troops were to be flown behind enemy lines to capture the eight bridges that spanned the network of canals and rivers on the Dutch/German border. An armoured corps would follow up, cross the captured bridges and pour into Germany. Montgomery was reluctantly given his head by the American Supreme Commander Eisenhower, who was won over at last by the political argument that V2 rockets launched from Holland were now landing in London.

The attack had to be planned in just six days, a rush contrasting with Montgomery's normal meticulous style. Success depended on the British assessment that the Germans were weak, disorderly and dispirited. However, the Dutch Resistance suddenly reported that SS troops were near Arnhem. They were right. Two crack SS Panzer divisions had arrived there to rest and regroup. A low-level Spitfire then photographed their camouflaged tanks. The operation should have been cancelled at once, but the intelligence officer who was trying to warn everyone was sent on sick leave to keep him quiet – perhaps because so many attacks had been cancelled and the airborne troops were thirsting to get on with it, 'restless, frustrated and ready for anything', as one officer later wrote.

Almost at once, the operation started to go wrong. The Irish Guards' problems were just part of it. The Dutch had long ago concluded that the narrow, exposed, elevated road would be a death trap for tanks and so it proved to be, with rows of burning vehicles blocking the road, predictable victims of the German lethal 88mm and 75mm anti-tank guns, and even of infantry with *Panzerfaust* rockets. So while the American paratroopers had captured the bridges at Nijmegen and Eindhoven, and the armoured corps had rolled across them, they were now stuck just a few miles from Arnhem, several days late.

At Arnhem, 'the bridge too far', it was even worse. The British airborne forces had landed 7 miles away to avoid the town's anti-aircraft flak – the one thing that never materialized. To reach Arnhem quickly, they needed speed and communications. But their reconnaissance jeeps did not arrive, and, incredibly, none of their radios worked. So they could coordinate neither with each other nor with Allied commanders.

Arnhem Bridge with the wreckage of the first German counter-attack. (David Shepherd / The Parachute Regiment)

Nobody knew what was happening or where the British forces were, so vital supplies were even falling into the hands of the Germans.

It was a catastrophe. The lightly armed airborne forces fought against German heavy tanks for eight days with incredible bravery. But, short of ammunition and supplies, they were killed or wounded or forced to surrender or to escape by night back across the Rhine. Out of 10,000 men, only 2,163 made it to safety.

Why did it all happen? Almost certainly everyone was blindly following the will of Montgomery. And Montgomery unfortunately was an egotistical and complex man. After the war, he was asked to list the three greatest commanders in history. Without hesitation, he named Alexander the Great, Napoleon – and himself. And he was not joking. Monty didn't make jokes.

Years later at Wellington School, he read the lesson and even managed to say: 'and God said unto the Israelites, and I have to say I agree with him'. Much more important than simple egotism, he was also suffering from a burning obsession which was to blunt his ability to rise to the occasion. Believing absolutely in his high opinion of himself, he resented the growing American dominance in the alliance and especially that other egotist US General George Patton, whom he had never forgiven for getting to Palermo in Sicily ahead of him. He also denigrated General Eisenhower, now his boss, as a 'hopeless amateur' as a hands-on commander. So he was determined to spite the Americans and pull off his own British victory, and was prepared to abandon all the cautious, detailed planning and attention to detail that usually served him so well, and to ignore any evidence that his plan was in danger.

It was a great tragedy, because he was probably right to opt for a single powerful push into Germany. If he had been less complex a personality, less driven by his anti-American obsession, and had got on rather better with his own side, he might just have pulled it off and won the war in 1944. The Russians might not have reached Berlin first and there might have been no Iron Curtain and no Cold War.

CRASSUS AND HIS THIRST FOR GLORY

Even by the brutal standards of Rome, Marcus Licinius Crassus was not a very attractive figure. His jealousy and greed would create one of the worst defeats in Roman history.

Crassus was born into a life of power and wealth, with his grandfather and father being consuls and censors, and his wealthy father dubbed *Dives* (rich). But the family was ruined by internal wars and young Crassus determined to get back both riches and influence, siding with Sulla and winning an important battle to enter Rome at the Colline Gate.

He then built up his wealth, first by 'proscribing' some of his fallen enemies and acquiring their wealth, then through silver mines and slave-owning. He was also a huge property owner, his portfolio augmented by his ownership of Rome's fire service and his cruel habit of turning up with his fire crews and negotiating very slowly while houses were burning, with the owners then forced to sell at knock-down prices.

The richest man in Rome, he too was now nicknamed *Dives*. And one of the ways he used his wealth was to finance an impoverished Julius Caesar. However, his political career was blighted by his rivalry with Pompey the Great, who he felt had been unfairly granted a 'triumph', which really rankled. His corrosive envy of Pompey was to have fatal consequences.

It was Spartacus and his slave revolt that gave Crassus his next chance for glory. Other Roman generals having been defeated, Crassus financed, equipped and led an army against the slaves. It did not go smoothly and he punished a retreating legion by 'decimation' (killing one in ten) which did not gain him affection from his soldiers, nor much respect from his countrymen. Eventually he won, and crucified 6,000 surrendering slaves along the Appian Way into Rome, leaving their bodies to rot as a gruesome example. Even then Pompey was partly credited with the victory, further fuelling Crassus' envy and hatred. Mediation through Julius Caesar led to the three of them ruling Rome as a secret and uncomfortable triumvirate.

Serving as a consul, with Pompey, Crassus was rewarded with Syria as 'his' province – a potential source of even more wealth. But it was not enough for him. He decided, aged 62, that he wanted final military glory, grand enough to rival Pompey, Julius Caesar and perhaps even Alexander the Great. Twenty years after his last taste of battle, once more at his own expense, he decided to create an occasion to rise to and invaded the kingdom of Parthia.

It was a very foolish decision, soon to be compounded by others. First he turned down an offer by the King of Armenia of 40,000 troops as long as Crassus went through Armenia. Then he learned nothing of the Parthian equipment and tactics, trusting that 35,000 Roman legionaries and 8,000 cavalry would be more than a match for anything the Parthians could muster. When he arrived at Carrhae he seemed vindicated when he was faced by a mere 10,000 cavalry.

What he did not bother to find out was that the Parthians used fearsome composite bows with arrows capable of penetrating Roman chain-mail armour. Another secret weapon was the *cataphracti*, heavily armoured horsemen who quickly ambushed his own cavalry and eliminated them from the battle. The Roman infantry were now subjected to endless barrages of arrows fired backwards by Parthian cavalry – the famous 'Parthian shot'. When they formed protective *testudines*, tortoise-like shield formations, the *cataphracti* smashed into them, and when they tried to charge, the horse archers kept raining arrows on them, constantly supplied by fresh arrows brought up by the camel-load. Crassus' son, Publius, was killed, and his head, displayed on a pike, did little for Roman morale.

Eventually, weakened by heat and thirst, the surviving Romans forced Crassus to go and parley with the Parthian general. There, he was seized and killed – some say by having molten gold poured down his throat 'finally to sate his thirst for wealth'.

Only Gaius Cassius Longinus, his quaestor, whose advice Crassus had constantly ignored, escaped with about 10,000 men (later he was more famous as one of Julius Caesar's assassins).

Crassus had lost 20,000 dead, 4,000 wounded and 10,000 captured. He had managed to create one of the worst and most humiliating Roman defeats, rivalling Varus and his 'lost Legions' in Germany.

His death, by removing the balancing force between Pompey and Caesar, led to civil war between them, the loss of the Republic and the creation of the Roman Empire.

GEORGE PATTON AND HIS TEMPER

To his countrymen of more modern times, George Patton would appear something of an anachronism. Like Douglas MacArthur, he seemed to belong to the 19th century – or even earlier. Born into a rich, landed and military background, he had longed to be a soldier since his father had read him Homer. He could read a military map at age seven. At West Point he became an expert fencer and polo player, and his football aggressiveness earned him three broken noses and two broken arms.

Patton even came fifth in the Modern Pentathlon at the 1912 Stockholm Olympics, missing a bronze medal by insisting on using a big military .38 revolver for the shooting part. His stint at the French Cavalry School at Saumur made him so expert at fencing that he became the 'US Army Master of the Sword', and even designed the army's new cavalry sabre.

When World War I started, he tried to enrol with his friends in the French cavalry but had to content himself with joining 'Black Jack' Pershing's expedition against Pancho Villa in Mexico, where he personally shot a general with his revolver.

America's entry into the war in 1917 saw Pershing promote Patton to lead the new tank arm, and after many daring and gallant actions in France, he was wounded as the fighting ended.

Montgomery (right) enjoys a joke (if only for the cameras) with his rival George Patton. (Imperial War Museum)

Between the wars he learned to fly and honed his military knowledge with 600 books which he carefully annotated, from Caesar, Alexander the Great and Napoleon right up to works by his future Panzer foes, Guderian and Rommel.

Indeed, it was Rommel's vicious blooding of the US 2nd Corps at Kasserine in February 1942 that saw Eisenhower giving the corps to Patton, who ruthlessly gripped its inexperienced, battered and demoralized troops.

He also started to dress extremely flamboyantly, with full medals and ivory-handled revolvers. He would arrive with sirens wailing; 'A man of diffident manner will never inspire confidence,' he said. His revived 2nd Corps helped to throw the Axis out of Africa, and then his 7th Army in Sicily beat Montgomery to Messina, starting a poisonous and childish rivalry between them.

But it was not just the strange and obsessive Montgomery or more amenable British commanders who disliked the talented but intemperate Patton. His American colleagues also resented the flashy profanity and even the successes of 'Old Blood and Guts'.

However, even his successes could not save Patton from a huge setback, all of his own making. Often men who rise to the occasion will have a special flaw – impetuosity. In the case of George Patton, it was compounded by a sudden temper.

While visiting a field hospital in Sicily a tense Patton slapped an unwounded but shell-shocked soldier, calling him a 'coward'. A few days later in another hospital he did it again. When news leaked out in the American newspapers, he was forced to apologize publicly. It was an embarrassing shock for such a proud man, but the long-term results were much worse. In spite of the support given to 'Georgie' by his old and exasperated friend Dwight Eisenhower, the supreme commander, he was effectively demoted, and Omar Bradley, his cautious subordinate, became his boss. Patton did not land on D-Day. Instead, he was ordered to show himself all over Norfolk and eastern England inspecting a fictitious army. Actually, it did a lot of good because the Germans refused to believe that the Americans had disciplined and sidelined their best combat general for such a tiny offence and were therefore more easily convinced by the elaborate phantom First US Army Group led by the 'Patton Bogeyman' which appeared to be about to attack at Calais. The Germans held back huge forces north of the Seine to receive him.

In fact, after participating in this useful deception, Patton had been given the 3rd Army and was placed south of the 'action' in Normandy. He then made his army into one of America's greatest fighting forces and broke out and thundered across France, advancing 600 miles in two weeks. But his supplies kept running out, often diverted (to Patton's fury) to Montgomery further north. Several times in the drive towards Germany he was held back by the cautious Bradley and Eisenhower, allowing the off-balance Germans to reorganize.

There are some who argue that if Patton had not lost his temper and slapped the two soldiers, he would have been commanding a whole army corps and, with his reckless courage and drive, he might well have cut right into Germany in 1944. Thus, no Russians in Berlin, no Iron Curtain and perhaps millions of lives saved.

MARK ANTONY AND HIS DANGEROUS LOVER

Among the normal reasons for military defeat and failure, love does not feature often. Of course, there have been occasions. Helen 'launched a thousand ships' at Troy, but that may have been less about love and more about a trade war. Attila's death on honeymoon certainly saved Rome, and Paraguay was comprehensively wrecked by Emperor Francisco Lopez and his Irish lover, Eliza Lynch (see page 269). But centuries before, when Rome was the military and political centre of the world, there was another soldier who allowed love to dominate his actions. Mark Antony should have known better.

After the assassination of Julius Caesar, two men appeared to have delivered the Roman Republic from its seemingly endless cycle of civil war. Both had been close to Julius Caesar – Octavian, his great nephew, and Mark Antony, his good friend. They pursued Brutus and Cassius, Julius Caesar's killers, and avenged his death at the battle of Philippi in 42 BC. The Roman world was carved up among Antony, Octavian and the nonentity Lepidus. Loosely speaking, Octavian controlled the west and Antony the east.

But, unfortunately, instead of peace, trouble for the Romans was not over. The world would once again be turned upside-down, this time not by the murder of a dictator, but by a love affair, one of the most famous and destructive in history. Antony, during his command in the east, fell for the Egyptian Queen Cleopatra. As Shakespeare put it: 'The triple pillar of the world transformed into a strumpet's fool'.

Cleopatra was famed for her powers over men. She had only recently won the heart of an even greater Roman, Julius Caesar, mothering his child,

Cleopatra, as portrayed here by Liz Taylor. In reality, she was probably not as beautiful, but just as irresistible to men. (Corbis)

Caesarion. Indeed, the affront caused by the Egyptian interloper may have been one of the causes of his assassination.

While we have seen her portrayed by beautiful actresses like Elizabeth Taylor, in reality her beauty was questionable. There was plainly something more, as Shakespeare has Enobarbus describe:

> Age cannot wither her, not custom stale
> Her infinite variety; other women cloy
> The appetites they feed, but she makes hungry
> Where most she satisfies; for vilest things
> Become themselves in her.

It is obvious that her intelligence was more attractive than her physical charms. She spoke nine languages and was a trained mathematician. Some have seen the relationship as a political one – Cleopatra providing Antony with ships and men. But she did bear him three children and his dedication to her even when the relationship was politically disastrous reveals the romantic truth. He really was prepared to throw it all away for love.

Back in Rome, the revelations of this new affair involving Cleopatra were causing increasing outrage, especially due to the couple's reported debauched lifestyle, which Octavian's propaganda machine did much to highlight: 'too besotted with lust and drink to think either of his friends or of his enemies'.

Conflicts between the two previous allies escalated. Even the attempted reconciliation at the Treaty of Brundisium, including the political marriage of Antony to Octavian's sister, Octavia, was not enough to prevent the inevitable.

Antony then broke two taboos. He married Cleopatra, thus publicly rejecting Octavian's sister. He also arrogantly celebrated a 'triumph', the most sacred of Roman military processions, in Alexandria.

Octavian seized on such insults, pushed aside Lepidus, who had always been closer to Antony, and put the final nail in the coffin of Antony's public image by reading his will publicly. It stated that he wished to be buried in Egypt, even if he died in Rome. It was also claimed he wanted to move the capital from Rome to Alexandria.

Events came to a head in open conflict. Attempting to return to the safety of Egypt, Antony and Cleopatra were cornered, low on supplies, at Actium, off the promontory of Akri in north-west Greece. While both sides had plenty of troops, Antony elected to fight a naval battle. Evenly matched, each side had about 450 galleys.

After several hours of stalemate, some of Octavian's ships broke through the line, but instead of committing her carefully placed reserve ships, Cleopatra panicked, turned her ships round and rowed away. Mark Antony then did something militarily unforgivable. He, too, sailed away, to be with her. He abandoned his brave men at the height of the battle, which they then lost, surrendering to Octavian's fleet.

The couple fled to Egypt and Antony was defeated outside Alexandria. With the Roman Army closing in, Mark Antony stabbed himself to death. Cleopatra, true to form, tried to seduce Octavian, but this time it did not work. Facing the certain humiliation of being paraded through Rome in chains, she smuggled in an asp, and the snake bit her to death.

For his love, Antony had lost the support of the Roman people, and thrown away his share in the known world. Octavian became its undisputed ruler, being granted the name Augustus. By his victory at Actium, he had destroyed the Roman Republic and created the Roman Empire.

CHARLES LINDBERGH AND 'AMERICA FIRST'

By almost any yardstick, Charles Lindbergh rose to the occasion for most of his life – becoming the most famous man in the world. But at a critical moment in his country's destiny he failed to do so, all part of a pattern of extraordinary triumph and tragedy.

Charles was born in Detroit on 4 February 1902, but lived in rural Minnesota. His father, Congressman C. A. Lindbergh, had become a strong advocate of keeping America out of World War I, even voting against the arming of American merchant ships to protect them against U-boats. He became ever more unpopular as war grew closer. History was to repeat itself.

From the moment he was taken up in a plane, young Charles could not get enough of flying. He became a dare-devil 'barnstormer', even riding on the wings of the planes. In March 1925, Charles graduated first in his class from the Advanced Flying School and became a second lieutenant in the Air Service Reserve Corps – but there were no flying duties to be had. So, he spent time in flying circuses, the first time that the name 'The Flying Fool' was applied to him.

He then joined the pioneering Air Mail Service, and twice he had to parachute from rickety, crashing planes. By now he was the most famous member of the 'Caterpillar Club', those saved by jumping, and the nation's only one to have been saved *four* times.

In 1927 his restless ambition made him plan something really spectacular. He determined to be the first to fly non-stop from New York to Paris. Needing 400 gallons of petrol for the 3,600-mile flight, he decided to fly alone. On the side of the huge extra fuel tank blocking his forward vision was painted SPIRIT OF ST LOUIS in recognition of the city whose businessmen had backed him. While other pilots threatened to beat him to it, the media took to this brave, shy, good-looking 'Kid Flyer', also calling him the 'Human Meteor'.

Lindbergh realises he is nearly there. From the painting *Hallelujah! Fishing boats* by Roger Middlebrook, GAVA.

At 7.54am on 20 May 1927, the 2-ton flying fuel tank staggered into the air. After hours desperately trying to stay awake, he spotted fishing boats. 'Which way Ireland?' he shouted, circling. No answer. But soon the coast of Dingle Bay appeared out of the mist. At 10.39pm, after 33 hours 39 minutes, he rolled to a stop at Paris, Le Bourget, thunderstruck by the 150,000 people flooding onto the airfield. Overnight he was the most famous man in the world.

France went mad for Lindbergh, led by Prime Minister Raymond Poincaré. Then it was King Albert of the Belgians, before

Charles Lindbergh, soon to be one of the most popular people of the time, poses with the *Spirit of St Louis.* (Library of Congress)

landing at Croydon to be greeted by an ecstatic, cheering crowd of 150,000 normally reticent British. George V and Queen Mary presented him with the Air Force Cross, Britain's highest peacetime honour, and the House of Commons rose in spontaneous applause. Winston Churchill said it all: 'From the little we have seen of him, we have derived the impression that he represents all that a man should say, should do and should be.'

But all this foreign praise merely made America more desperate for his return. A cruiser was even sent to collect him. 'Lucky Lindy' was the first of 200 songs churned out by Tin Pan Alley, and the 'Lindy Hop' dance was already the rage as he arrived, accompanied by four destroyers, two airships and 40 aircraft. President Calvin Coolidge was one of a crowd of 250,000 people waiting in Washington, presenting him with the first Distinguished Flying Cross, with the prophetic words, 'He has brought unsullied fame home.' The Post Office issued the first stamp in honour of a man still living. Five million New Yorkers gave him an ecstatic ticker-tape parade, while millions of Americans wrote letters to him and sent him cables and gifts. The grateful city of St Louis greeted him with half a million of its citizens, the first of 82 cities he flew to, all of which bestowed on him the same ceaseless adulation.

Hermann Goering pins a Nazi medal on Charles Lindbergh, something which was to haunt Lindbergh in the future. (Herman Goering Collection / Library of Congress)

It is hard for us now to cast our minds back and appreciate or even believe just how famous Charles Lindbergh was. It was like combining Princess Diana, the Beatles, the Pope and about ten others into the fame of a tall, handsome, shy boy from Detroit.

The picture of 'The American Dream' seemed complete when Lindbergh fell for Anne Morrow, the beautiful daughter of a distinguished ambassador and senator. Married in May 1927, she obtained a pilot's licence and went off with him all over the world as co-pilot and navigator – 'The First Couple of the Skies'. Popularity only grew with the happy domestic news of the arrival of Charles Junior, 'Baby Lindy' or 'The Eaglet'.

Then any chance that their hysterical public fame would dissipate was eliminated by a dreadful event. The 'Lindbergh Baby' was kidnapped. When the infant disappeared from their New Jersey house, Lindbergh tried to rise to the occasion by bringing his cool headed and methodical approach to bear – ultimately to no avail. The world watched, with horrified fascination, the desperate search, the ransom drama, the discovery of the little body and, two and a half years later, the trial of the suspected murderer.

It was during this troubled time that Lindbergh made a long-term enemy. In February 1934, President Roosevelt cancelled all the mail contracts, on which the airlines relied to break even, including Lindbergh's TWA. The president ordered the US Army to fly the mail, a job for which they were not equipped. It was a disaster. Only a fraction of the mail was carried and 12 army pilots died in crashes. Lindbergh threw his whole weight publicly against the decision. An angry Roosevelt was soon forced to back down, but neither he nor Lindbergh ever forgot – or forgave.

In spite of immense public sympathy about the baby, it was a gruelling, publicity-filled period, which made the Lindberghs leave for England and Europe. There, he made several visits to Germany, where he plainly admired her technical aviation skills. So, at an American Embassy dinner on 18 October 1938, the ambassador and his guests were not unduly surprised when Reichsmarschall Hermann Goering presented Lindbergh, 'By order of the Führer', with the *Verdientskreuz Deutscher Adler*, the Service Cross of the German Eagle, for his services to world aviation and his 1927 flight. It was a golden cross with four small swastikas, on a red ribbon. Charles Lindbergh returned and showed it to his wife, Anne, who glanced at it casually and then remarked, both enigmatically and prophetically, 'The Albatross'. For the moment, they thought no more about it.

But just two weeks later came *Kristallnacht* – the burning of synagogues, the wrecking of Jewish shops, the arrests and street attacks, the first public pogrom against the Jews in Germany. This opened the world's eyes to the true nature of the Nazis. Suddenly the medal indeed looked like an albatross.

Now the stubborn and opinionated hero followed in his father's footsteps, using all his popularity and prestige in an attempt to keep the United States out of the war. He became America's symbol of neutrality, now publicly equated with being defeatist or pro-Nazi. He led the 'America First' movement, to the growing fury of President Roosevelt, with whom he had quarrelled over the airmails in the past, and who now said unfairly, 'I am convinced Lindbergh is a Nazi.' Having resigned his US Army colonel's commission, he was then constantly pilloried by public opinion for stubbornly not giving back the Nazi medal, and dubbed 'The Knight of the German Eagle'. With Poland and Western Europe over-run and heroic RAF pilots fighting the Battle of Britain in the skies right above his old home in England, his popularity slumped further.

Roosevelt's Secretary of the Interior, Harold Ickes, was particularly bitter in his denunciation: 'I have never heard Lindbergh utter a word of a word of pity for Belgium or Holland or Norway or England. I have never heard him express a word of pity for the Poles or the Jews who have been slaughtered by the hundreds of thousands by Hitler's savages. I have never heard Lindbergh say a word of encouragement to the English for the fight they are so bravely making for Lindbergh's right to live his own life in his own way, as well as for their own right to do so.'

Lindbergh stubbornly ignored such warnings from the government and prepared his strongest speech, 'Who Are the War Agitators?' He named them as 'the Roosevelt administration, the British and the Jews'. His wife Anne could see the anti-Semitic danger and went into a 'black gloom'. She was absolutely right to fear the worst.

His well-meaning naïvety meant that 'The Lone Eagle' was transformed from 'Public Hero Number 1' into 'Public Enemy Number 1'. Columnist Walter Winchell sneered, 'His halo has become his noose.' Even his wife's sister admitted that he had gone 'from Jesus to Judas'.

Everything suddenly changed with the treacherous Japanese attack on Pearl Harbor. Lindbergh immediately closed down 'America First' and tried to rise to the occasion once more and to rejoin the colours. But Roosevelt said, 'I'll clip that young man's wings' and spitefully blocked it, and even used his power to stop any commercial war-effort appointments by Lindbergh's friends at companies like PanAm. With Lindbergh now miserable at these rejections, at last the eccentric Henry Ford stepped in.

Lindbergh hurled himself into his work at Ford, whose plants were soon turning out one B-24 Liberator bomber every hour. He radically improved aircraft like the P-47 Thunderbolt. In the Far East, he so extended the range of the P-38 Lightning that General Douglas MacArthur sent for him to thank him. He even secretly flew 50 combat missions and downed a Japanese plane.

When Roosevelt died, Lindbergh was somewhat rehabilitated and joined a technical mission to Europe. There he saw, with horror, the real results of aviation under the Nazis, in the appalling conditions in the tunnels of Camp Dora where thousands of prisoners had perished building the V1 and V2 rockets.

Charles Lindbergh was always a decent man, but a man of very firm convictions. One of those convictions cost him dear.

4

TREACHERY AND RANK DISOBEDIENCE

LORD CHELMSFORD, SIR BARTLE FRERE AND THE ZULUS

They had been friends since their days in India – one a soldier and the other a colonial civil servant. Both had experienced the horrors of the Indian Mutiny and both were now driven by their obsession that a powerful 'native' army would be a threat to their ambitions for a British South Africa.

They had followed fairly conventional careers. Frederick Thesiger, soon to become Lord Chelmsford, had been commissioned into the Rifle Brigade, but had then purchased a transfer to the Grenadier Guards. He had been 'mentioned in despatches' in the Crimea, and transferred to command the 95th (Derbyshire) Regiment in India. He was now a lieutenant-general commanding the forces in South Africa.

Sir Bartle Frere had been one of the tiny band of colonial administrators who ran the huge subcontinent of India. He had started as a 'writer' in the Bombay Civil Service, then became assistant collector in Poona and later chief commissioner at Sind. His competent actions during the Mutiny had earned him the thanks of both Houses of Parliament, and Queen Victoria had made him a Knight Commander of the Bath. Now he was High Commissioner of South Africa.

In 1878, it became apparent that these two men were trying to engineer a war against the Zulus, a friendly and allied kingdom. Colonial Secretary Sir Michael Hicks

Lord Chelmsford, whose reputation was tarnished forever by his unauthorized attack on the Zulus. (Michael Grimsdale)

Beach saw the danger and ordered Frere, 'By the exercise of prudence and by meeting the Zulus in a spirit of forbearance and reasonable compromise, it will be possible to avert the very serious evil of a war.' In any case the written instructions for a high commissioner stated: 'He is not to declare war or to make war against any foreign state.'

Not only were they about to act in direct disobedience to British government instructions, their iniquitous intentions were obvious to many worried British officials in Africa. Trying to avert disaster, Sir Henry Bulwer convened a boundary commission in 1878 at Rorke's Drift on the Buffalo River, a place soon to become very famous indeed.

Frere was mortified when, after five weeks the commission ruled in favour of the Zulus. So he locked up the report. The Zulus were then summoned to Rorke's Drift on 11 December, expecting a favourable verdict, and were dismayed to have read out to them a written ultimatum from Frere insisting that, among other strong demands, they dismantle their military machine, an impossible demand that had huge social implications. This clause, significantly, was left out of the copy sent to Hicks Beach.

One remarkable man, Shaka, had created the Zulu nation with its 50,000 warrior army (see page 213). It was he who transformed inter-tribal warfare from the equivalent of village cricket to ruthless conquest. He had also trained his men to manoeuvre smoothly in regiments, with the tactics of the 'head' and the 'enveloping horns', and the 'loins'. Furthermore, he had imposed mortal discipline that no African (or European) had ever known.

Then there were the 'age-sets' of his regiments, recruited by age and not by location or family. Crucially, men were only allowed to marry when they were well over 30, and then only after 'the washing of the spears', proof of bravery in battle.

Fifty years later, it was fundamental threats to this Zulu way of life, as Bartle Frere and Chelmsford well knew, that caused the meeting at Rorke's Drift to break up and forced Cetshwayo, crowned Zulu king with the approval of Queen Victoria and a British ally for decades, reluctantly to order his army to resist.

Nevertheless, Cetshwayo sent seven peace messages to Chelmsford. All were ignored. Frere and Chelmsford should have known better than to underestimate the Zulus militarily, but now they were on a mission.

It was once again at Rorke's Drift, on 12 January 1879, that an illegal invading British Army under Frere's confident accomplice Lord Chelmsford crossed into Zululand. Chelmsford, an energetic, likeable and well-respected officer, was convinced that not even the Zulus would face European firepower. A quick and easy victory could surely be achieved. The classic military mistake of underestimating the enemy was about to take its toll.

Under the mountain at Isandlwana, the British made camp, and Chelmsford made his first slip, overruling his officers and not bothering to dig trenches and 'laager' the wagons in a defensive circle, in direct contravention of *Regulations for the Field Forces in South Africa*. As one officer noted, 'It was as defenceless as an English village'. In one sense, he was actually wrong. For riflemen, the houses and walls of a village would have provided better defence than the sprawling open camp.

The next day Chelmsford made his second fatal error. He divided his command and took half his army to seek out the Zulus, who he was anxious 'would not give battle'. He need not have worried. At noon, firing from back at the camp alerted him that something was wrong, although telescopes revealed that 'bodies of men were moving about and the tents were standing'. But at 3pm, in galloped Commandant Lonsdale with dreadful news. Despite their discipline and courage and the firepower of their Martini-Henry rifles, backed by artillery and rockets, the 1,700 defenders at Isandlwana had been overwhelmed by 25,000 well-coordinated Zulus in less than an hour.

Now, for the third time, would come Rorke's Drift's final and greatest claim to fame. Actually, the Zulus never intended to invade Natal, merely to block the invasion of their homeland. But as one Zulu later laconically stated, 'the Undi and Udhloko regiments went to Rorke's Drift to plunder the post, and failed and lost very heavily after fighting all afternoon and night'.

That evening, fighting from the walls and buildings, a handful of men beat off the attacks of thousands of Zulus, a truly heroic action which caught the public's imagination and somewhat mitigated the earlier disaster.

Eleven of them were awarded the Victoria Cross, the most ever awarded for one battle. Seventeen men had lost their lives. The heroism of this most remarkable of battles has been famously recorded in the film *Zulu*, starring a young Michael Caine and Stanley Baker, and has one of the great understated lines of the cinema. Colour-Sergeant Bourne (Nigel Green) orders one very frightened soldier, staring at 4,000 advancing Zulus, 'Do up your tunic lad! Where do you think you are?'

Chelmsford, in spite of the fact that he had just been relieved of command, did eventually defeat the Zulus deep in their own homeland at Ulundi. But it did not really redeem his reputation, nor that of his friend Frere. They would always be regarded as the pair who caused the greatest Victorian military defeat and, in hindsight, the deliberate and squalid destruction of a great nation.

MARK CLARK AND HIS VERY OWN CITY

Listeners to the BBC on 5 June 1944 woke up to apparently wonderful news:

> The people of Rome have crowded onto the streets to welcome the victorious Allied troops. The first American soldiers, members of the Fifth Army, reached the centre of Rome late last night. The people have been celebrating. Shops have closed and huge crowds have taken to the streets, cheering, waving and hurling bunches of flowers at the passing army vehicles.
>
> Rome is the first of the three Axis powers' capitals to be taken and its recapture will be seen as a significant victory for the Allies and the American commanding officer who led the final offensive, Lieutenant-General Mark Clark.

It may have seemed a victory – and a triumph. It *was* a triumph for Mark Clark, but in reality it was a disaster for the Allies, for the Italians and for the whole world.

By 1944, the realities of the Anglo-American alliance had changed. The Americans were becoming ever more numerous and the more experienced British commanders were having to work with some American subordinates who were far from ideal. Even his US colleagues thought that Clark had risen too fast, promoted two grades in 1941 from lieutenant-colonel to brigadier-general and less than a year later to major-general. Some suspected that it was because he was a cousin of the US chief of staff, General George Marshall. Now he commanded the 5th Army in Italy. He was brave, and a first-class planner and organizer, but his character as a senior officer was flawed with conceit, ambition, vanity and envy. He employed 50 public-relations men, demanded that he should only be photographed from his 'good side' and that all press releases had to feature his name three times on the first page. It was not just rather reserved British colleagues who objected to him. American General Omar Bradley later wrote, 'I had serious reservations about him personally. He seemed false, somehow, too eager to impress, too hungry for the limelight, promotions and personal publicity.'

George Patton, no publicity wallflower himself, found him 'too damned slick' and 'more preoccupied with bettering his own future than winning the war'. How right he was.

Mark Clark's immediate superior could not have been a greater contrast. For those who were lucky enough to know him, Field Marshal Alexander was one of the nicest people you could meet. Winston Churchill regarded him as 'the personification of the British officer and gentleman'. But in Italy and with Mark Clark, 'Alex' was probably much too nice.

The younger son of an earl, Harold Alexander joined the Irish Guards in 1911; and in the slaughter of the trenches of the Western Front he was several times decorated for bravery and, aged just 24, rose to command their 2nd Battalion, soon to be a brigadier at 27. Two decades later, commanding the rearguard at Dunkirk, he was famously the last man off the beach.

He was once again to taste the bitterness of retreat in the face of superior odds in Burma against the Japanese in 1942. But only months later, he was Commander in Chief of the Middle East, and as Montgomery's supportive superior, masterminded victory over Rommel in North Africa. There were many who served with Alexander who felt strongly that he was overshadowed in the media by his egotistic, publicity-seeking deputy, Montgomery – probably because of 'Alex's' legendary modest and gentlemanly charm. King George VI once visited Alexander and Monty in their desert headquarters. After an hour of declaiming how exactly he was going to use 'his' troops, Monty was briefly called away. 'Alex' quietly apologized to his monarch that neither had been able to get a word in, commenting ruefully, 'I'm afraid he may be after my job.' 'Thank God for that,' replied His Majesty, 'I thought he was after mine!'

In many ways, 'Alex' and the Allies' Supreme Commander Eisenhower shared the same crucial skill of leading vast armies from different nations while containing, with great diplomacy, the ambitions and rivalries of prima donnas like 'Monty', George Patton and Mark Clark, who behind his back called 'Alex' a 'peanut' and a 'feather duster'.

Now, in their hard, slogging fight up Italy, in what should have been the 'soft underbelly of Europe', Alexander had under him a disloyal Mark Clark as the commander of half his forces. Twice Clark was to ruin Alexander's bold plans to speed up the advance.

When Mussolini was deposed by the Italian king, the Germans had reacted decisively, invading Italy and blocking the Allies with their Gustav Line, especially at the pivotal point of Monte Cassino, where assault after assault had failed to dislodge them. Thousands had died in stubborn fighting and miserable conditions reminiscent of World War I. Alexander decided to outflank the Germans with a bold amphibious landing from the sea further north at Anzio, designed to make them withdraw from Cassino. However, the Anzio commander, Major-General John Lucas, was a feeble and indecisive officer. Clark virtually ensured that Lucas would not achieve the aim of a breakout by secretly advising him, 'Johnny, don't stick your neck out' – exactly what he was meant to do.

Thus the Allies, having achieved complete surprise and landing unopposed, simply sat in their crowded beachhead. The Germans were able furiously to counter-attack them without having to withdraw from the Gustav Line. At Anzio, the Allies were trapped for five long, bloody months. Churchill bitterly complained that he had hoped to 'land a wildcat' and all he got was 'a beached whale'.

So now Alexander planned a breakout designed to trap the German forces and to end the war in Italy. Operation *Diadem* did catch out the Germans brilliantly, and did indeed smash at last through the Gustav Line, also allowing the Anzio forces to break out. After two weeks, just as Alexander had planned, US General Lucian Truscott was approaching Valmontone and was poised to close the escape route for the whole German 10th and 14th Armies. Suddenly, he received a very strange order from Mark Clark. Truscott was to split his forces and head north-west for Rome, which would leave far too few troops to trap the Germans. Knowing the implications, Truscott was dumbfounded and appalled, and he challenged the order. But his demand to speak personally to Mark Clark by radio was refused. He was obliged to obey. So American troops were welcomed by cheering crowds in the undefended city.

The conquering hero, Mark Clark, is greeted by the ecstatic crowds in Rome, while a few miles away whole German armies are escaping. (Imperial War Museum)

The broadcaster Alan Whicker, as a war correspondent the first and only British officer in Rome, still recalls his contempt at watching Mark Clark preening himself for photographers. An embarrassed Truscott was heard to say, 'I am anxious to get out of this posturing and to get on with the business of war.' Meanwhile the Germans were escaping north to fight another day – or, rather, what turned out to be 330 bloody and bitter days. American military historian Carlo D'Este summed up the views of most people in the know, 'It was as militarily stupid as it was insubordinate.'

Driven by envy, Mark Clark had become obsessed with upstaging his colleagues both in Italy and in England, and had decided to reap the 'glory' of taking Rome – just before the D-Day landings in Normandy would make Italy a publicity backwater – and especially ahead of the British, who had, of course, actually no intention of going near Rome. Clark denied that he had disobeyed orders, but later revealed to a journalist that he had even ordered his men to shoot at the British if they threatened to upstage him.

The result of Clark's disobedience in pursuit of personal glory was disastrous. It condemned the Italians to a year of brutal occupation, their partisans to huge losses and the Allies to a year of warfare. It prevented them from reaching Austria months before the Soviets and perhaps ending the war much earlier, with huge human and political benefits.

A seething Churchill confined himself to calling the event 'unfortunate'. Alexander, nice as ever, never let his true feelings be known, but his family have revealed how bitter and disappointed he was to have his war-winning strategic move wrecked for such selfish reasons.

In some armies, German, Japanese and Russian, Mark Clark would have been dismissed or even shot for such an act of fatal disobedience. As it was, he was promoted and went on to a distinguished military career, his picture even appeared on the cover of *Time* magazine three times.

LORD SACKVILLE AND MINDEN

In 1760 at London's Horse Guards, a court martial handed down one of the most devastating verdicts ever made on a senior British officer, not only upholding his recent dismissal but adding the damning ruling that 'he was unfit to serve his Majesty in any military capacity whatsoever'. This was even read out to every regiment in the British Army.

The court was referring to Lieutenant-General Lord George Sackville and his lamentable and strange behaviour at the battle of Minden. Amazingly, however, after his dismal performance during a now-forgotten European war, he was later to be rehabilitated and was then, unfortunately, to be in a position to damage British interests on a far larger and longer-lasting scale.

George Sackville's background was fairly typical of a privileged, 18th-century aristocrat. He was the third son of the Duke of Dorset, who was the Lord Lieutenant of Ireland, and he graduated from Trinity College, Dublin, in 1737 before entering the British Army.

Before Minden, he actually had quite a good military career. During the War of Austrian Succession, he was wounded leading an infantry charge at Fontenoy, and was captured, treated and returned by the French. He then took a break to become an Irish MP and returned to action, rising to lieutenant-general in the Seven Years' War. Furthermore, he was the senior British commander in the Hanoverian/British alliance under the command of Prince Ferdinand of Brunswick.

On 1 August 1759, at Minden in Westphalia, a 37,000-strong Anglo-German army faced 44,000 French. Three brigades of British infantry, wearing roses plucked from the hedgerows in their hats, were ordered to advance 'on the beat of the drum', meaning, of course, on a drum signal. However, language problems meant that this was misunderstood, and they set off, initially unsupported, against the French line 'to the beat of the drum'. As they advanced, the French cavalry confidently charged three times to destroy them, but with superb control, the British waited until they were only ten yards away before unleashing devastating volleys. The French Marshal de Contades later wrote bitterly, but admiringly, 'I never thought to see a single line of infantry break through three lines of cavalry and tumble them to ruin.'

Lord Sackville returned to power to create more mischief in America, despite facing court martial after the Minden fiasco. (Michael Grimsdale)

With the rest of his army – British and German, infantry and artillery – performing superbly, Prince Ferdinand then ordered Sackville to complete the victory by charging with his five powerful cavalry regiments. Four times, and with mounting urgency, did the prince send the order – and four times did Sackville stubbornly refuse to move.

Desperate with shame and frustration, his deputy, Lord Granby, tried to advance, but was ordered to halt by Sackville. It is said that Sackville and Granby hated each other and that Sackville did not want Granby to 'get the credit for a victory' – the kind of petty personal squabble that occurred between Lord Lucan and Lord Cardigan a century later and helped to cause the fiasco of the 'Charge of the Light Brigade'.

At Minden, Sackville's unprecedented disobedience and failure to rise in any way to the occasion was immediately recognized as having cost a decisive victory. He was duly cashiered in the field and sent home. Foolishly, he then demanded a court martial – and got it – resulting in that damning ruling that he should 'never serve in any military capacity whatsoever'.

And that, you might think, was that.

But no, 15 years later the new king, George III, quietly returned him to the Privy Council. Sackville, still an MP, then allied himself to Lord North and at the death of his mother-in-law, Lady Elizabeth Germain, became a rich man and, in compliance with her will, changed his name to Lord George Germain.

In 1775, he was given a disastrous appointment by Lord North – Secretary of State for the American Department. This made him responsible for suppressing the revolt, caused by Lord North's taxes, which had broken out in the colonies. Now, he was unfortunately once again 'serving in a military capacity', able to appoint or dismiss British generals and to control their supplies.

Three thousand miles from the action, with no concept of either the terrain or the spirit and skills of the 'enemy', he made disastrous false assumptions: first, that the Americans, even on their home ground, would not be able to withstand British professional soldiers. Indeed he sneered, 'These country clowns cannot whip us'. Then, after their 'inevitable' defeat, he seemed to imagine that they would return docilely to the British fold. 'The rabble ought not to trouble themselves with politics, which they do not understand'. Apart from his contemptuous attitude, his meddling from a distance and confused orders contributed to the British defeat at the turning point of Saratoga and five years later to the loss of Yorktown – and, of course to the final loss of America.

When Lord North's disastrous ministry ended, Lord George Germain also resigned. The king made him Viscount Sackville, and he retired to his estates.

Every 1 August 'Minden Day' is still celebrated, and those British infantry regiments that had covered themselves in glory proudly parade with symbolic wild roses in their caps. For some inexplicable reason, also on that day, red roses are delivered anonymously to the British Consulate in Chicago.

There is no such honoured remembrance for Lord Sackville. He had been either a disobedient fool or a coward at Minden. Even more extraordinary was that he was allowed to be a bigger fool over America.

LORD LOUIS MOUNTBATTEN AND HIS RAID

There are two names that arouse bitterness among veterans who fought for the British Empire in two world wars. For Australians it is 'Gallipoli', and for Canadians it is 'Dieppe'. And it was not those Germans successfully defending Dieppe who made the Canadians feel bitter, but another German. He was born 'His Serene Highness Prince Louis von Battenberg', the son of Prince Louis von Battenberg and Princess Victoria von Hesse und bei Rein. By 1942, he was better known as Admiral Lord Louis Mountbatten, Britain's Chief of Combined Operations.

Not that anyone would question his family's loyalty to Great Britain. His father had been First Sea Lord. He had been forced by public anti-German sentiment to resign in 1914 and to change his German name to Mountbatten – just as his cousins, the British Royal Family, had changed their name from Saxe-Coburg-Gotha to Windsor.

By 1942, Captain Lord Louis Mountbatten was a young and glamorous naval officer with the looks of a film star, friends in Hollywood and a rich and royal cousin on the throne. As a dashing destroyer captain, he was a hero and just what Winston Churchill needed after a string of military reverses. He therefore personally promoted Mountbatten three grades, and made him Chief of Combined Operations.

Handsome and nonchalant, Lord Louis Mountbatten's reputation would never be quite the same following Dieppe. (Imperial War Museum)

'Dickie' Mountbatten was very ambitious and keen to prove himself. The initial 'combined operations' successes, like the raid on Bruneval to capture Germany's radar secrets, were actually initiated by his predecessor Roger Keyes and were not enough for him. Mountbatten needed something bigger, and visibly his own. So in 1942 Operation *Rutter*, the raid on Dieppe, was conceived. It had three theoretical goals: to see if a port could be held for a short period, to obtain intelligence and to gauge German reaction. Unofficial aims, however, were to bolster Churchill's weak position, to draw up the Luftwaffe and hit it hard, and to give the highly trained and bored Canadians something better to do than cause ructions in the towns and villages of southern England. Lord Haw Haw, Germany's infamous radio propagandist, had even said 'Why not give the Canadian soldiers each a bottle of whisky and a motorcycle, declare Berlin an open city, and they will be there in a week.'

In May 1942, the chiefs of staff approved *Rutter*, although the navy and the army chiefs remained uneasy, especially Montgomery. On 7 July, because of bad weather, the raid was cancelled and the seasick troops returned to southern England. Everyone was convinced that Dieppe was off forever. There was, from top to bottom, a sigh of relief.

Mountbatten then did something very strange. With a small staff, he furtively reinstated the Dieppe operation under the new codename *Jubilee*, and kept its planning secret from the chiefs of staff. As he said on television in 1972, 'I made the unusual and, I suggest, rather bold decision that we would remount the operation against Dieppe.' It *was* unusual, to say the very least. At two meetings, the chiefs had turned down the idea. But the plans proceeded in secret, which meant that the normal up-to-date intelligence information could not be requested, nor was the raid cleared with the Inter Service Security Board.

The Royal Air Force was an enthusiastic supporter of the raid. They had no fewer than 70 fighter squadrons available which had little to do but conduct so-called 'Rhubarbs', sweeps designed to bring up the Luftwaffe, which, mostly committed in Russia, had been reduced in the west to a mere two fighter wings. However, they had retained some of their best pilots and their finest new fighter aircraft, the Focke-Wulf Fw190. Dieppe was meant to be the RAF's biggest and most successful 'Rhubarb'.

When, on 19 August 1942, the raid went ahead, it turned into a murderous fiasco. The Allied ships blundered into a German coastal convoy, and the resulting 'firework display' fully alerted the defenders of Dieppe. There, the Canadians were shot to pieces by the hidden guns and machine guns on their flanks, while 27 Churchill tanks scrabbled helplessly on the huge pebbles of the beach. Only 15 reached the esplanade, and then became stuck in front of the new tank traps – all of which up-to-date intelligence would have revealed.

Before they could be stopped, the French-Canadian reserve arrived to enter a 'blizzard of firing'. Of 600 of them, only 125 made it back to England.

In just a few hours, out of 6,090 men, 1,027, mostly Canadians, were killed and 2,340 captured. The casualty rate was actually higher than the Somme. And for the RAF it proved to be its single worst defeat, with the loss of no fewer than 112 fighters to only 44 of the Luftwaffe in one day – a 'Rhubarb' indeed.

Field Marshal Sir Alan Brooke was away in Moscow with Churchill visiting Stalin. General Nye, his deputy, and, as the vice chief of the Imperial General Staff, the most senior officer in Britain, was furious that he knew absolutely nothing of the attack until the signals started streaming in on that very morning.

There was an immediate cover-up, but Churchill's explanation in the House of Commons did not ring true. 'Dieppe was a reconnaissance in force – to which I gave my sanction.' Indeed, most would have been more likely to agree with the

The wreckage on the beach after the disaster at Dieppe. (Imperial War Museum)

German defenders' battle report: 'This affair mocked all rules of military strategy and logic.' Canadian opinion was, understandably, rather more bitter and personal.

The Allied rationalization of how vitally useful this bloody experience was for the Normandy invasion two years later does not hold water. To learn such elementary lessons, why did so many men have to die?

Curiously, however, the disaster had three beneficial effects, albeit completely unintended. It finally convinced the Americans that an invasion before 1944 was not possible. It made the Germans *sure* that the Allies would try to secure a port. However, it caused the Allies to decide just the opposite. When they invaded Normandy in 1944, rather than try to capture a heavily defended port, they took one with them – the artificial concrete 'Mulberry Harbour'.

As for Mountbatten, he got away with his strange behaviour over Dieppe. But many would never trust him again. The words 'Tricky Dickie' were applied to him years before anyone had heard of Richard Nixon.

He was always very defensive about Dieppe, but nevertheless went on to be a 'British hero', the last British viceroy of India, a mentor to his great-nephew Prince Charles, and, in spite of his flaws, considered a great man. And he certainly did not deserve to be murdered in old age by the IRA.

GEORGE ARMSTRONG CUSTER AND THE LITTLE BIG HORN

It was one of his mentors, General McClellan, who unconsciously summed up the virtues and vices of George Armstrong Custer, when he wrote admiringly, 'He was simply a reckless, gallant boy, undeterred by fatigue, unconscious of fear.'

The son of a blacksmith and a fifth-generation descendant of German immigrants called Küster, he had always wanted to be a soldier. In 1857 he entered the United States Military Academy at West Point, aged 17. 'My career as a cadet had but little to recommend it, unless as an example to be carefully avoided.'

He was, indeed, constantly in trouble, an irrepressible adolescent, always playing practical jokes, always close to expulsion by earning so many 'demerits'. Once he allowed a fight between cadets to continue, and, under arrest, admitted to the commandant, 'The instincts of the boy prevailed over the obligations of an Officer of the Guard.' It was to sum up his whole life.

After sadly watching his Southern friends depart to fight for their states against the Union for which they had all trained, he at last graduated – 34th out of 34. Joining the Army of the Potomac, Custer led an impromptu attack in the Peninsular campaign, capturing 50 Confederates – 'a very gallant affair', said a watching General George McClellan. Later, McClellan wondered aloud how deep a river was. Nobody moved, but Custer spurred his horse across, and shouted, 'That's how deep it is, General!' He was promptly rewarded with promotion to captain and a place on the general's staff.

Custer had a brilliant Civil War, fighting enthusiastically in innumerable battles, having a dozen horses shot from under him, always in the limelight, never wounded or even ill – when more Union soldiers were dying of dysentery than gunshots. He was very lucky, while the men he led into action so often were not. His reckless bravery, especially at Gettysburg, resulted in some of the highest cavalry losses of the war.

At 23, he was promoted to brigadier-general, the youngest general in the history of the US Army. 'The Boy General with his flowing yellow curls', enthused the *New York Herald*. Indeed, part of his quest for publicity was Custer's style of clothing, 'like a circus rider gone mad'. His outfit included shiny jackboots, tight olive corduroy trousers, a wide-brimmed slouch hat, tight hussar jacket of black velveteen with silver piping on the sleeves, a sailor shirt, with silver stars on his collar, and a red cravat. He wore his hair in long glistening ringlets liberally sprinkled with cinnamon-scented hair oil.

In September 1863, after a year of resistance from her wealthy father, Judge Bacon, the war hero's proposal of marriage to Elizabeth Bacon was accepted and 'Libbie' became an essential part of Custer's life. Still only 26, he ended the war as major general, witnessed Lee's surrender at Appomattox Court House and was even given the table on which it was signed as a gift for his gallantry.

Thus we have a vivid picture of a young, immature, brave, impetuous officer, unaffected by danger or fatigue, who plainly regarded military rules as applying only to others. He was also bound to be spoilt by public attention, a 'media personality' or a 'celebrity' in modern terms, often taking journalists to witness his feats, one of the most photographed Americans of the period. No wonder that the frustrating years

Custer, always brave, reckless and flamboyant. (Corbis)

fighting the tribes of the Plains, who were trying to protect their homelands and hunting grounds, were likely to be turbulent.

Actually, Custer was somewhat sympathetic to the 'Plains Indians', as the Native Americans living in the Great Plains were called. Certainly, he did not share the attitudes of generals like Sherman, who once reprimanded Custer for leniency, or Phil Sheridan, with his infamous remark, 'The only "good Indian" I ever saw was dead.'

Two incidents of this period are revealing. On a march against the Cheyenne, Custer spotted antelope, decided to hunt them and impetuously galloped away from his 7th Cavalry, together with his greyhounds. Now miles away, he then decided to hunt a big bull buffalo, but managed to shoot his own horse in the head and was found, very luckily, hours later by the column, alone, on foot and lost. The fact was that for frivolous reasons he had deserted his command. He was to do something similar when he left a fort under attack and took a column on a 150-mile forced march just to be with his beloved Libbie. This time he was court-martialled and lost command and pay for a year. But the 'Fetterman Massacre' had occurred (see page 176) and Custer was needed again. He returned to duty in 1868, the same year that a formal treaty was signed with the tribes – a treaty soon to be broken.

At the Washita River, Custer controversially attacked the camp of the friendly White Kettle and his Cheyenne, killing some warriors but also women and children. Apart from accusations of lack of reconnaissance, Custer was also condemned by some of his regiment for abandoning 20 cavalrymen, later found dead. To say that he was now unpopular with some of his officers and men was putting it mildly.

In 1874, it was Custer who entered the sacred Black Hills and trumpeted the presence of gold. Any chance that the 1868 treaty would be honoured was scuppered by the recent financial 'panic' that had shaken the whole country. The gold was needed to shore up the economy and nobody now cared enough about the rights of a few 'savages'. The scene was set for a tragic showdown.

Custer himself was being courted by the Democrats and even revealed to his Crow scouts that he might soon be 'the Big White Father', the president. A victory over the Sioux would seal his candidacy.

After a political fight with President Grant, and only after the pleading of General Sheridan, Custer was allowed to lead his beloved regiment against the Sioux. He was ecstatic. 'I could whip all the Indians on the Continent with the Seventh Cavalry.' (Now where have we heard that kind of talk before?)

In order to take possession of the Black Hills and their gold, the government set a deadline of 31 January 1876 for all Plains Indians to report to reservations or to be considered 'hostile' and be rounded up by the US Army. In reaction, Sitting Bull called together the largest gathering of Native Americans ever witnessed. They camped beside a river called the Little Big Horn.

On 21 June, General Alfred Terry called a council of war with General John Gibbon and Custer to plan how they could encircle and trap their adversaries. Custer, who was meant to be just one part of this encircling movement, then behaved exactly as we would expect.

He was going to 'rise to the occasion', but unfortunately in his own way. So, did he accept Terry's offer of Gatling machine guns, or even of four troops, nearly 200 men, of the 2nd Cavalry? No, he turned them down, confident in his own men (and perhaps unwilling to share glory). When the columns parted and Gibbon called out, 'Now, Custer, don't be greedy, but wait for us,' did he obey these orders? No, he was determined to go it alone. Did he keep his men and horses fresh for the coming battle? No, incapable of feeling fatigue himself, and perhaps with his own secret political timetable, he forced the pace so much that the Indians later described his exhausted men as 'swaying with fatigue, like the limbs of trees in the wind, scarcely able to hold their rifles'. Did Custer listen to his Crow scouts who feared that they faced the greatest force that they had ever seen, 'enough for three days fighting'?

No. He smiled and said he could do it in a day. Did he know his enemies' strengths and fighting ability? No, he thought he might face 1,500 retreating warriors, when there were twice that number – many excellently armed with repeating Winchesters. Did he keep his 611 men together to give them a fighting chance to use their firepower? No, he split them into three forces, his, Major Benteen's and Captain Reno's, none of them strong enough.

Looking down, he could only see part of the huge camp. Perhaps sensing an easy victory like Washita, he cried, 'We've caught them napping. We've got them this time, boys!' He sent a messenger to tell Benteen to hurry and then, without waiting, plunged his exhausted 225 men down towards the camp. Suddenly, out of the dust galloped Gall and 1,500 Hunkpapas, blocking his way. Custer must have realized in a flash that he was no longer the attacker – but now faced a fight for survival. Desperately, he tried to lead his men to the top of the hill behind him, to dig in and wait for reinforcements – Benteen or, perhaps the next day, Gibbon.

But as they struggled up the hill, fighting off Gall, they suddenly faced a terrible sight. There, on the very crest they so needed to reach, appeared Crazy Horse with 1,000 Cheyenne and Sioux, men and ponies magnificent in war paint. Crazy Horse, with his single feather and his Winchester, had ridden his warriors right round Custer, the second jaw of a trap worthy of Napoleon. He paused for a moment and then thundered down the hill and crushed Custer and his 225 doomed men, including Custer's two brothers, his brother-in-law and his cousin.

George Custer fought to the last. Sitting Bull described how 'he laughed as he fired his last shot'. Perhaps Custer recalled his own words, written years before:

When I was verging on manhood, my every thought was ambitious – not to be wealthy, not to be learned, but to be great. I desired to link my name with acts and men, and such a manner as to be a mark of honor – not only to the present, but to future generations.

Custer's ideas of how to rise to the occasion had indeed ensured that few people would forget his name.

BENEDICT ARNOLD AND WEST POINT

On the battlefield of Saratoga, there is one of the world's strangest military monuments. It depicts, in stone, a boot to commemorate a wounded foot, and bears the inscription: 'In memory of the most brilliant soldier of the Continental Army, who was desperately wounded on this spot, winning for his countrymen the decisive battle of the American Revolution, and for himself the rank of Major General.' And just as with another memorial to the same man at the United States Military Academy, there is no name.

The reason is that this American hero became one of the country's greatest villains, the epitome of treachery – Benedict Arnold.

The youngest son of a failed and alcoholic businessman, young Benedict had to leave school at 14, and a year later enlisted in the Connecticut Militia. He witnessed the British surrender of Fort William Henry to the French invaders from Canada and the subsequent massacre by their Indian allies of hundreds of British men, women and children. It was to make him distrust the French forever.

Arnold became a successful merchant, but was one of the victims of the oppressive British taxes which nearly ruined him. When the riot involving the shooting of five Americans called the 'Boston Massacre' occurred in 1770, his revolutionary fervour stirred him to write, 'Good God, are the Americans all asleep and tamely giving up their liberties, or are they all turned philosophers that they don't take immediate vengeance on such miscreants?'

When news of the opening battles of the revolution, at Lexington and Concord, reached Boston, Arnold became captain in a company of Connecticut Guards. Realizing that Fort Ticonderoga held many cannons vital to the revolution, he organized a force and was instructed to link up with Ethan Allen and his 'Green Mountain Boys'. Together they took the Fort, but both disputed the other's overall command.

Soon, a new force arrived, and by orders of the Continental Congress, Arnold was placed under the new commander. Benedict Arnold was furious. It was the first slight that was to change his life, prompting him to resign his commission and go home. It was already obvious that his military virtues were more than balanced by his faults. He was ambitious, vain, arrogant, greedy and selfish.

But he was soon back in action, this time as a colonel commanding a force attacking Quebec City. It was unsuccessful, but Arnold fought and commanded well and he was wounded in the leg. At another battle, Ridgefield, his wounded horse crushed his leg again. Soon politics intervened and officers junior to him were promoted above him. In anger, he resigned his commission again, but his friend George Washington asked for him, and Arnold now played a decisive role in the battle of Saratoga, which saw the British General Burgoyne being forced to surrender. Again he was wounded in that same leg. In view of his subsequent disastrous career, he later wryly said that 'it would have been better to have been shot in the chest'.

Arnold had shown military brilliance and courage in cutting off Burgoyne's retreat, but he received no credit because his superior, General Horatio Gates, disliked him, calling him 'a pompous little man'.

He spent several agonizing months in hospital, burning with both resentment and pain. His left leg now two inches short, he emerged to find that his own victory at Saratoga had ironically convinced King Louis XVI to commit French forces to help the Americans – something he bitterly opposed. Then Congress also refused to repay the funds he had personally paid for his force in Canada. Extravagant, he slid into further debt and was court-martialled for corruption and 'malfeasance'. He complained to George Washington, 'Having become a cripple in the service of my country, I little expected to meet such ungrateful returns.' The scene was set for treachery.

Benedict Arnold now deliberately sought and obtained the command of West Point, a strategic fort on an escarpment overlooking the Hudson River, whose guns prevented the British from sailing north and connecting with their forces in Canada. By May 1779, he was spying for the British and regularly receiving money for useful information, some even gleaned at the dinner table of his friend George Washington.

He then embarked on something truly decisive and cynically treacherous. He would betray West Point itself, together with his own garrison. He secretly negotiated with the British General Clinton, demanding as his reward £20,000 ($1 million today) and the rank of brigadier-general in the British Army. Clinton appointed his own head of intelligence, Major John André, as the go-between.

A Huguenot by birth, André was a charming, charismatic man, artistic and musical, and master of four languages. After months of haggling negotiation by letter, they decided that they needed to meet personally, and André came up-river on the British sloop *Vulture* and was rowed ashore. But, in the night, the *Vulture* was fired on by American artillery and was forced to sail back down the river, stranding André in dangerous American-controlled country. The next day he was stopped, riding alone in civilian clothes, in neutral territory at Tarrytown, by three militiamen whom he mistook as British. Incriminating plans and documents from Arnold were found hidden in his boot and he was arrested. George Washington convened a board of senior officers and eventually, to their great sadness, they were forced to sentence him to death. Alexander Hamilton wrote, 'Never perhaps did any man suffer death with more justice, or deserve it less.' Washington's own opinion was that he 'was more unfortunate than criminal'.

Meanwhile, Benedict Arnold had received his report of André's capture just before George Washington had and so had time to escape downstream on the *Vulture*. He did indeed soon become a brigadier-general in the British forces and was quite successful against his old comrades, who now regarded him as the most odious of traitors, motivated by greed and spite. He once asked a young captured American officer what would happen if he himself were captured. 'We'd cut off your left leg, bury it with full military honours, and then hang the rest of you from a gibbet!'

Nor was he much liked or appreciated by his new comrades. Indeed, when he was recalled to

One positive legacy of Benedict Arnold's treachery is the United States Military Academy, based at West Point since 1917. (United States Military Academy)

England, Edmund Burke in the House of Commons stridently urged the government not to put him in command, 'lest the sentiments of true honour, which every British officer holds dearer than life, should be affected'.

West Point went on to become the site of America's famed Military Academy, and John André's remains were eventually sent back home and re-interred with honour and ceremony under a Robert Adam marble monument paid for by George III, in London's Westminster Abbey.

By contrast, Benedict Arnold died through illness and in poverty, disliked by the British and hated forever by Americans.

Apart from those strange, anonymous monuments in the United States, there is a blue plaque on his old house in London's Gloucester Place. It reads 'American Patriot', which seems a little generous, to say the least.

5

A STREAK OF CRUELTY

SIR JOHN MAXWELL AND HIS FIRING SQUADS

Just days after the outbreak of World War I, a small group of the Irish Republican Brotherhood (IRB) met secretly at 25 Parnell Square in Dublin. The Home Rule Act, giving Ireland her freedom, had been passed in 1914 and was about to become law. However it had been shelved when war broke out. Exasperated by just one more delay, the IRB planned an armed insurrection, sometime before the end of the war. They had little hope of a real 'victory', but had three more limited objectives: to declare a republic, to claim a place at any post-war peace conference and to revitalize the spirit of the people and arouse separatist fervour.

Little did they realize that they would achieve the third objective only too successfully, thanks to the brutal behaviour of Lieutenant-General Sir John Maxwell, one of a long line of Englishman who did not understand the Irish and also one of a long line of soldiers who *thought* they were rising to the occasion.

If you were looking for early signs of Maxwell's arrogant and callous indifference to those he despised, the Sudan and the battlefield of Omdurman in 1878 would provide them. There, in belated revenge for the death of 'Gordon of Khartoum', 26,000 Mahdists Dervishes had been killed or wounded, with only 48 British fatalities. This was the result of firepower, because, as Rudyard Kipling wrote:

Whatever happens we have got
The Maxim gun and they have not.

A young Winston Churchill, who had just taken part in one of the world's last cavalry charges, vehemently objected to Major Maxwell's orders not to help the wounded Dervishes, but to 'finish them off or let them die'. Maxwell contemptuously replied, 'A dead fanatic is the only one to extend any sympathy to.' Eighteen years later Maxwell was to indulge himself again, but with more far-reaching effects.

Maxwell had actually enjoyed quite a good military career; awarded the DSO in the Sudan after the 1886 battle of Ginnis (the last time the British Army wore scarlet), he had been mentioned in despatches several times. In March 1916, he asked to return from the 'backwater' of Egypt. It was a pity because he was soon to be propelled to real fame, or notoriety, by what he was to do in Ireland that Easter.

The Rising was planned to take place under cover of 'manoeuvres' by the Citizen Army and the Irish Volunteers. For months, the British authorities had stood aside as these armed and uniformed men had drilled, just as the 'loyalist' Ulster Volunteers drilled in the North. The government was apprehensive, but felt matters were under control, especially as Parliament had passed the Home Rule Act in 1914 – to be implemented once the presumably short war with Germany had ended. The nationalist cause lacked broad popular support, and indeed hundreds of thousands of Irishmen were fighting loyally for the British Empire in a world war 'for the freedom of small nations'.

Yet the previous week the Royal Navy had apprehended the *Aud*, a merchant ship packed with German arms headed towards the coast of south-west Ireland. Soon after, prominent nationalist leader Sir Roger Casement was arrested as he landed from a German submarine. The military felt the crisis had passed. With Casement's capture, the worried leader of the Irish Volunteers, Eoin MacNeill, then tried to stop things by placing a notice in *The Sunday Independent* to cancel the 'Easter manoeuvres'. The stage was set for tragic failure.

However, plans were too far advanced to halt, and few saw or heeded the warning. Thus the Rising proceeded as planned. A force of some 1,200 men and women would seize prominent strong points from which to pin down military barracks and hold off reinforcements. These included the Four Courts (the law courts on the quays of the River Liffey), Jacobs' biscuit factory and Boland's Flour Mills, the latest of those to guard canal crossings against troops arriving from the port of Kingstown. The General Post Office (GPO) was to be the headquarters of the Rising.

Up until the last moment, the British did not suspect a thing. It was Easter Monday, the Fairyhouse Races were on and only about 400 soldiers were on duty. On 24 April,

Irish volunteers fight on from the General Post Office in Dublin. Overwhelmed by superior British forces, they surrendered and their leaders were shot after secret and illegal courts martial, quickly turning Irish sentiment against the British. (*Easter 1916*, Thomas Ryan RHA)

at the GPO, armed men suddenly expelled the staff and customers and took over the building, barricading the windows and preparing to resist attack.

Padraig Pearse, impressively styled 'Commandant-General and President of the Provisional Government of the Irish Republic', formerly a patriotic schoolmaster with an unhealthy interest in blood sacrifice, read out a proclamation to a somewhat bemused crowd. 'Irishmen and Irishwomen,' he announced, 'In the Name of God and of the dead generations from which she receives her old tradition of nationhood, Ireland through us summons her children to her flag and strikes for freedom.' Some lancers and their mounts trotting down Sackville Street were among the first casualties, apparently unaware of the danger.

Martial law was quickly declared by the Lord Lieutenant, Lord Wimborne, which allowed court trials of anyone breaching the Defence of the Realm Act of 1914. Four days into the Rising, Sir John Maxwell arrived to take 'firm charge', promising maximum severity with indifference to damage.

Once the British had recovered their composure and poured in 30,000 reinforcements, an armed cordon slowly tightened around the city centre. They brought in artillery, with fire directed from the roof of (loyal) Trinity College. An armed fishery protection vessel on the Liffey also bombarded the GPO and other strong points. By Thursday, thousands of soldiers were able to concentrate on the Post Office with machine guns and artillery. On Friday, the insurgents tunnelled out from the burning building and set up positions in nearby houses. By early afternoon of the Saturday, to avoid any more loss of life, they surrendered. Eighty-two rebels were dead, along with 256 civilians and 157 soldiers, and 2,600 were injured. Whole areas of Dublin had been destroyed.

As the firing died away, the feeling among Dubliners was that these men and women were at best misguided and at worst traitors to the thousands of Irish fighting for the British against the Germans. Indeed the prisoners being marched off to be shipped out to England were cursed by the crowds and pelted with vegetables.

However, rising to the occasion, as he thought, General Maxwell was soon to change all that. He arrested 3,430 men and 79 women. He then convened 'Field General Court Martials'. Maxwell ignored the Defence of the Realm Act ruling that such courts should be in public, with 13 members, a professional judge and proper defence lawyers. Rather, they were held in secret with Maxwell and his officers as judge and jury. On 2 May, 90 people were condemned to death. The next day, at Kilmainham Gaol, firing squads started shooting the leaders one by one. James Connolly, who had been hit, ironically, by a marksman from the 3rd Royal Irish Regiment, was too wounded to stand up and was shot strapped to a chair. James Plunkett was executed ten minutes after being married to his fiancée. It was the Countess of Fingall, a leading figure in Dublin society, who coined the famous phrase, 'It was like watching a stream of blood coming from beneath a closed door.' And one night, dining with her, even one of Maxwell's officers, General Blackadder, the President of the Court Martial, revealed his grave misgivings. Speaking of Padraig Pearse, he said, 'I have just done one of the hardest things I have ever had to do. I have had to condemn to death one of the finest characters I have ever come across. There must be something wrong in the state of things that makes a man like that a rebel.'

The news caused mounting horror on both sides of the Irish Sea, together with real political problems. John Redmond and John Dillon of the Irish Party at Westminster both stood up in Parliament and asked Prime Minister Herbert Asquith to stop the shootings. Dillon, in his despair, even reflected Lady Fingall's passion. 'You are washing out our whole life's work in a sea of blood.' Behind the scenes, the Cabinet was beginning to panic.

But it was too late. By the time the shootings were stopped on 12 May, with 15 dead, the mood in Ireland had changed from apathy to revulsion. W. B. Yeats captured the mood in his memorable poem *Easter 1916*, in which he described how all was 'changed, utterly changed'.

Yeats later wrote a letter to warn the British about Ireland's passionate and shifting emotions, quoting a neighbour who had said, 'The young men are mad jealous of their leaders for being shot.'

When they did not get their promised Home Rule, the Irish decided to fight. In 1919, the first shots were fired in the war to liberate Ireland. It was the same year, ironically, that another callous British general decided to 'teach the Indians a lesson', shooting 1,200 men, women and children at Amritsar (see page 261).

In Ireland, after four years of fighting, killing and repression, in 1922 one of the survivors of the Rising, Michael Collins, helped to negotiate the Irish Free State (see page 75). Another survivor, Eamon de Valera, fought a tragic civil war to repudiate the compromise partition of Ireland, the results of which live with us to this day.

By now, Sir John Maxwell, promoted to full general, had comfortably retired. He may or may not have realized that his hasty, brutal and illegal actions had not only alienated Ireland forever but had started the slow unravelling of an empire.

STALIN AND HIS COUNTRY RETREAT

If you are likely to have to face the world's most aggressive military power, it is probably not a good idea to kill most of your *own* commanders and officers in advance. And if you are about to be invaded, it is probably also not a brilliant idea to ignore all those who are trying to tell you exactly when and where the blow will fall. Joseph Stalin managed to do both.

There has never been anyone quite like Stalin. A cunning, sinister, pock-marked Georgian, Joseph Djugashvili had worked his way to the top of the Russian revolutionary party and was soon called Stalin, or 'Man of Steel'. It was an apt name. He was to kill more people in 30 years than the tsars in four centuries. A dying Lenin had warned his colleagues not to give Stalin power. Nikolai Bukharin, one of Lenin's closest aides, correctly predicted, 'Stalin is a Genghis Khan who will kill us all.' Apart from wiping out millions of his own citizens, in the 1930s Stalin ruthlessly eliminated all political rivals for power. He turned on his former friends and colleagues, who were tortured before public 'show trials' condemned them to be shot or sent to the *gulags* (camps) – together with their families. Of Lenin's last Politburo, soon only Stalin and Leon Trotsky were still alive. Sure enough, even Trotsky, exiled to distant 'safety' in Mexico, was hunted down by an assassin and killed with an ice pick.

Then, in his paranoia, Stalin in 1938 decided that the Red Army was the next threat. First to go was its head, Marshal Mikhail Tukhachevsky, Stalin's rival since the Civil War, 'a refined nobleman, handsome, clever and able'. Tortured, his written confession of 'being a German spy' was spattered with blood. 'I feel I'm dreaming', the broken marshal murmured. He wasn't. Three out of five marshals were shot, 15 out of 16 army commanders, 60 out of 67 corps commanders, all 17 political commissars and no fewer than 37,000 other officers down to major level.

Stalin had decapitated his own armed forces. What is more, he had instilled such fear in the survivors that no senior officer would in future dare to take an initiative without personal orders from Stalin.

And all the while, Nazi Germany was getting stronger, with Hitler's published and never retracted intention to obtain *Lebensraum* (living space), for the German people, and to destroy Communism (where else but the Soviet Union?).

To the world's amazed shock, Stalin bought time in 1939 with his cynical non-aggression pact with Hitler. Days later, they conquered and divided up Poland, the NKVD and Gestapo working together to kill their enemies. Germany was free to unleash *Blitzkrieg* on Western Europe, leaving only Britain unconquered, but isolated.

Stalin knew in his heart that it was only a matter of time before his 'partner' would return to his original intentions, but he thought that he could buy that time – at least until 1942. In spite of his fury over Hitler's encroachments in the Balkans, he neither protested, nor did he slow down the massive shipments of Russian raw materials that were propping up Germany's war effort.

Stalin's appeasement did not work. In December 1940, Hitler signed Directive 21, the secret plans for Operation *Barbarossa*. 'The German armed forces must be ready, before the end of the war against Great Britain, to defeat the Soviet Union by means of *Blitzkrieg*.'

In France, the invasion of Britain had been 'postponed' and German troops started to roll east, leaving the Luftwaffe reduced to just two wings. Difficult to conceal entirely, huge forces were massing on Russia's borders. Suddenly Mussolini, determined for once to 'score off Hitler', managed to spoil this methodical build-up by incompetently invading Greece. Hitler had to rescue him and send forces to take out Greece and Crete and vengefully to punish Yugoslavia. So *Barbarossa* was delayed a fatal five weeks, giving Stalin, theoretically, even more time to prepare.

However he did not, in spite of the mounting evidence of Hitler's

Stalin's official portrait was the first thing after the war that people saw as they entered East Berlin from the West. But Stalin was lucky to be the final victor after his disastrous performance at the beginning of the war. (Imperial War Museum)

impending treachery. In Tokyo, the spy Richard Sorge sent his first alert (see page 136). In January 1941, another spy in Germany, Harro Schulze-Boysen, sent the complete plans to Moscow. In February, Leopold Trepper of the 'Red Orchestra' spy ring supplied the first potential date, 15 May. President Roosevelt also tipped Stalin off, but his warnings were dismissed as 'capitalist provocation'. In May, Sorge now reported that 150 German divisions were in place, the same month that the anti-Nazi German ambassador in Moscow, Count Friedrich Schulenberg, tried to warn the Russians. 'So, disinformation has now reached ambassadorial level,' sneered Stalin. Richard Sorge, who had been so accurate and helpful in the past, now told the precise date. Stalin retorted, 'There's this bastard who's set up factories and brothels in Japan and even deigned to report the date of the German attack as 22 June. Are you suggesting I should believe him too?'

Churchill, armed with 'Ultra' intercepts of German Enigma messages, sent a personal letter to Stalin, via Stafford Cripps, his ambassador. Stalin ignored it. He was sure of his political instincts.

When German reconnaissance flights increased, Stalin mused, 'I'm not sure Hitler knows about those flights.' And when a Soviet spy called 'Starshina' at Luftwaffe headquarters confirmed the final decision for the attack, Stalin scrawled crudely on the message, 'Tell this Luftwaffe "source" to f**k his mother! This is no source but an informer.'

On 20 June, 25 German ships suddenly left Riga, some not yet unloaded. 'A provocation', shrugged Stalin. Ambassador Schulenberg was asked why the German Embassy was burning papers and why all the diplomats' wives had left. He tried to dissemble. 'Not all, my wife is still in town.'

At midnight on 21 June, one of the German deserters who had crossed over to warn the Russians, a young Berlin Communist called Alfred Liskov, had even swum the River Pruth to bring the news. He was ordered by Stalin to be shot, 'for his disinformation'. Events were to save him. Three hours later the Germans struck on a 1,000-mile front, with three million men, backed with 3,600 tanks, 600,000 vehicles, 2,500 aircraft and 625,000 horses.

For the Russians, the beginning of the war was an unmitigated disaster: 1,500 Russian planes were destroyed on the ground in the first nine hours. Millions of troops would be cut off and surrounded, together with their commanders – paralysed by fearful indecision, more scared of Stalin than of the Germans.

As the news got worse, a few days later a very depressed Stalin decided to drive back to his country retreat. As he got in his car, he muttered, 'Everything's lost. I give up. Lenin founded our state, and we've f**ked it up!' He said that he 'resigned as leader'. He was certainly not rising to an occasion that he had done so much to create. He did not return to Moscow, but shut himself in his dacha for a full ten days, not even answering the telephone, leaving a gaping chasm of indecision.

Eventually, his shaken ministers, made wary by years of arbitrary terror, summoned up the courage to visit him. A thinner, haggard and gloomy Stalin received them, appearing, when he saw them, to 'turn to stone'. He plainly thought that they had come to arrest him (as he would have done in their place, of course). He was mightily relieved when they asked him to return 'as their leader'.

He recovered, and did eventually lead them to victory in a four-year, ruthless and bloody 'Great Patriotic War'.

But Stalin's own self-delusion and incompetence would mean that another 20 million or so would be added to the 20 million of his own citizens that he had killed before the war had even begun.

AMRITSAR AND THREE IRISHMEN

In the cool of one early morning in the summer of 1917, my grandmother went to look out over the Punjabi countryside. She was surprised to discover an old Baluchi fakir with greasy love locks, sitting in the Buddha position at the end of the veranda. 'I'm sorry. You are not meant to be in the compound,' she ventured. 'Salaam, memshiba, salaam,' said this disconcerting figure. 'All I really want, darling, is a bath.'

It was her husband, Lieutenant-Colonel Aubrey O'Brien, brilliantly disguised, who had been absent for several weeks listening in the bazaars for when the next raid from Afghanistan might come. When he died, *The Times of India* recalled:

> His remarkable power of work, inexhaustible mental and physical energy, intimate knowledge of the people, their problems and their languages gave him enormous personal influence in the districts of which he held charge.

Sadly, in 1919 there were other, less sympathetic Irishmen serving in the Punjab. It was, admittedly, a difficult time. Over one million Indians had served as soldiers and labourers during World War I. Over 36,000 had died. Indians now wanted recognition for their loyalty and some kind of independence. What they got were high taxes and harsh laws against any form of sedition. Mahatma Gandhi now began to emerge as a formidable leader.

The Punjab was a hotbed of unrest, and acts of sabotage were appearing. The lieutenant-governor of the Punjab was Sir Michael O'Dwyer, born in Tipperary. He was determined that he was not going to allow anything like a second Indian Mutiny to develop. But from the start of his rule seven years earlier in 1912, he had exasperated the people of the Punjab. He now convened a secret meeting at

Government House in Lahore, with the objective of 'teaching the Punjabis a lesson which they will never forget, and striking terror throughout Punjab'.

His chosen instrument was Brigadier Reginald Dyer. This officer had gone to school in County Cork, but he had lived most of his life in India. Born just after the Indian Mutiny, he too had always had a fear of another great armed uprising. In many ways, the two men's relationship had the same ominous results as that of Lord Chelmsford and Sir Henry Bartle Frere in Zululand (see page 231).

When two of the Punjab's nationalist leaders were arrested after addressing mass rallies, their sympathizers marched on the deputy commissioner's bungalow and were fired upon. English banks were attacked, and several rioters killed. Dyer's suspicions and fears became almost hysterical when, on 9 April 1919, a missionary doctor, Miss Marcia Sherwood, was attacked by a mob. A curfew and ban on public meetings was announced.

A few days later, nearly 10,000 Indian pilgrims, having set off from miles away and days before any travel bans were imposed, arrived for Baisaki, a festival celebrating the harvest and the Sikh new year. They gathered in an open park called the Jallianwala Bagh near the sacred Sikh Golden Temple in Amritsar. Unfortunately, in the same park there was also a protest meeting by extremists, largely ignored by the bulk of the disinterested pilgrims. Dyer had heard about the protest meeting and regarded it as an affront to the law and to himself.

There were four very narrow entrances to the park, and a fifth from which Dyer suddenly emerged with 90 Gurkha soldiers. As soon as he arrived, Dyer, without addressing the crowd or giving them any chance to disperse, ordered his men to open fire. Some soldiers, naturally enough, at first fired into the air. But he shouted, 'Fire low! What have you been brought here for?' The steady rifle fire continued for ten minutes, with Dyer carefully directing it at places where the frantically escaping crowd was thickest. One witness at a window reported, 'The worst thing was, the firing was directed towards the exit gates where people were running out. Many were trampled to death. Even those lying flat were fired upon.'

In desperation, many tried to survive by jumping into a well – 120 bodies were found there later. Dyer's troops fired 1,650 rifle rounds. His two armoured cars with their machine guns luckily could not get through the narrow entrances – otherwise the toll would have been even more appalling.

The 'official' death toll was 379, including a baby, with 200 wounded. However, most sources, both British and Indian, claimed well over 2,000 casualties in all.

Dyer marched his men away, reporting to Lahore that he had seen off 'a revolutionary army' and 'taught the Punjabis a moral lesson'. Michael O'Dwyer sent back a telegram, 'YOUR ACTION IS CORRECT. LIEUTENANT GOVERNOR APPROVES.'

However, the rest of the world very much did not approve. A few days later, Dyer showed quite how mad and racist he really was. He designated the spot where Miss Sherwood was assaulted as 'sacred'. Daytime pickets were placed at either end of the street. Anyone wishing to proceed down the street during the day was made to crawl the 150 yards on all fours, lying flat on their bellies. The effect of this 'crawling order' on the Indian community can be imagined.

However bad the original shootings' effect was on public opinion, it was made worse by Dyer's unfeeling and self-centred testimony when facing the subsequent Hunter Inquiry. He showed no remorse. 'I think it quite possible I could have dispersed the crowd, but they would have come back and laughed, and I would have made a fool of myself.'

When asked if he had tried to help the wounded, he retorted, 'Certainly not. That is not my job. Hospitals were open, and they could have gone there.' (This ignores the curfew, which meant the wounded lay unattended all night.)

At the inquiry my grandfather, Aubrey O'Brien, with his deep knowledge of the locals, firmly stated that 'there was no rebellion to be crushed'.

Dyer was condemned on four counts and was stripped of his command and forced to resign. Disgracefully, on his return to England, the pro-Imperialist *Morning Post* newspaper raised the then huge sum of £26,000 for him. However, others understood what a terrible and dangerous event it had been. In the debate in the House of Commons which censured Dyer, Winston Churchill, then Secretary of State for War, called it 'an episode without precedent or parallel in the modern history of the British Empire. An extraordinary event, a monstrous event which stands in singular and sinister isolation.' Former Prime Minister Herbert Asquith observed, 'there has never been such an incident in the whole annals of Anglo-Indian history, nor I believe in the history of our Empire since its very inception. It is one of the worst outrages in our whole history.'

Dyer died of illness only two years later, unable to sleep or to admit that he had done anything wrong.

Michael O'Dwyer, who had also been forced to resign, lasted much longer, but met a much more dramatic end. In 1940, after giving a lecture in London's Caxton Hall, he was shot dead by a Sikh, who stated that he had 'waited 21 years to obtain revenge for Amritsar'.

It is an ironic thought that the British Empire, which took dedicated officials like my grandfather 300 years to build up, was helped to its eventual destruction by the callous actions of an Englishman, Sir John Maxwell, killing Irishmen after the 1916 Dublin Easter Rising (see page 253) and, three years later, two Irishmen killing Indians.

WILLIAM CALLEY AND HIS MY LAI ORDERS

History records some spectacular and horrible acts of murderous barbarism by soldiers on unarmed, helpless civilians. Most were in the distant past, with 'barbarians' like Genghis Khan, Attila the Hun or Tamurlane. More recently we can blame the worst type of Nazi Germans for Oradour and Lidice, or the Japanese for Nanking.

In the good old days, America, founded by people fleeing the entanglements, persecutions and wars of Europe, generally tried to keep out of wars, and, if forced into them, brought a rather moralistic attitude to the business. But November 1969 changed all that. Suddenly American screens, newspapers and magazines were full of something dreadful that had occurred 18 months earlier in far away Vietnam in a little village called My Lai.

They were right to be shaken. The massacre at My Lai was carried out by ordinary, young Americans. A few hours of collective madness was to lose America any of its rights to morality, to weaken its resolve to continue the Vietnam War and to begin years of self-doubt.

A woman from My Lai, one of the few survivors, summed it up: 'The first time the Americans came, they gave our children sweets. The second time we gave them water. The third time, they killed everybody and destroyed everything.'

By 16 March 1968, when C Company of the 11th Light Infantry Brigade of the Americal Division entered My Lai, the Americans were frustrated. They had been fighting an undeclared war in Vietnam for 13 years. Despite growing protests back home, more than 500,000 young Americans were now in Vietnam, part of eight million who passed through, with the sole justification that they were saving Vietnamese civilians from Communism.

The pressure to draft so many into what was an undeclared war meant a serious drop in officer quality. The lawyer Jerome Walsh, later part of the official inquiry, pointed out: 'We were getting officers who were below the minimum everything. Calley was only at the minimum height, 5 foot 4, and, more serious, had an IQ of only 115.'

William Calley at his trial, November 1970 – March 1971. (Corbis)

Young Americans who had never before left home faced a hidden enemy, often lost in the local rural population, who were themselves caught helplessly in the middle. Brutal methods crept in. Most of My Lai's neighbouring villages had been razed to the ground. As war reporter Jonathan Shell admitted, 'Calling them "free-fire" zones meant that villages were just ground up – so the idea of killing civilians was hardly novel.'

Coming right from the top, the need to produce 'kills' was felt by every soldier. A Marine described the atmosphere: 'Our mission was not to seize positions or win terrain, but simply to kill. Victory was a "high body count", defeat a "low kill ratio", war a matter of arithmetic. The pressure on unit commanders to produce corpses was intense, and they in turn communicated it to their troops. It is not surprising, therefore, that some men acquired a contempt for human life and a predilection for taking it.' As one American infantryman also put it, 'They were gooks, spooks, Charlie. We never looked at them as being other human beings.' So here we have Americans talking just like SS men on the Russian Front in 1944.

'Charlie' Company did not have the excuse of being bitter, war-weary troops. It was an above-average unit, with good results in training, but inexperienced. It had been just four months in Vietnam under its commander, Captain Ernest 'Mad Dog' Medina. When he briefed his men, Medina ordered that everything in 'heavily fortified' My Lai should be destroyed. No prisoners. The company had lost men recently, to mines and booby traps, and Medina hinted that they 'could get their revenge'.

Leading the assault would be Lieutenant William Calley, in civilian life a failed diner cook, car wash attendant, insurance clerk and railway ticket collector – somewhat dubious officer material. Also to take part by chance were photographer Sergeant Ron Haeberle and reporter Jay Roberts, to record the action for the brigade's newspaper.

In My Lai on that warm morning, in a beautiful little village so far untouched by war, children were playing, women cooking, men going off to the fields. Suddenly high explosive and phosphorous artillery shells slammed into the village. Moments later Charlie Company, having landed in helicopters, came marching through the paddy fields, already shooting. Photographer Haeberle testified later:

> A woman's form, a head, appeared from some brush. All the other GIs started firing at her, aiming at her, firing at her over and over again. She had slumped over so that her head was a propped-up target. There was no attempt to question her or anything. They just kept shooting. You could see bones flying in the air chip by chip.

Looking through his viewfinder, he suddenly saw a little child flipping back through the air. 'I looked up, shocked and asked, "Why?" The soldier just turned away.' The soldier was Private Fred Widmer, who admitted years later how horribly out of control he became. 'I killed 25 people, cutting throats, scalping them, cutting off hands and tongues.'

One woman survived because of the sheer numbers killed. 'I pushed my little son into the paddy field. "Don't cry, they are killing everyone." We were protected by the corpses on top of us.'

In the village itself, it was even worse. Charlie Company moved from hut to hut, grabbing terrified inhabitants by the hair, shouting 'VC? VC?' and then murdering them. In the middle of the village, Calley gathered 45 civilians and, when his men hesitated, manned the M-60 machine gun himself. There were many soldiers who refused to join in the killing, one even shooting himself in the foot. But many did, in what became collective madness. 'It was carnage, with bodies lying everywhere. Some of the soldiers were even killing the water buffaloes with their bayonets. The weirdest thing, a freakout.'

Private Paul Meadlo then also helped Calley kill another 75 men, women, children and babies in a ravine. A woman survivor recalled: 'We were herded like ducks, landing headfirst in the ditch. People cried "Have pity". Tiny children crawled along the edge until they were shot. It broke my heart.'

Jay Roberts saw it happen. 'Just outside the village … there was this big pile of bodies. This really tiny little kid – he only had a shirt on, nothing else – he came over to the pile and held the hand of one of the dead. One of the GIs behind me dropped into kneeling position and killed him with a single shot.'

The troops stopped for lunch, 'finishing off some people in a pile near by who were moaning', before continuing their grisly work. One of the few heroes was Hugh Thompson, a helicopter pilot who landed by the ditch full of bodies. Thinking they had been killed by accident, he said to a sergeant, 'We've got to help these people.'

'The only way to help them is to kill them.' 'I thought he was joking. As we took off my crew chief pointed at the same guy firing into the ditch.' Thompson later even threatened to open fire on the Americans and managed to save some women and children.

Worse than 'just' killing occurred. Scalping, mutilation and rape. One of Ron Haeberle's photographs was to go round the world. A 13-year-old girl had been stripped and hid behind her mother. Haeberle's presence stopped the rape, but when he looked away, seconds later the whole group of women and children were machine gunned to death.

In fact it was B Company who did most of the raping in the sister villages of My Khe and Binh Tay, where 90 died. One little girl in Binh Tay recalled with horror: 'This American was raping my sister, she had no clothes. He then stood up and shot her.'

The rape did not stop even when disquiet at the indiscriminate killing began to creep in. Private Dennis Bunning tried to intervene. 'When we got a radio call to stop the killing from Captain Medina, the raping did not stop of 15, 16-year-olds – even 12. I tried to stop them but five guys turned to me: "Look Bunning, leave us alone or we're going to kill you."'

The body count at My Lai was one American, three Vietcong and 504 civilians. Everyone was ordered to keep quiet, as it had been touted as a triumph by the Army. Commander in Chief General Westmoreland had even sent a telegram of congratulations. But a GI, Ron Ridenhour, then met a friend, Private 'Butch' Gruver, in a bar who quite casually mentioned what had happened, saying they'd been told to 'cover our asses'. After asking around and finding out more, on 29 March 1969, a full year after the massacre, Ridenhour wrote a detailed and damning letter to incoming President Nixon, General Westmoreland and dozens of others in the military and government. Many could not believe it.

At first the army tried to make out that there had been a real battle, with civilians caught in cross-fire. But not for the first time, the media flushed out the story. CBS, magazines and newspapers ensured that an inquiry took place, with Sergeant Haeberle's photographs providing horrific evidence and eliminating all doubt.

A very honourable officer, Lieutenant-General William Peers, tried to rise to the occasion. In his highly detailed inquiry, initiated by the US Army, he soon discovered that the massacre was initiated by orders from the top. C and B companies had both been ordered to 'shoot anything that moves'.

He also discovered that senior officers had ignored the evidence. Colonel Warren Henderson, the brigade commander, had been told by pilot Hugh Thompson that 100 civilians had been killed, but had shrugged it off, merely congratulating his men on 'a job well done'.

After collecting 20,000 pages and 400 hours of recorded testimony, General Peers, stating 'the Army and the country were on trial', wanted a top-down court martial of at least 30 officers. However, only five junior ranks were court-martialled, finally focussing on Lieutenant William Calley, initially indicted for killing 102, then charged with a 'specimen' 22. His defence was that he was 'only obeying orders'. Colonel Henderson and all the other officers were acquitted. Jerome Walsh reiterates that 'General Peers was very disappointed. He was very much behind bringing charges against those people. It was disgusting, a fiasco of military justice.'

In the end, General Peers was effectively gagged by the Pentagon, forced to reduce what President Nixon had admitted was a 'massacre' to a 'tragedy of major proportions'.

Calley was sentenced to hard labour for life. Three days later he was released from prison on the orders of President Nixon and went to work in a jewellery shop in Georgia. He has never expressed remorse, although some of his men have gone through agony. At least one has even committed suicide.

It was probably scant satisfaction for the victims of My Lai, which now has a museum with lists of exactly who died and where, including Ron Haeberle's famous photographs.

There were many in the US Army, it is fair to say, who did not rise to the occasion – either before, during or after that terrible day.

FRANCISCO LOPEZ AND HIS IRISH MISTRESS

In 1855, Francisco Lopez was in Paris on a buying trip. It was not for the things you normally shop for in Paris. Under orders from his father, the military dictator of Paraguay, he was there to buy arms and munitions, together with river steamers. He was also trying to build a railway and even to encourage a French colony in his country.

One day, needing some relaxation, he dropped in on a beautiful, blonde courtesan with a gorgeous figure, Eliza Lynch. It was a visit that would cost half his countrymen their lives.

It is fair to say that among all the 'Wild Geese' who have left Ireland to escape poverty and oppression and to seek their fortunes abroad, none was to prove as destructive as Eliza Lynch.

Eliza had arrived in Paris in 1849 soon after the Irish Famine and was married off to a French army officer at just 15. After three boring years in Algiers, she returned to Paris alone and was soon successfully selling her statuesque body to rich and influential men. She decided to attract a foreign 'sugar daddy', and into her salon one night came a rather ugly, short man with brown teeth and a cigar. It was Francisco Lopez, and he fell in love with her. He told her of his 'paradise' in Latin America, and she agreed to go back with him to Paraguay.

Arriving with crates of Parisian gowns, china, furniture and even a piano, Eliza was shocked to find a hot, humid and run-down capital, Asunción, whose aristocratic women plainly regarded her as the 'Irish Whore'. But she bore him six children, and they built a 'palace' – the first two-storey building in Paraguay. When his father died, Lopez became president and demanded that his mistress be accorded the courtesies due to a wife. All this was rather petty and provincial. He could have then settled down to be a normal corrupt, incompetent Latin American dictator of the period.

But Lopez had inherited his father's worries that tiny Paraguay, with a population of just half a million, could be swamped and dismembered by its two large neighbours, Brazil and Argentina, and even by Uruguay. He was probably right but, unfortunately for his country, it was the last thing he was right about. His paranoia was not helped when Eliza filled his strange mind with grandiose ideas of military glory and of how they could become emperor and empress of the whole of South America.

Now with the largest army in South America, 30,000 men, but with no proper officers and no reserves, he escalated some boundary and tariff problems into full-scale war. He ordered an attack on a Brazilian steamer and on it captured the Governor of Mato Grosso, whose province he then invaded. He next quarrelled with Argentina, seizing two ships and attacking a border town.

By May 1865, he had managed to force his neighbours into a triple alliance against him. His forces were now outnumbered ten to one, but poor coordination among the allies meant that the wars dragged on for four years.

Eliza tried to help by recruiting 'Amazon' regiments of women with lances, leading them into battle on a white horse. Even more in character, she took great pleasure in confiscating the jewels of her rivals, ostensibly 'for the cause', and promptly shipping them out of the country and off to Paris for her future private plans.

By now Lopez was a hugely fat megalomaniac and it rapidly became more dangerous to be his friend than his enemy. His armies were destroyed by continuous suicidal attacks, and then he turned on his own elite. Suspecting a conspiracy, he ordered the killing of his two brothers, his brothers-in-law, cabinet ministers, officers, bishops, policemen and even hundreds of the diplomatic corps.

When his mother revealed that Lopez was actually illegitimate and therefore had no right to be president at all, he cracked – ordering the population of Asunción into the jungle like Pol Pot in Cambodia a century later. He also demanded to be recognized as a saint and simply shot the 23 bishops who disagreed. Worse, he even ordered what remained of the national treasure of gold to be thrown off a cliff, and then killed all the witnesses.

He had his mother flogged in public, before she, too, was to be executed. She was, however, saved by his final military collapse. With only a handful of troops, he was attacked in northern Paraguay and was finally killed by a Brazilian grenadier as he waddled into the water and tried to swim a river.

Eliza Lynch, the beautiful Irish girl who persuaded her lover Francisco Lopez to attack Paraguay's three neighbours, ruining the country.

He had managed to reduce Paraguay's population from 525,000 to 221,000, of which only 28,000 were adult males – a feat unmatched by Hitler, Stalin or even Genghis Khan. Paraguay's neighbours duly took great chunks of the country. As an attempt to rise to the occasion, it was one of the most disastrous performances in history.

However, Eliza did rise to the occasion in her own way. Typically now under the gallant protection of a Brazilian general, she managed to make it back to Paris, where she lived in comfort on the proceeds of her rivals' jewels.

Amazingly, generations later, Paraguay's dictator Alfredo Stroessner tried to rehabilitate both her and Lopez, bringing her body back from Paris and proclaiming her a 'national heroine'.

However, most people would agree that, for a poor emigrant girl from Cork, she had been able to do an amazing amount of damage.

SELECT BIBLIOGRAPHY

Ackroyd, Peter, *London, The Biography*, London, 2000

Alexander, Bevin, *Korea, The Lost War*, London, 1986

Ambrose, Stephen, *Crazy Horse and Custer*, New York, 1975

Babington Smith, Constance, *Evidence in Camera*, London, 1957

Baigent, Michael with Richard Leigh, *Secret Germany*, London, 1994

Beevor, Anthony, *Berlin*, London, 2002

Beevor, Anthony, *Stalingrad*, London, 1998

Berg, A. Scott, *Lindbergh*, New York, 1998

Bierman, John with Colin Smith, *Alamein*, London, 2002

Blandford, Edmund, *Fatal Decisions*, Shrewsbury, 1999

Bolin, Luis, *Spain, the Vital Years*, London, 1967

Bredin, A. E. C., *History of the Irish Soldier*, Belfast, 1987

Brendon, Piers, *The Dark Valley*, London, 2004

Brown, Dee, *Bury My Heart at Wounded Knee*, London, 1998

Bryson, Bill, *Made in America*, New York, 1989

Butler, Rupert, *Gestapo*, Wisconsin, 1996

Chamberlain, Joshua L., *The Passing of the Armies*, New York, 1915

Churchill, Winston, *The Second World War*, London, 1952

Cohen, Stan, *East Wind Rain*, Montana, 2001

Cole, J. A., *Lord Haw Haw*, London, 1964

Coltrane, Robbie, *Engines that Turned the World*, London, 1997

Connely, S. J., *The Oxford Companion to Irish History*, Oxford, 1998

Coogan, Tim Pat, *The Irish Civil War*, London, 1999

Coogan, Tim Pat, *Wherever Green is Worn*, London, 2000

Cowley, General Sir John, *Memoirs*, London, 1998

Cowley, Robert, *What If?* London, 2000

Cronin, Vincent, *Napoleon*, London, 1994

SELECT BIBLIOGRAPHY

David, Saul, *The Homicidal Earl*, London, 1997

David, Saul, *Military Blunders*, London, 1997

Deighton, Len, *Blitzkrieg*, London, 1979

Deighton, Len, *Blood, Tears and Folly*, London, 1993

Dillon, Richard, *North American Indian Wars*, Greenwich, CT 1983

Doherty, Richard, *Irish Generals*, Belfast, 1993

Dorril, Stephen, *Blackshirt*, London, 2007

Dunnigan, James, *Dirty Little Secrets of World War II*, New York, 1994

Durschmied, Erik, *The Hinge Factor*, London, 1999

Eastlake, Keith, *World Disasters*, Chicago, 2001

Esposito, Vincent, *Military History and Atlas of the Napoleonic Wars*, London, 1996

Evans, Harold, *The American Century*, London, 1998

Froissart, Sir John, *The Boy's Froissart*, New York, 1906

Ford, Brian, *German Secret Weapons*, London, 1966

Ford, Roger, *The Grim Reaper, Machine Guns and Machine Gunners*, London, 1996

Fraser, David, *Alanbrooke*, London, 1992

Fraser, George McDonald, *Quartered Safe out Here*, London, 1992

Frost, David, *The Rich Tide*, London, 1986

Fuller, J. F. C., *Decisive Battles of the Western World*, London, 1954

Gibbon, Edward, *Decline and Fall of the Roman Empire*, London, 1979

Goldhagen, Daniel, *Hitler's Willing Executioners*, London, 1997

Greaves, Adrian, *Rorke's Drift*, London, 2002

Grehan, Ida, *Irish Family Histories*, Dublin, 1997

Hall, Allan, *War Crimes*, Leicester, 1993

Harcup, Guy, *Code Name Mulberry*, London, 1977

Harrison, Salisbury, *The 900 Days*, London, 1969

Hart, Peter, *Mick, the Real Michael Collins*, London, 1979

Harvey, Robert, *Clive*, London, 1998

Hastings, Max, *Das Reich*, London, 2000

Hastings, Max, *The Korean War*, London, 1987

Haythornthwaite, Philip, *Die Hard*, London, 1996

Hill, Maureen, *Women in the Twentieth Century*, London, 1991

Hofschröer, Peter, *The Waterloo Campaign, A German Victory*, London, 1999

Hogg, Ian, *Weapons of the American Civil War*, London, 1987

Holmes, Richard, *Redcoat*, London, 2001

Holmes, Richard, *The Oxford Companion to Military History*, Oxford, 2001

Holmes, Richard, *The Western Front*, London, 1999

Holmes, Richard, *Tommy*, London, 2005

Holmes, Richard, *War Walks*, London, 1996

Horne, Alistair, *How Far from Austerlitz?* London, 1996

Howarth, Stephen, *Henry Poole*, London, 2003

Hughes-Wilson, Col John, *Military Intelligence Blunders*, London, 1999

Irving, David, *The War between the Generals*, London, 1981

Jackson, Robert, *Aerial Combat*, London, 1976

Jackson, Robert, *Suez, the Forgotten Invasion*, Shrewsbury, 1996

Jenkins, Roy, *Churchill*, New York, 2001

Johnson, Paul, *A History of the American People*, London, 1997

Johnson, Paul, *Ireland Land of Troubles*, London, 1980

Jones, R. V., *Most Secret War*, London, 1978

Josephus Flavius, *The Jewish War,* Rome, 75 AD, translated by Thomas Lodge, London, 1602

Kahn, David, *The Codebreakers*, London, 1977

Keeler, Christine, *The Truth at Last*, London, 2001

Keneally, Thomas, *The Great Shame*, London, 1998

Knight, Ian and John Laband, *The Anglo-Zulu War*, London, 1996

Koch, H. W., *The Age of Total Warfare*, London, 1983

Kostof, Spiro, *America by Design*, New York, 1987

Kurlansky, Mark, *Salt, A World History*, London, 2002

Lagrange, Bruno, *Napoleon*, Paris, 2003

Lamb, Christian, *I Only Joined for the Hat*, London, 2007

Lamb, Richard, *Mussolini and the British*, London, 1997

Lamont-Brown, Raymond, *Kamikaze*, London, 1997

Lanning, Michael, *100 Most Influential Military Leaders*, London, 1997

Large, David, *Berlin, A Modern History*, London, 2001

Lawrence, Russell, *The Mammoth Book of Battles*, London, 2002

Laxton, Edward, *The Famine Ships*, London, 1996

Leavitt, David, *The Man Who Knew Too Much*, London, 2006

Lewis, Jon E., *The Mammoth Book of Heroes*, London, 2002

Lichfield, Patrick, *In Retrospect*, London, 1998

Lomax, Eric, *The Railway Man*, London, 1995

Longford, Lord, *Abraham Lincoln*, London, 1975

SELECT BIBLIOGRAPHY

Lossin, Yigal, *Pillar of Fire – The Rebirth of Israel*, Jerusalem, 1983

MacArthur, General Douglas, *Reminiscences*, London, 1964

MacDonald, John, *Great Battlefields of the World*, London, 1984

Mackay, James, *Michael Collins. A Life*, Edinburgh, 1996

Macmillan, Harold, *War Diaries. The Mediterranean 1943–45*, London, 1984

Mailer, Norman, *Miami and the Siege of Chicago*, New York, 1968

Manchester, William, *Goodbye Darkness*, New York, 1945

Manchester, William, *The Arms of Krupp*, London 1955

Massie, Robert K., *Castles of Steel*, London, 2007

Mayor, S. L., *The Rise and Fall of Imperial Japan*, London, 1976

McCormack, Goran with Hank Nelson, *The Burma Thailand Railway*, Thailand, 1993

McMurty, Larry, *Crazy Horse*, London, 1999

Mitcham, Samuel W., *Hitler's Field Marshals*, London, 1988

Morgan, Chris, *Facts and Fallacies*, Exeter, 1981

Morgan, Ted, *FDR*, London, 1997

Moxham, Ray, *The Great Hedge of India*, London, 2001

Moynahan, Brian, *The British Century*, London, 1999

Murray, Williamson, *The Luftwaffe, Strategy for Defeat*, London, 1986

Norton, Bruce, *Secret Warfare*, London, 1989

O'Brien, Donough, *Banana Skins*, London, 2006

O'Brien, Donough, *Fame by Chance*, London, 2003

O'Brien, Donough, *Fringe Benefits*, London, 2000

O'Brien, Donough, *Numeroids*, London, 2008

O'Brien, Edward Donough, *Big 3 or Big 2½?* London, 1945

O'Brien, The Hon. Donough, *History of the O'Briens*, London, 1949

O'Brien, The Hon. Grania, *These Are My Friends and Forebears*, Clare 1991

O'Connor, Ulick, *The Troubles*, London, 1975

Owen, Dr David, *In Sickness and in Power*, London, 2008

Preston, Anthony, *Sea Combat off the Falklands*, London, 1982

Preston, Anthony, *Send a Gunboat*, London, 1967

Price, Alfred, *Battle over the Reich*, Surrey, 2005

Read, Anthony with David Fisher, *The Fall of Berlin*, London, 1992

Readers Digest, *Illustrated History of South Africa*, Cape Town, 1989

Readers Digest, *The World at Arms*, London, 1989

Rees, Laurence, *Horror in the East*, London, 2001

Regan, Geoffrey, *Air Force Blunders*, London, 1991

Regan, Geoffrey, *Great Military Blunders*, London, 2000

Regan, Geoffrey, *Heroes in Battle*, London, 2000

Regan, Geoffrey, *Military Blunders*, London, 1991

Regan, Geoffrey, *Someone Has Blundered*, London, 1987

Rhodes, Anthony, *Propaganda*, New York, 1976

Ridley, Jasper, *Mussolini*, London, 1999

Ripley, Tim, *Bayonet Battle*, London, 1999

Roseman, Mark, *The Villa, the Lake, the Meeting*, London, 2002

Saint Exupéry, Antoine de, *Flight to Arras*, London, 1943

Saint Exupéry, Antoine de, *The Little Prince*, London, 1944

Sampson, Anthony, *Anatomy of Britain*, London, 1969

Schama, Simon, *A History of Britain*, London, 2002

Sebag Montefiore, Simon, *101 World Heroes*, London, 2007

Sebag Montefiore, Simon, *Stalin*, London, 2003

Shirer, William, *The Rise and Fall of the Third Reich*, London, 1960

Sifakis, Carl, *Encyclopaedia of Assassinations*, New York, 1993

Simpson, Ivan, *Singapore, Too Little, Too Late*, London, 1970

Spears, Edward, *Liaison 1914*, London, 1968

Spellmount, *Irish Guards, The First Hundred Years*, Staplehurst, 2000

Summers, Anthony, *The Secret Life of J. Edgar Hoover*, London, 1993

Swimson, Simon, *Kohima*, London, 1978

Taylor, Colin, *The Plains Indians*, London, 1997

Taylor, Peter, *Provos*, London, 1997

Thatcher, Margaret, *The Downing Street Years*, London, 1993

Thomas, Gordon, *Ruin from the Air*, London, 1977

Time Life, *WWII*, New York, 1989

Toffler, Alvin, *Future Shock*, London, 1970

Toffler, Alvin, *The Third Wave*, London, 1980

Touhill, Blanche, *William Smith O'Brien*, Missouri, 1981

Travers, Tim, *Gallipoli*, Stroud, 2001

Tsuji, Masanobu, *Singapore, The Japanese Version*, London, 1951

Twiss, Miranda, *The Most Evil Men and Women in History*, London, 2002

Urban, Mark, *Generals*, London, 2005

Verney, Peter, *The Micks. The Story of the Irish Guards*, London, 1970

SELECT BIBLIOGRAPHY

Vincent, Edgar, *Nelson, Love and Fame*, Yale, 2003

Ward, Geoffrey, *The Civil War*, New York, 1990

Ward, Geoffrey, *The West*, London, 1996

Warry, John, *Warfare in the Classical World*, London, 1980

Wier, Hugh, *Brian Boru,* Clare, Ireland, 2002

Wilson, Harold, *A Prime Minister on Prime Ministers*, London, 1970

Wood, Derek, *The Narrow Margin*, London, 1969

Woodham-Smith, Cecil, *The Great Hunger*, London, 1962

Yeager, Chuck, *Yeager*, London, 1986

York, Alvin, *Sergeant York, His Own Life Story and War Diary*, New York, 1928

Zamoyski, Adam, *1812*, London, 2004

INDEX

INDEX

INDEX